AF477873

The Language of Police Interviewing

The Language of Police Interviewing
A Critical Analysis

Georgina Heydon
Monash University

First published 2005 by
PALGRAVE MACMILLAN
Houndmills, Basingstoke, Hampshire RG21 6XS and
175 Fifth Avenue, New York, N.Y. 10010
Companies and representatives throughout the world

PALGRAVE MACMILLAN is the global academic imprint of the Palgrave Macmillan division of St. Martin's Press, LLC and of Palgrave Macmillan Ltd. Macmillan® is a registered trademark in the United States, United Kingdom and other countries. Palgrave is a registered trademark in the European Union and other countries.

ISBN 1–4039–1726–4 hardback

This book is printed on paper suitable for recycling and made from fully managed and sustained forest sources.

A catalogue record for this book is available from the British Library.

Library of Congress Cataloging-in-Publication Data
Heydon, Georgina, 1970–
    The language of police interviewing : a critical analysis / Georgina Heydon.
        p.   cm.
    Includes bibliographical references and index.
    ISBN 1–4039–1726–4 (cloth)
    1. Police questioning—Australia.   2. Criminal investigation—
    Australia—Language.   I. Title.

    HV8280.A3H49 2004
    363.25′4′0994—dc22

                                                        2004053944

10   9   8   7   6   5   4   3   2   1
14   13   12   11   10   09   08   07   06   05

Printed and bound in Great Britain by
Antony Rowe Ltd, Chippenham and Eastbourne

Contents

List of Tables

Preface

It is my intention that this book will provide a framework for the critical analysis of police interview discourse. To this end I have applied a number of analytical tools to the data which first illuminate the minutiae of police–suspect interactions and then combine to reveal assumptions underlying the police approach. The fact that these tools are drawn from Interactional Sociolinguistics and Conversation Analysis may be considered controversial, especially by proponents of the latter methodology. However, I believe that by undertaking this detailed analysis of my own data, I can demonstrate that these tools have a powerful role in critical discourse analysis which should in no way diminish their value in the study of conversation.

The book is organised according to the approach taken to the data analysis. Following an introduction to the theoretical and methodological background to the study, the next two chapters are concerned with the interview structure (Chapter 3) and the construction of police and suspect versions of events (Chapter 4). Participant roles are central to the analysis of structure, while topic management is the key to analysing competing versions of events. The approach taken by police trained to interview child witnesses under the Victoria Police Video and Audio Taping of Evidence scheme is presented in the following chapter (Chapter 5) and provides a useful comparison with police behaviour in interviews with adult suspects. In Chapter 6, the results of the detailed analyses are integrated and considered in relation to three 'myths', or underlying police beliefs, about discursive behaviour in interviews with suspects. Chapter 7 examines the findings and presents a critical view of police discourse, the relationship between police power and institutionality, and the impact of police institutional discourse on the interview process. I have included some suggested directions both for future research and police interview practice, as it is my sincere hope that this project will benefit law enforcement bodies as well as providing a framework for critical analysis of police interview data.

My desire to see a practical benefit for police officers stems from my own experiences in dealing with the police both as a citizen and a researcher. In relation to the latter, I have always found police members to be highly sensitive to the institutional requirement to combine due process with effective interviewing and enthusiastic about research which might shed light on this difficult task. As for the former, one experience in particular was the catalyst for my decision to undertake this research: on a Saturday night in October 1997, I found myself debating the finer points of police institutional discourse with a bemused sergeant at a Melbourne police station. The poor man was attempting to write a witness statement on my behalf relating to the recovery of my stolen car and I must confess that, as I was in the middle of a dissertation on police language, I may have been slightly more opinionated than expected on the subject of what was or was not the most appropriate way to represent my version of events. As I suggested that the phrase 'I located the vehicle' might be replaced with 'I saw my car', it occurred to me that the negotiation of various versions of events in a police interview would indeed require further investigation.

This book is the culmination of several years' work, during which time a large number of people have contributed their insights and support. My thanks firstly to Brian Paltridge, Alastair Pennycook, Keith Allan and Joanne Winter for insights and inspiration during the preparation of an earlier version for submission as a doctoral thesis. I am especially grateful to Jo Winter for her continued support through periods of leave and for her co-operation in the struggle to overcome the tyranny of distance.

I am grateful to the Department of Linguistics and Applied Linguistics, University of Melbourne and the staff of the Linguistics Programme, Monash University, for their practical assistance and continued interest in my research throughout the project. My thanks also to the School of Languages, Cultures and Linguistics for providing vital research funds, giving me the opportunity to incorporate earlier research involving police–child interviews into the discussion of police-suspect discourse.

In the final stages of preparation I have had the pleasure of working with the very capable editing team at Palgrave Macmillan and my thanks in particular go to Jill Lake and her assistants for being flexible enough to accommodate the vagaries of early motherhood.

I wish to acknowledge the lawyers whose co-operation made it possible for me to obtain the necessary data and I also extend my thanks to the staff at the Policy and Research Division of the Victoria Police for their support of the project.

My thanks of course to my friends and family for having faith that I would actually bring it all together and to Greg for being a committed partner and father throughout the sometimes painful process of juggling work and family life. Finally I am dedicating this book to Declan, whose arrival threw every completion timetable out of the window but who gave me the greatest motivation to finish.

Georgina Heydon

Transcription Conventions

As described in section 2.3.2, the conventions used in the transcription of data for this study are based on those outlined in Levinson (1983). The list of conventions below is intended as a guide for the convenience of the reader. Details about the transcription methodology can be found in section 2.3.2.

A1.1   List   of transcription conventions used in data extracts from police-suspect interviews

Symbol	Description
//	overlapping speech commences
*	overlapping speech ends
=	latching
(0.6)	silence measured in seconds
(.)	micro-pause of less than 0.2 seconds
(..)	pause more than 0.2 seconds, less that 3 seconds (VATE interview extracts only)
°word°	softer than surrounding speech
WORD	louder than surrounding speech
<u>word</u>	syllables having greater stress than surrounding sounds
↑	high rise intonation
∧	low rise intonation
⇒	level intonation
↓	falling intonation
::	the sound is lengthened by one syllable for each colon
-	truncated word
h	audible outbreath
.h	audible inbreath
(h)	explosive aspiration (as in laughter)
(word)	uncertain transcription
( )	incomprehensible utterance, no transcription attempted
(( ))	transcriber's remarks, including comments on voice quality or non-verbal sounds

Abbreviations

The table below is intended as a convenient guide to the abbreviations used in the transcriptions and the text.

Abbreviation	Description
	Data: Interviews and Participants
INT1	Interview 1
SPT1	Suspect participant in interview 1
pio1	Primary interviewing officer in interview 1
sio1	Secondary interviewing officer in interview 1
tio12	Tertiary interviewing officer in interview 12
VATE	Video and Audio Taping of Evidence (scheme)
V-INT1	VATE interview 1
VPO1	VATE interviewing police officer in interview 1
CH1	Child witness in interview 1
	Theoretical Frameworks
CDA	Critical discourse analysis
CA	Conversation analysis
S3R	Participation framework where the author, principal and animator roles are allocated to the suspect
P3R	Participation framework where the author, principal and animator roles are allocated to the police interviewer (primary or secondary)
PI2R	Participation framework where the author and principal roles are allocated to the police institution
P2RA	Participation framework where the author and animator roles are allocated to the police interviewer and the principal role is allocated to the suspect

1

Police Institutional Discourse

> We as police officers are obliged to detail to you the observations which we have made and the facts that we have uncovered during the course of our investigation and we are obliged to put any allegations arising from that to you.
>
> (Police officer speaking in an interview with a suspect, recorded in rural Victoria, Australia, 1994)

1.1 Introduction

The confession of a suspect obtained in a police evidentiary interview comprises the key piece of evidence in almost every criminal case in Australian courtrooms. It is crucial to the successful prosecution of a defendant that the confession is voluntary and not a product of threats or physical violence and that any written confession is a true and accurate record of the suspect's words during the interview. In Australia, as in many parts of the world using similar interview procedures, the introduction of tape-recorded police interviews has eliminated some of the more obvious problems associated with ensuring that all these criteria are met. Contested police statements alleging a confession by the suspect can now be checked against the audio tape of the interview, which is made in accordance with guidelines designed to maximise the integrity of the recording itself.

Despite these advances, the police interview process remains problematic for a number of reasons. For instance, it is not always clear when pressure is being brought to bear on the suspect to conform to a police version of events due to the subtlety of power play in discourse. British research in criminology has identified serious gaps in the understanding of the interview process by even experienced police officers (see for instance Baldwin 1993), but such claims have not yet been substantiated by analyses of the actual language used to construct an interview.

Exposing assumptions and beliefs underlying the discursive practices of participants in the interview is an important process in understanding how apparently voluntary confessions can be influenced and guided by the police institution, represented by the interviewing officer. Prior studies have identified mythologies underlying various kinds of institutional discourse that can subvert the intentions of institutions in their interactions with the public. However, such an approach has not yet been taken in the analysis of police interview data, where it could prove crucial in providing an insight into the construction of the confession by the participants.

Nonetheless, linguistic research and opinion has made, and continues to make, a valuable contribution to legal proceedings and contested evidence. For example, in Australia there have been many cases where the validity of records of interview is disputed when the suspect is not a native speaker of English and an interpreter is not provided. The need for an expert opinion in these cases has introduced many linguists to the field of language and the law and there is now a growing body of research in this area commonly referred to as Forensic Linguistics.

As it currently stands, studies of language and the law generally, and police interviews in particular, are being approached from two ends of a spectrum. At one end, forensic linguistic research is driven by the need to respond to particular, problematic cases and these studies are supplemented by background research into police behaviour, often in disciplines other than linguistics. At the other end, there exist a number of studies which are primarily concerned with language use and discourse structure but which happen to draw on police interview data for their analyses. Between these bodies of research, there remains a gap. Research is needed which is not based on a specific court case but which seeks, through the expansion of the current understanding of police-suspect interviews, their structure and linguistic features, to provide a critical analysis of police behaviour in evidentiary interviews. Furthermore, such research should result in the provision of feedback to the relevant institutions and as such become part of the knowledge resources available to participants in these interactions, both lay and professional. Research which focuses on the analysis of legally undisputed or unproblematic interview data can highlight the linguistic features we might ordinarily expect to find, and how these construct or are constructed by the institutionality of police discursive practices in the interview.

Thus it is the need to draw the two ends of the research spectrum together with a comprehensive understanding of the beliefs that inform the discursive practices of participants in police interviews that drives the research presented in this book. More specifically, this book provides a detailed investigation of the role of police institutional discourse in the construction of a police-suspect interview, both in terms of the negotiation of power relations between participants and the successful fulfilment of institutional requirements.

In order to carry out this investigation, the analysis is divided into three stages, each stage providing a basis for subsequent analysis and all three building a framework for the critical examination of police discursive practices. Firstly, the analysis will provide a descriptive framework of police-suspect interviews based on linguistic devices and interactional features used in recordings of actual police interviews with suspects. Secondly, we will analyse this description of the interviews and reveal the discursive practices of participants as they negotiate the various functional requirements of the interviews. The final phase will aim to expose the process through which underlying beliefs of the police participants routinely affect the construction of the police interview both as an interaction in time and space and as a socially and culturally situated activity.

1.2   Approach to the analysis

An important goal in writing this book is to present a framework for the detailed and systematic analysis of texts which can be used to support a critical sociolinguistic study of institutional discourse. For the first two parts of the research, analytical approaches are employed using participation frameworks as advanced by Erving Goffman, and Conversation Analysis, based on the work of Harvey Sacks and developed by Gail Jefferson, Emanual Schegloff and others. The critical analysis that forms the core of the project is based on the investigation of mythologies in institutional discourse as proposed by Ruth Wodak within a Critical Discourse Analysis framework. The decision to combine tools from Interactional Sociolinguistics and Conversation Analysis to underpin a broader sociolinguistic investigation may be considered controversial, given the commitment of Conversation Analysts to studying the organisation of talk in interaction (see for instance Schegloff (1991)). However, I am convinced that the analysis of turn structure and topic management in the police-suspect interviews is powerfully revealing and essential to the critical inquiry into participants' orientations to their talk. I will revisit these methodological issues in Chapter 2 where the analytic framework is described in greater detail.

In the remainder of this chapter, I will introduce some of the main features of police interview discourse and discuss the way in which it functions as part of the broader legal and judicial institution. Prior research in the area of institutional discourse more generally and language and the law specifically, as well as appropriate theoretical frameworks for the analysis of interview data will be the focus of the next chapter. The analysis of the discursive institutional structure of the interviews is the focus of Chapter 3, while in Chapter 4 the analysis is focused on the production of turns and turn sequences and the distribution of interactional resources. The findings presented in Chapters 4 and 5 provide the basis of the analysis in Chapter 6 where several key aspects of the interview are considered in relation to discursive behaviour that constitutes a police mythology about interviewing suspects. Chapter 7 draws together the findings of the various levels of analysis and discusses the features of police institutional interviews that result in apparently counterproductive police discursive practices. Concluding remarks are presented in section 7.5, together with a discussion of the implications of the findings for the police and legal institutions and some suggested directions of further research in this area.

1.3   The police interview as institutional discourse

Although the police interview is a highly regulated form of discourse that is structured around legislative requirements, its 'institutionality' is constructed through the participants' interaction as they negotiate the organisational goals. That is, while aspects of a police interview, especially the beginning and end of the interview, are dictated by legislation and police regulations, the way in which each police interview is constructed as belonging to police institutional discourse is negotiated through the interactions. The differences in the way that men and women approach police work (McElhinny 1995) indicate that operating within the same set of legal requirements does not result in identical interactions. Nonetheless, adhering to the formal requirements of a police interview is bound to influence the resulting talk to some extent. Prior research into the impact of legal talk in a police interrogation has tended to focus on the role of cautions in protecting the suspect's rights (Ainsworth 1993; Shuy 1997; Cotterill 2000) and clearly the special properties of police cautions as 'a creative speech which brings into existence that which it utters' (Bourdieu 1991: 42) are worth considering in a broader sense. Because of this power of certain legal language to 'create' what is stated, it is important to know when such language is being used in the inter-action under investigation.

As in other nations and states where the law enforcement authority supports an adversarial justice system, in the state of Victoria, Australia, an investigation of interview procedures can be supported by reference to the Crimes Act (1958) which informs the Operating Procedures con-tained within the Victoria Police Manual. For instance, the Crimes Act (1958) S 464A (3) states that

> Before any questioning (other than a request for the person's name and address) or investigation under sub-section (2) commences, an investigating official must inform the person in custody that he or she does not have to say or do anything but that anything the person does say or do may be given in evidence.

This is then represented in the Operating Procedures as follows:

> Before any such questioning or investigation commences, inform the person that they:
>
> . . .
>
> – do not have to say or do anything but anything that they do say or do may be given in evidence.[1] (Victoria Police Manual (CD-ROM, version issued 11–07–03) s. 112–3, 4.2.1)

For the analyst, this provides the institutional background for the use of particular utterances as in the following extract from Interview 1[2]:

Extract 1-1 INT1

25. pio1[3]:   °yeah°⇒ (0.6) before I <u>do</u> this I must <u>inform</u> you

26.   that you are <u>not</u> obliged to say or do anything

27.   but anything you say or <u>do</u> (0.3) may be given in <u>evidence</u>

28.   do you understand <u>that</u>↑

This example demonstrates how legislation enacted in the Crimes Act, via police regulations articulated in the Police Manual directly influences the utterances produced by the police interviewer. There are several similar types of utterances in the data which can be traced back to the legislative requirements, such as utterances concerning the suspect's contact with a friend or relative, and a solicitor, and the requirements concerning fingerprinting at the conclusion of the interview.

However, the same legal sources reveal less specific influences over the interactions in an interview. Perhaps the most critical of these is the legislation concerning the voluntary nature of any confession. The Crimes Act itself is relatively non-specific about this issue. S464J (b), for instance, makes reference to the existence of 'the onus on the prosecution to establish the voluntariness of an admission or confession made by a person suspected of having committed an offence'; however, a great deal more information about voluntary statements can be found in the case material, which forms a commentary to the Act, and in the Victoria Police Standing Orders, about which more will be said shortly.

The Crimes Act, for instance, in Section 568.50.8, cites *R v Bueti* (CCA(SA), 12 December 1997, unreported), stating that '[t]he onus is on the prosecution to show that any admissions made by the accused were made voluntarily. Voluntariness involves the exercise of free choice.' The point being made is that merely failing to give a caution in an interview may not, at the discretion of the trial judge, render the evidence obtained in the interview inadmissible. This position is further supported in Section 568.50.8, which comments on the guidelines intended to protect the rights of Aboriginal and non-English speaking suspects and concludes that '[t]he legal question will always be whether the confessional statement was voluntary in the sense in which that expression is used by the relevant authorities' (*Gudabi v R* (1984) 52 ALR 133 at 145).

The Victoria Police Standing Orders were current until the earlier 1990s when they were superceded by the Operating Procedures of the Victoria Police Manual. The Standing Orders tend more towards interpretation of regulations and substantive advice for officers than do the Operating Procedures and as such they provide a useful source of commentary on police behaviour. A 'sense' of the expression 'voluntary', as referred to above, is provided by Section 8.5 of the Standing Orders, where it is stated that a confession may be defined as 'voluntary, not in the sense that it is made spontaneously or that it was volunteered, but in the sense that it was made in the exercise of a free choice to speak or be silent.' Thus, the use of a caution by police officers to advise suspects of their right to remain silent is a step which in itself is intended to render any subsequent confession or admission voluntary. However, the Police Standing Orders in subsequent sections demonstrate that voluntariness is not endowed upon a confession that follows a caution as a matter of course. Indeed, police officers are instructed to avoid certain discursive practices that may jeopardise the voluntariness of any confession or admission. For instance, Section 8.8(a) prohibits interviewing officers from any action which may 'endeavour to force any such person [i.e. an interviewee] into making any admission of guilt' and Section 8.8(g) states that 'where such person makes a confession [a member of the Force shall not] attempt, by further questioning, to break down answers[4] to which unfavourable replies have been received …'. In other words, although a confession may have been offered that would ordinarily be deemed voluntary by virtue of having been made by a suspect who is aware of his or her right to remain silent, the approach taken by the police officers in the elicitation of such a confession may still render the confession involuntary. Both the legislation and the Standing Orders recognise that, for suspects faced with coercive police behaviour in an interview, merely knowing that they can remain silent is not considered sufficient protection against forced confessions.

Furthermore, the two studies of cautions mentioned earlier (Ainsworth 1993; Shuy 1997) both find that in an inherently coercive situation, the use of a verbal caution can only go so far to protect the suspect's rights. Shuy (1997) outlines ten linguistic issues around the 'Miranda rights' (the right to remain silent and the right to an attorney) that he presents as possible topics for further research, among them the issue of coercion in a speech situation that has a question – answer structure. In a detailed study of police interrogations in the United States of America, Ainsworth (1993) finds that the linguistic tools required to successfully invoke the Miranda rights belong to a category of talk that Ainsworth labels 'assertive speech'. Drawing on linguistic research into features of 'powerless' speech and a 'female register' (primarily Lakoff 1975), she finds that women and ethnic minorities are disadvantaged by the requirement to use assertive speech in such situations and that their access to constitutional rights under Miranda is severely compromised as a result. The findings of her study can be generalised to the legal systems of Australia or Britain where a similar approach is taken to reading suspects their rights at the beginning of a police interview.

In relation to the suspect's right to remain silent, the Standing Orders reinforce at a general level the importance of adhering to institutional requirements and recognise the relationship between respecting the suspect's rights and conducting a successful interview:

> Every member of the Force, therefore, when questioning any person, shall use his [sic] utmost endeavours to obtain the free and voluntary co-operation of that person, so that the discharge of the important responsibility cast upon him [sic] of crime prevention and detection

shall not be thwarted by a refusal, on the part of the person being interviewed to answer questions put to him [sic]. (Victoria Police Standing Orders, Section 8.3)

Thus, reference to these key institutional documents provides an understanding of the legal parameters within which the police interviews are produced. We have been able to identify in the Crimes Act and the Victoria Police Manual the origin for several utterances produced by police officers as well as a number of requirements pertaining to the voluntary nature of a confession obtained within a police interview. In particular, it is possible to establish that the suspect's access to silence as a response to a question must be actively maintained by the police interviewer in the course of the interview. It is not sufficient to provide the suspect with the standard caution prior to questioning if the suspect is later submitted to police coercion or force to obtain a confession. Furthermore, if a confession has been produced that is in some way 'unfavourable', the police interviewer is prohibited from attempting to 'break down the will' of the suspect and elicit changes to the confession by using continued questioning relating to the confession.

This examination of the legislative and institutional requirements reveals two key points relevant to this research. Firstly, it is evident that the judicial system recognises the potential for police interviewers to disregard the rights of the suspect through their conduct in the interview and that should this occur, the decision to include the interview recording as evidence will be made in court. That is, it is recognised that concerns about the behaviour of the police interviewer will be addressed at the time of the court case, not at the time of the interview.

Secondly, this section has highlighted an institutional awareness that, by failing to maintain the rights of the suspect, police interviewers risk the integrity and successful completion of their investigation. This includes, but is not limited to, the co-operation of the suspect and the acceptance of the interview as evidence in court. Thus, recognition of the potential for interviewing officers to engage in conduct which ultimately may be self-defeating is embedded in the legislation and institutional regulations that govern police discursive practices.

In relation to the first point above, the legislation acknowledges that expert opinions regarding police interviewing techniques may be included as part of the court proceedings. Accordingly, section 2.2.1 discusses the contributions of linguists working within the judicial system as expert witnesses or consultants to the defence council in cases that address concerns about police interview conduct.

Regarding the second point, we can identify at an institutional level a basis for concerns about police behaviour in interviews that may conflict with the efficient and successful execution of police duties. That is, the legislation itself recognises the potential for inconsistency between what the police officers believe may be helpful in an interview and what will actually further the goals of the interview. This police behaviour bears a strong resemblance to the promulgation of 'myths' by members of institutions identified by Wodak (1996a). The analysis of an institutionally based mythology about police discourse will be discussed further following a summary of research pertaining to police institutional discourse and police interviewing in section 2.2.2.

In summary, the legislation concerning police interviewing acknowledges that the inappropriate use of language by police interview participants has the potential to invalidate evidence. Instances of misconduct by police officers or a failure to correctly adhere to the legislative requirements of a police interview may be addressed in court, as mentioned above, and if such instances are concerned with the use of language, then it may be appropriate to involve a linguist as an expert witness. As mentioned, section 2.2.1 describes the work of such linguists, often referred to as 'Forensic Linguistics', and considers the relationship between this work and related research into language and the law produced within the broader linguistic community. Prior to this discussion of forensic linguistics, the following chapter will expand upon earlier descriptions of the analytic frameworks used in the study, including an introduction to the concepts of power, discourse and structure as they relate to the research.

2
Tools for the Analysis of Police Interviews

2.1 A framework for the analysis

The approach to the analysis described in this chapter was specifically designed as a multi-layered or 'staged' response to the aims of this book. Thus, in subsequent chapters, we will be using the analytic tools described here in order to:

- provide a descriptive framework of police-suspect interviews based on linguistic devices and interactional features used in recordings of thirteen police interviews with suspects;
- analyse this description of the interviews and reveal the conversational strategies used by participants as they negotiate the various functional requirements of the interviews; and
- expose the process through which underlying beliefs of the police participants routinely affect the construction of the police interview both as an interaction in time and space and as a socially and culturally situated activity.

The identification of an interview framework based on linguistic devices and interactional features provides a platform for the subsequent micro-analysis of participants' discursive practices. The resulting description of the turn-by-turn construction of the interview will then contribute to the investigation of myths in a police institutional setting and the role of police institutional discourse in the construction of a mythology.

The approach that I have developed for the first two parts of the analysis involved participation frameworks (Goffman 1981) and Conversation Analysis or CA (Sacks, Schegloff and Jefferson 1974; Schegloff and Sacks 1973). The former is used as a tool to uncover the structure of the interview by identifying shifts in participation roles that aligned with shifts in interview goals. CA provides resources for the micro-analysis of the participants' discursive practices as they negotiate participation frameworks and interview goals. These two theoretical frameworks are discussed in sections 2.1.3 and 2.1.4 respectively.

Following these two stages of analysis, we will be in a position to consider the results from a critical perspective such as exemplified by Critical Discourse Analysis (CDA) (Fairclough 1989; Fairclough and Wodak 1997; van Dijk 1996). Section 2.1.2 describes the contribution made to this research by CDA. As mentioned, we will examine the findings for the presence of a mythology in institutional discourse, as discussed by Wodak (1996a) (see also Barthes 1972). It will then be possible to focus the discussion on the impact that such myths may have on the goals of the interview, and of police institutional discourse more generally.

As the ultimate goal of this book is to investigate the role of police institutional discourse through an analysis of the negotiation of power and institutional goals, this research is shaped by the understanding of three key concepts: power, discourse and structure. In the next section, I will explain how these concepts can be understood through work of researchers in a variety of fields, including philosophy, sociology and, of course, linguistics.

This chapter will conclude with a description of the data and a brief discussion of some methodological issues. This will provide readers with some background information which will better enable them to contextualise the many interview extracts featured in the analysis.

2.1.1 Power, discourse and structure

The approach to issues concerning power in the research is informed by an understanding of power as a subject for analysis and explanation, rather than a given whose existence in language must be demonstrated. Foucault (1980) suggests that we analyse power by 'starting … from the infinitesimal mechanisms, which each have their own history, their own trajectory, their own techniques and tactics, and then see how these mechanisms of power have been – and continue to be – invested, colonised, utilised, involuted, transformed, displaced, extended, etc., by ever more general mechanisms' (p. 99).

As A. I. Davidson (1986) explains, we must 'write a micro-physics of power; this will lead one to view power not as the homogenous domination of one group or class over another, but as a net-like, circulating organization' (p. 226). In this study, I attempt to uncover the 'net-like, circulating organisation' of power in the relationship between the police institution and citizens as it is manifested in the police interview. In the specific context of policing, Settle (1990) draws on Weber (Gerth and Wright Mills 1970) who defines power as 'the chance...to realise [one's] will in a communal action even against the resistance of others participating in the action' (Gerth and Wright Mills 1970: 180) and contrasts this with Weber's definition of authority as 'the exercise of power within a framework of a legally-binding set of rules/mutual obligations' (Settle 1990: 3). Importantly, I understand power not as something that resides 'outside' language, nor as something that is socially predetermined prior to the interaction, but rather as potentially residing within language, forming part of the interaction. Such a relationship between power and discourse is proposed by Giddens who finds that:

> Anyone who participates in a social relationship, forming part of a social system produced and reproduced by its constituent actors over time, necessarily sustains some control over the character of that relationship or system... In all social systems there is a dialectic of control, such that there are normally continually shifting balances of resources, altering the overall distribution of power. (Giddens 1982: 198–9)

His view of participants as 'knowledgeable, capable agents' (Giddens 1982: 199) is related to his theory of 'structuration' which will be discussed in more detail below. However, the concept of a 'dialectic of control' is an extremely useful one in the formation of a working definition of 'power'. The conceptualisation of power not as a given, but as a part of the discourse which requires explanation is complementary, in my view, to Giddens's dialectic of control. Giddens explains that the mere fact of participation in an interaction is sufficient to grant a person access to some form of control over the interaction. He gives examples of extreme forms of social control, such as a gaoler and a prisoner, and shows that even in the case of solitary confinement, the prisoner still has access to resources which enable some level of control – such as the choice to begin a hunger strike – and therefore the power in the interaction is not distributed completely in favour of the gaoler. It is a fluctuating force that depends upon the actions – some of which may be discursive actions (see below) – of the participants. Of course, most social interactions do not involve anything approaching this level of inequality. All participants in police interviews, for example, have access to some resources that facilitate control over the interaction. Suspects may manipulate the information gathering process by withholding responses to questions. That is not to say that such an action would grant the suspect absolute power in the interaction – under the definition of power being developed here, it is not something to be considered in 'zero-sum' terms. As one participant increases their power relative to other participants, those other participants do not necessarily 'lose' power. One participant may access resources that will increase her or his control over the interaction, but other participants can make use of their own available resources to consolidate their power. To return to the example of the police interview, should a suspect increase his or her control over the interaction by refusing to answer a question, the interviewing officer may bolster his or her own power using access to information known only to the police which may persuade the suspect to produce a response. Thus, the power relationship throughout such an interaction does not seesaw from the suspect to the police officer, rather it changes relative to the participants' access to resources which provide control over the interaction.

It is important to note, however, that access to resources that facilitate power may be limited by more than the speaker's role in the interaction. The work of Critical Discourse Analysts (e.g. Fairclough 1989; van Dijk 1996; Wodak 1996b: see section 2.1.2) addresses to some extent the different levels of access that members of a society have to such resources on the basis of their social class, education and cultural background. This problematises the view of power expressed by Giddens (1982, 1984) who appears to take a comparatively a-critical approach to the description of social power relations.

Nonetheless, it is useful to consider a view of the relationship between power and discourse in which 'discourse transmits and produces power; it reinforces it, but it also undermines and exposes it' (Foucault 1990: 101). We cannot assume that there is a static relationship between the participants' roles and their power over the interaction. Rather, we need to explore the relationship between participant roles and access to interactional resources. Then by analysing the allocation of interactional resources as well as how and when they are accessed by participants, we can begin to understand the power relations in the discourse.

It should be noted here that a common objection to Foucault's approach to the analysis of power, and one which is reiterated by Wodak (1996a), is that it does not allow that the results of any analysis might be used to emancipate participants from oppressive discourses of society since 'power continues to exist – and even better hidden than before' (Wodak 1996a: 26). The criticism offered by Wodak exemplifies the 'instructive contradiction' which Habermas (1986) finds inherent in the work of

Foucault, who, Habermas claims, 'contrasts his critique of power with the "analysis of truth" in such a fashion that the former becomes deprived of the normative yardsticks that it would have to borrow from the latter' (p. 108). Such criticisms are more broadly criticisms of postmodernism – that such a stance is self-defeating because it is never possible to achieve a position 'outside' the discourse from which one might conduct an 'objective' analysis.

This interpretation of Foucault's views might be usefully compared with the notion of 'problematising practise' identified by Dean (1994), who advocates the critical analysis of underlying assumptions or 'givens' as part of a Foucauldian approach to discourse. This does not imply that Foucault considers critique of social practice to be a 'lost cause', but rather that such critique must be rigorously critical, even of itself. It must never be assumed that one's position as analyst gives a view of discourse as undistorted by the social forces that reside within, and are recreated by, the discourse.

As mentioned, the specific understanding of power and language as it is used by proponents of Critical Discourse Analysis will be discussed in the following section, but first it is important to establish some of the features of language as discourse.

Thus far we have used the term 'discourse' in at least two ways: either as though it were roughly equivalent to 'talk in interaction' (as in 'institutional discourse' discussed in section 2.2.4), or to indicate sets of expressions forming a field of understanding or a body of knowledge (as in 'the discourse of legal institutions' discussed in section 1.3). However, it is important to note, especially when dealing with research emanating from the fields of philosophy and sociology, that the former is by no means a commonly accepted definition. Furthermore, even the latter definition does not seem to include the productive element found in Foucault's use of the term which Mills (cited in Pennycook 2001: 83) describes as, 'something which produces something else (an utterance, a concept, an effect) rather than something which exists in and of itself and which can be analysed in isolation'. Wodak (1996a) notes that the term is used in linguistic analyses with a great deal of diversity in its intended meaning and that 'frequently it is unclear whether a short text sequence is meant or a whole variety of text, or whether a very abstract phenomenon is to be understood under this heading' (p. 12).

Through his discussion of discourse as social practice, Fairclough (1989) illustrates that the way we understand discourse as a concept is central to the way we approach 'discourse analysis'. Therefore the concept of discourse, particularly in relation to social practices, will be discussed further in the following section. However, to summarise Fairclough's understanding of discourse, he begins by drawing a distinction between discourse and text, whereby a text is 'a product of the process of text production' and discourse refers to 'the whole process of social interaction of which a text is just a part' (Fairclough 1989: 24). His distinction between 'orders of discourse', 'types of discourse' and 'actual discourses' is perhaps less clear-cut. Orders of discourse are described as the networks or sets of conventions that underlie and determine actual discourses, which seems consistent with the Foucauldian sense of discourse described by Mills and indeed Fairclough (1989) acknowledges this connection (p. 28). However, Fairclough (1989) goes on to state that the term 'discourse' can be used to refer either to 'discoursal action' (e.g. talking or writing) or to 'a convention, a type of discourse (e.g. the discourse of police interviews)' (p. 29). Fairclough relates these three levels of discourse to social order and social practice so that 'an order of discourse is really a social order looked at from a specifically discoursal perspective'. I will return to the relationship between discourse and social practice in the context of the CDA approach in the section below.

It is clear that a definition of 'discourse' for linguistic study remains elusive. The Foucauldian sense of 'discourse' as 'something which produces something else', though offering a broad scope, can be problematic for a linguistic analysis, if only because it does not encompass an understanding of discourse as stretches of text or instances of language use. Perhaps the only practical solution is that offered by Fairclough (1989) whose somewhat flexible approach to the definition of 'discourse' permits a kind of homonymity to exist, and the intended meaning is invoked by reference to the context. I will use the term 'orders of discourse' to describe sets of conventions that underlie discourse (Fairclough 1989: 28) and 'discourse types' to describe a particular convention (e.g. the discourse of police interviews) (Fairclough 1989: 29). Together with the use of 'discursive practice' to describe instances of actual discourse (e.g. talk in interaction) these terms will assist in the identification of different understandings of 'discourse' and they will be drawn upon and explained further as required.

Finally, as mentioned above, our understanding of power and discourse can be augmented by an understanding of 'structure' drawn from Giddens's work on social practice (Giddens 1982, 1984). Central to Giddens's work is the observation that 'the rules and resources drawn upon in the production and reproduction of social action are at the same time the means of system reproduction (the duality of structure)' (Giddens 1984: 19). The present research seeks to describe the discursive practices that 'produce and reproduce' the 'order of discourse' within which a particular interaction – a police-suspect interview – takes place. As a part of this undertaking, this research seeks to identify the interactional resources available to each participant which enable him or her to draw upon and thus reproduce the set of applicable rules for a police interview. This is consistent with Giddens's view that social practices are structured by agents using resources available to them to reproduce sets of rules, even as they engage in social practices 'which "make a difference" to the world in some way, no matter how small' (Cassell 1993: 11).

In reference to the institutional definition of the rules mentioned above, it is important to note that Giddens's 'structuration' approach does not exclude the possibility of institutionalised properties of an interaction's setting being accepted as 'given'. Rather, he claims that 'to treat structural properties as methodologically "given" is not to hold that they are not produced and reproduced through human agency. It is to concentrate analysis upon the contextually situated activities of definite groups of actors' (Giddens 1984: 288). He then goes on to suggest important considerations for the analysis of strategic conduct such as 'the need to avoid impoverished descriptions of agents' knowledgeability; a sophisticated account of motivation; and an interpretation of the dialectic of control' (p. 289).

Some of the central issues raised by structuration theory are taken up in my analysis of shifts in 'participation frameworks' which seeks to demonstrate that the structure of the interview is constructed both by the institution and by the participants. I then proceed to the level of the production of a narrative as an ongoing process shaped by the conversational mechanisms (questions, answers, formulations and accusations) that are used by conversationalists. This investigation, based on Conversation Analysis (see below), has the potential to reveal 'how things work at the level of on-going subjugation' (Foucault 1980: 97), and it is this revelation that is the aim of the research.

The perspectives on power, discourse and structure outlined above will be expanded and contextualised throughout this chapter. In the following section, I will discuss some of the issues raised by prior research which have helped to shape my critical approach to discourse analysis.

2.1.2   Critical Discourse Analysis

The theoretical issues raised above concerning the relationship between power, discourse and structure are highly relevant to the establishment of a critical framework for the analysis of police interview discourse.

Critical Discourse Analysis (hereafter CDA – see Fairclough 1989; Fairclough and Wodak 1997; van Dijk 1997; and Wodak 1996a) considers the (re)production of power relations through language as a central concern for investigation. CDA aims to expose 'the ideological loading of particular ways of using language and the relations of power which underlie them [that] are often unclear to people' (Fairclough and Wodak 1997: 258). To take a politically based example, Fairclough (2000) analyses the use of language in British politics focusing on the discourse of 'New Labour' under Prime Minister Tony Blair. Fairclough describes the analysis as 'within the tradition of critical social science – it seeks knowledge for purposes of human emancipation' (p. 16) Similarly, CDA has been used to expose racist ideologies underlying public discourse (van Dijk 1987; van Dijk 1996; Wodak 1996b) with emancipatory aims.

The eight principles of CDA summarised below are proposed by Fairclough and Wodak (1997):

(1) CDA addresses social problems;
(2) power relations are discursive;
(3) discourse constitutes society and culture;
(4) discourse does ideological work;
(5) discourse is historical;
(6) the link between text and society, between the micro and the macro, is mediated;
(7) discourse analysis is interpretative and explanatory;
(8) discourse is a form of social action.

These principles suggest that the concepts of power and discourse as they were discussed earlier may require elaboration by reference to their use in CDA and their relationship with notions of ideology and social practice.

Fairclough's work on 'Language and Power', which provides a framework for undertaking CDA, focuses on 'the significance of language in the production, maintenance, and change of social relations of power' (Fairclough 1989: 1). This view is echoed by van Dijk (1997) who, in an introduction to work on 'discourse as social interaction', notes that there is an obvious significance for the 'concept of power in a critical discussion of the role of discourse in the reproduction of social inequality' (p. 35). However, van Dijk (1997) notes that such critical discussions cannot avoid a detailed analysis of the nature of the power involved and how it is 'enacted, expressed, or reproduced in text and talk' (p. 35).

For Fairclough (1989) the relationship between language and power is mediated by 'ideologies', or assumptions that are 'implicit in the conventions according to which people interact linguistically, and of which people are generally not consciously aware' (Fairclough 1989: 2). Thus in order to analyse 'the exercise of power', we might analyse 'the ideological workings of language' (1989: p. 2). The concept of ideology is also drawn upon to distinguish between power exercised through physical force and power exercised through the manufacture of consent: 'Ideology is the prime means of manufacturing consent' (p. 4).

The investigation of ideologies, as proposed by Fairclough (1989) is reiterated by Pennycook (2001), who suggests that we might consider the benefits of problematising 'givens' by 'turning a skeptical eye toward assumptions, ideas that have become "naturalized", notions that are no longer questioned' (Pennycook 2001: 7). This approach is advocated further by Dean (1994) in his discussion of Foucault's 'history of the present' where he notes that 'such a discourse remains critical as it is unwilling to accept the taken-for-granted components of our reality and the "official" accounts of how they came to be the way they are' (p. 4). Clearly, through its engagement with issues of power and ideology in discourse, CDA is well situated theoretically to take up the challenge of 'problematising practice' (Dean 1994).

Regarding the concept of discourse as social practice, Fairclough (2000) emphasises that 'although language is always an element of a social practice, it can be a more or less important element, a more or less salient part of the practice' (p. 156). Fairclough (2000) avoids the over-generalisation that all aspects of social life can come to be described as 'just discourse'. Thus, he defines social practice itself as 'a particular area of social life which is structured in a distinctive way involving particular groups of people in particular relations with each other' and notes that 'language is just one element of any practice' (pp. 143–4). The others are identified as physical, sociological and psychological, though all four are considered interrelated and not discrete, and language may be 'internalised' as a discourse residing within other elements.

Keeping in mind the conceptual understanding of power, discourse and structure outlined above, I propose a path of exploration that, while self-reflexive in its criticism, still retains the potential to uncover sociocultural assumptions that underlie the negotiation of power relations by participants in the institutional interaction. In the context of this research, such a path will seek to identify the macro-level mythologies embedded in patterns of language use at the micro-level. In other words, the analytical framework used in this project attempts to respond to 'the crucial challenge of combining post-structuralist discourse theory with detailed analysis of text' (Pennycook 2001: 109) through the 'restive problematisation of the given' (Dean 1994: 4). Furthermore, this research acknowledges that the participants are 'knowledgeable, capable agents', in Giddens's sense, and thus rejects the structuralist view identified by Giddens that 'human agents are mere "bearers of modes of production"' (Giddens 1982: 199).

Finally, this research draws on a CDA-related concept of 'myths' (Barthes 1972; Wodak 1996a) within the discourse of institutions that function as 'a second reality, imposed by the dominant groups' (Wodak 1996a: 39). Barthes (1972) emphasises the 'naturalising' effect of myths and explains that the function of a myth is not to deny things but 'to talk about them; simply, it purifies them, it makes them innocent, it gives them a natural and eternal justification' (p. 143). For the purposes of this research, myths are understood to represent a 'second reality' where '[e]vents become linked in a quasi-causal way although they are not related to each other' (Wodak 1996a: 39) and this process is naturalised through discursive practices of participants in interactions. Mythologies are networks of myths that exist within a given institution and relate to a particular order of discourse.

In the following sections, I will present an overview of research that contributes to a framework for detailed text analysis in the present study.

2.1.3 Participation frameworks

Although the concept of participation frameworks (Goffman 1981) is central to the analysis of the data in this study, it is useful to consider the theoretical backdrop against which this concept has been developed by researchers. This particular aspect of Goffman's work has come to form part of a broader approach to the study of language in society known as Interactional Sociolinguistics (sometimes abbreviated as IS) and primarily associated with the work of John Gumperz (Gumperz 1981, 1982, 1999).

In his book *Discourse Strategies*, John Gumperz (1982) proposes a theory of communication that goes beyond merely explaining the production of well-formed sentences, and takes into account the way in which participants in a conversation are able to infer meaning from each other's situated utterances. Thus, Gumperz develops a view of language as a culturally determined symbol system which is used by interactants to signal both their group identity and status and their position or beliefs at a particular moment. Signalling devices, which he calls 'contextualization cues' (Gumperz 1982: 5), enable the accurate inferencing of what is meant by indicating the background knowledge necessary to form contextual presuppositions about what is said. Gumperz describes this method of analysis as the 'careful examination of the signalling mechanisms that conversationalists react to, [whereby] one can isolate cues and symbolic conventions through which distance is maintained or frames of interpretation are created' (Gumperz 1982: 7). Here we find a link to Goffman's notion of 'frames' (Goffman 1974) in that the contextualisation cues indicate to hearers the frame being employed by speakers as they participate in a linguistic exchange.

Goffman (1974) introduces the notion of 'frames' as a way of addressing the need for a concept which will be of use in explaining people's perceptions of reality. Importantly, Goffman's tool is intended to reveal the way in which people engaged in social interaction are able to identify the appropriate social context for the interaction. For Goffman frames are used to define 'the principals of organization which govern events – at least social ones – and our subjective involvement in them' (pp. 10–11). Thus a frame is a way of structuring experience such that the use of a particular frame by a speaker can indicate whether the speaker is joking, recounting a past event, making a prediction and so on.

Gumperz's contextualisation cues can therefore be understood as the ways that speakers indicate to hearers the appropriate frame within which their utterances must be interpreted. Thus, a change in frames during an interaction can indicate to the participants that there may be a change in the function of the language being used. The importance of the notion of frames in a study such as this one is that it provides a description of the different stages of an interaction as they are recognised and negotiated by the interactants themselves. The negotiation of frames is an important consideration in the present study as the interviews are divided into different parts and each part can be seen as having a separate set of goals which must be understood by both parties (see Chapter 4). The analysis of frame negotiation provides a tool with which we can identify and differentiate the different parts of the interview as they are recognised by the participants, rather than assuming the presence of a predetermined discourse structure in the data.

Another way of describing participants' alignments is by reference to the related concepts of 'footing' and 'participation frameworks'. The concept of participant roles is introduced by Goffman (1974) as a way of describing the different statuses allocated by participants in talk when referring to themselves or others. Throughout an interaction, participants are found to display various alignments or 'footings' to what is being said. To explain how these different footings are managed by people in conversation, Goffman proposes that participants in talk be identified as having four possible roles: *principal, animator, figure* and *author*. Goffman (1974) describes the *principal* role as 'the party who is held responsible for having wilfully taken up the position to which the meaning of the utterance attests' (p. 517) and the *animator* role as producer of an utterance, 'the current, actual sounding box from which the transmission of articulated sound comes' (p. 517). The role of *figure* can be occupied by anyone or anything that can be spoken of or animated by another, while the role of *author* is one who creates or 'writes' an utterance. Goffman proposes that when people interact, they assume one or more of these roles forming a network of participant roles. This framework is referred to by Levinson (1988) as a 'production format' (p. 169) and the term 'participation framework' is reserved for the roles taken up by recipients of talk (e.g. addressed and unaddressed ratified recipients and unratified overhearers, bystanders and eavesdroppers (p. 169)). However, I am using the term 'participation framework' to refer to the collection of participant roles taken up by speakers relative to their utterances, as outlined by Schiffrin (1994: 104).

The participation framework indicates to other participants the footing to which speakers are aligned at any given time. Thus, Goffman's (1981) notion of footing provides a link between the sociological aspects of the participation framework and Gumperz's sociolinguistics of interpersonal communication. Footing concerns 'the alignments we take up to ourselves and the others present as expressed in the way we manage the production or reception of an utterance' (Goffman 1981: 128). Thus shifts in footing and alignment are signalled through the management of the production of an utterance and this includes signals such as Gumperz's contexualisation cues. Speaker roles in participation frameworks are conceptually linked to notions of dialogic 'voice' proposed by Bakhtin (Holquist 1981), in particular the 'double-voicedness' that expresses both 'the direct intention of the character who is speaking, and the refracted intention of the author' (p. 324). Furthermore, a view of roles that is closely related to the construction of 'identity' is described by Roberts and Sarangi (1999), who explain that 'identities are negotiated through the differentiation and delineation of role expectations. But the latter are also confirmed or reconfirmed through situated identity work' (p. 228). The construction of identity is an important part of the discussion in Chapter 7 which responds to the primary research aim: investigating the role of police institutional discourse in the construction of a police-suspect interview.

Taken together, the concepts developed by Goffman and Gumperz provide a framework for the analysis of interactions that can reveal the ways in which interactants signal to each other that they are shifting their footing and adjusting their alignment to utterances as they are produced. The frames employed throughout an interaction can therefore be understood as negotiated by the participants and indicated by their uptake of various participant roles. Shifts from one frame to another are achieved interactively and participants demonstrate their awareness of such shifts through the use of contextualisation cues. Thus, an analysis of the data which maps the invocation of participation frameworks by speakers to shifts in the frames of the interaction does not impose a set of rules on the discourse in a top-down manner, but rather reveals how the participants themselves draw upon the conversational resources available to them to respond to frame shifts and related phenomena. In this way the 'rules' of the interaction are (re)produced through the participants' actions and oriented to demonstrably in their exchanges.

This final point has been a central issue in the development of Conversation Analysis and it will be further discussed in the following section.

2.1.4   Conversation Analysis

A research pathway such as described above in section 2.1.1, which leads in an upward and outward spiral, may appear to be inconsistent with the recognised goals of Conversation Analysis (CA), used here as part of the micro-level analysis. CA is generally regarded as focusing on the mechanics of how people achieve successful interactions and not the social relationships and structures which may be (re)produced through that interaction. However, if we examine the roots of CA, and in particular the role played by ethnomethodology (Garfinkel 1967), we will see how the use of CA may provide an appropriate response to the key concerns of the research framework identified at the start of this section. For instance, Garfinkel demonstrates that participants achieve understandings of their circumstances through interaction and in doing so produce a sense of order. Thus a central concern for ethnomethodology is 'a member's knowledge of his [sic] ordinary affairs, of his [sic] own organised enterprises, where that knowledge is treated by us as part of the same setting that it also makes orderable' (Garfinkel 1974: 17). Knowledge about social conduct and circumstances is therefore produced and reproduced through participants' actions (Schiffrin 1994: 233).

CA has in common with ethnomethodology this understanding of participants' production and reproduction of the ordering of social action through their interaction. Importantly, CA rejects the quantitative techniques common to contemporary sociological analysis and 'the arbitrary imposition on the data of supposedly objective categorisations' (Levinson 1983: 295). This aspect of CA proves crucial to the types of data that CA proponents gather and the method they use to analyse them. Indeed, the coining of the term 'Conversation Analysis' reflects the choice by sociologists, primarily Harvey Sacks, of naturally occurring conversations as the most appropriate type of data for analysis. In conversation, participants can be found to produce a sense of social order by drawing upon the rules specific to talk in interaction. Through his lectures (Sacks 1992b) and published work (for example Sacks et al. 1974; Sacks 1972, 1974, 1987; and Schegloff and Sacks 1973) Sacks developed an approach to the analysis of naturally occurring conversational data which enabled him to observe phenomena as they were recognised and oriented to by the participants themselves. His approach was taken up and expanded by several like-minded sociologists, notably Gail Jefferson and Emanuel Schegloff, and a great deal of research since has identified many such features of conversation both in ordinary conversation (for example Bilmes 1988; Button and Casey 1984; J. Davidson 1984; Drew 1984; Drew and Holt 1988; Goldsmith 1999; Heritage 1984; Heritage and Watson 1979; Jefferson 1978, 1979, 1980, 1984a, 1984b, 1985, 1987, 1988, 1989; Jefferson and Lee 1980, 1992; Michaud and Warner 1997; Polanyi 1985; Pomerantz 1980, 1984a, 1984b, 1984c, 1986; Pritchard 1993; Schegloff and Sacks 1973) and in a range of institutional settings: for example in medical settings (Frankel 1990; Tracy 1997); in legal settings (Atkinson 1984, 1992; Atkinson and Drew 1979; Clayman 1992; Drew 1985; Greatbatch and Dingwall 1998; Pomerantz 1987; Sacks 1972); in news interview settings (Greatbatch 1988; Heritage 1985; Pritchard 1994); and in general institutional settings (Drew and Heritage 1992; Drew and Sorjonen 1997).

Fundamental to the CA approach is an understanding that each utterance produced by a speaker can be understood as comprehensible by reference to prior utterances, and specifically the immediately preceding turn. Hence the importance to CA of the 'turn-taking system' (Sacks et al. 1974) which governs the order in which speakers take the floor to speak through a set of rules, oriented to by speakers as they construct their interactions. The system described by Sacks et al. (1974) accounts for the orderly transition from one speaker to another and provides a set of rules which can be drawn upon by conversationalists in any circumstances to decide the crucial question of who should speak next. The rules, reproduced below, provide for the 'projectability' of a 'transition relevance place' (TRP) by participants in an interaction.

> Rule 1 – applies initially at the first TRP of any turn
>
> (a)   If C [current speaker] selects N [next speaker] in current turn, then C must stop speaking, and N must speak next, transition occurring at the first TRP after N-selection
> (b)   If C does not select N, then any (other) party may self-select, first speaker gaining rights to the next turn
> (c)   If C has not selected N, and no other party self-selects under option (b), then C may (but need not) continue (i.e. claim rights to a further turn-constructional unit)
>
> Rule 2 – applies at all subsequent TRPs
>   When Rule 1(c) has been applied by C, then at the next TRP Rules (a)–(c) apply, and recursively at the next TRP, until speaker change is effected. (Levinson 1983: 298)

That is, Sacks et al. (1974) found that a place in the current speaker's utterance where it will be appropriate for the floor to pass to a new speaker, is predictable as the utterance is underway. Speakers, being able to anticipate such a place, can prepare to produce an utterance so that its commencement will coincide with this place, or TRP. Furthermore the rules stipulate that the same speaker may elect to produce a further utterance, having arrived at a TRP or may pass the floor to another speaker, either by permitting them to select themselves as the next speaker, or by overtly selecting them as the next speaker (by naming them, for instance). Finally, the rules control overlapping speech by stating that when another speaker has selected to speak, according to a hierarchy of permissible next speakers also covered by the rules, current speakers must stop speaking.

As CA is interested in phenomena which are oriented to by the participants in a conversation, utterance types such as questions and answers, which may previously have been described as kinds of speech act (Austin 1962) or in terms of their grammatical function (direct or indirect), are considered instead in terms of how they relate to the turn-taking system and how the organisation of turns makes a particular type of turn relevant at a particular moment in a conversation. Therefore, if a speaker produces a question, the next turn produced will be considered to be made relevant by that question. If the next turn is not an answer to that question, or some other permissible turn type, such as the first part of an insert sequence (see below), the answer to the question will be noticeable in its absence and some explanation will be expected by other participants in the conversation. Turn types which 'require' particular turn types to follow them in this fashion are therefore identifiable both by the participants in an interaction and by an observer. Such turn sequences are called 'adjacency pairs' (Schegloff and Sacks 1973) in reference to the requirement for the second pair part (e.g. an answer) to be supplied immediately following, or adjacent to, the first pair part.

Adjacency pairs are perhaps the fundamental unit around which conversations are organised (Levinson 1983) and given the nature of the data analysed in the present study, certain adjacency pairs such as question–answer pairs and accusation–response pairs are critical components in the interaction. It is important, therefore, that we have an awareness of the organisation of such adjacency pairs and in particular that we firmly establish an understanding of the notion of 'preference', which is central to the analysis of certain adjacency pairs.

I wish to stress that I am referring to preference as a technical CA notion, not in its everyday usage. I am drawing on Jack Bilmes's 1988 paper on the subject where he makes a clear distinction between these two conceptualisations. He reminds us that the purpose of CA, as already mentioned, is to provide a set of conversational rules which are 'conventional reference points that actors orient to and that give behaviour its particular intelligibility' and 'by which actors understand one another's behaviour' (Bilmes 1988: 162). In this context, Bilmes articulates the rule of preference by reference to a principle of ordering, which he identifies in Sacks's lectures on this topic (see Sacks 1987 and 1992b). Sacks (1987) focuses on the related phenomena of agreement and contiguity in question–answer adjacency pairs. He finds that questioners design their turns to exhibit a preference for some answers and that answerers design their turns to agree with this preference. Furthermore, questioners and answerers design their turns so that they maintain a 'contiguity' of the question and answer across the turn sequence. Sacks finds that the interaction between the preference for agreement and contiguity has an observable effect on the production of 'disagreeing' turns, which he articulates in his inimitable fashion:

> if an agreeing answer occurs, it pretty damn well occurs contiguously, whereas if a disagreeing answer occurs, it may well be pushed rather deep into the turn that it occupies. (Sacks 1987: 58)

Bilmes's definition of the technical notion of preference can be summarised thus: following utterances which comprise first pair parts of adjacency pairs (e.g. invitations, requests, accusations etc.) certain responses, or second pair parts, are 'preferred' over others by virtue of the fact that if there is no response, those 'preferred' responses will be noticeably absent. For example, following an invitation it is possible for the recipient to accept or refuse the invitation. However, if the recipient remains silent, it is the acceptance that is lacking, and a refusal is assumed to have been offered in its absence. In other words, preference is used by speakers to make inferences about responses that they receive. In his discussion of preference, Sacks (1987) elaborates on this phenomenon, demonstrating that speakers may use the inferences formed by reference to the rules of preference organisation to redesign their question turn so that it displays a preference towards an initially disagreeing answer turn. That is, upon perceiving that a disagreeing answer may be forthcoming, a questioner may reproduce the question displaying a preference for the anticipated answer. The phenomenon is demonstrated by Sacks using the following extract from a transcribed conversation:

Extract 2-1 from (Sacks 1987: 64)

A: They have a good cook there?

 ((pause))

 Nothing special?

B: No, everybody takes their turns.

This extract is described as showing that A initially designs the question to display a preference for a 'yes' response, but upon receiving a silence, A redesigns the questions to display the reverse preference. B is then able to supply an agreeing response and A can be seen as having oriented to obtaining agreement.

We see here an example of the kind of preference organisation that Bilmes (1988) described. The silence following A's initial question is assumed by A to indicate that B was unable to supply a preferred response. Of particular relevance to the present research is Bilmes's discussion of preference in the case of accusation first pair parts. Atkinson and Drew (1979) assert that following accusations, denials are preferred. Thus, accusations are designed by the speaker to display a preference for denial. Bilmes agrees with this assessment and notes that 'if one fails to deny an accusation, a denial is noticeably absent and is a cause for inference, the most common inference being that the accusation is true' (Bilmes 1988: p. 167).

Bilmes goes on to demonstrate that in fact this preference for denials following accusations is part of a broader type of preference – 'when A attributes some action or thought or attitude to B, in B's presence, there is a preference for B to contradict A *interruptively or immediately following* the turn in which the attribution was produced... When such attribution occurs without contradiction, a contradiction is relevantly absent' (Bilmes 1988: 167, my emphasis). Bilmes's observation that a contradiction is required as a first priority by the recipient of an attribution implies that contradictions provided by the recipient that are delayed by a pause or another utterance may still be considered 'absent' in some sense. Delayed contradictions, in other words, may not count as contradictions, or may not be as convincing or acceptable as those provided 'interruptively or immediately following' the attribution. Bilmes is able to demonstrate the strength of this argument using a number of examples of both contradicted and non-contradicted attributions (Bilmes 1988: 167).

This rule for preference in attributions and accusations has some clear implications for police interviewing, namely that interviewers are likely to interpret hesitations or delays following one of these first pair parts as an indication that the suspect agrees with them. If the suspect does not agree with the attribution or accusation, subsequent police turns may be based on a false assumption of guilt, especially given that the suspect has the right to remain silent.

In addition to the analysis of attribution-type adjacency pairs, the analysis of participants' discursive practices, which supports the subsequent identification of myths underlying the discourse, draws upon the CA understanding of topic. In particular, the analysis presented in Chapter 5 is concerned with topic initiation by participants and topic management and maintenance. The centrality of topic to discourse analysis is highlighted by Heritage and Watson (1979) who claim that 'all conversations can be seen as organised around topics' (p. 149). The contributions made to topic analysis by CA researchers is primarily concerned with the way that topics are introduced by speakers and taken up by recipients (e.g. Button and Casey 1984; Frankel 1990; Jefferson 1984a). For instance, Frankel (1990) is concerned with the different ways in which doctors and patients initiate topics during consultations, while Jefferson (1984a) describes the sequential positioning of talk about 'troubles' and the approaches taken to topic shift following such talk. Button and Casey (1984) investigate the use of turns labelled 'topic initial elicitors' as devices to generate a new topic at sequentially relevant points in a conversation, such as following a greeting exchange or prior to a closing sequence.

A further phenomenon which has been the focus of a variety of CA studies is the use of 'formulations' by speakers as a way of providing 'a gloss on "what we are talking about (or have talked about) thus far"' (Heritage and Watson 1979: 149). By formulating the gist of prior talk, and obtaining agreement to formulations, participants are able to check their mutual understanding of the talk's intended meaning. This is critical to the management of topics since the use of formulations becomes 'a built-in part of rendering conversations preservable and reportable, and it is in this sense that formulations may be said to "fix" what will have turned out to be a (the) topic' (Heritage and Watson 1979: 149). Formulations are described by Heritage (1985) as 'relatively rare in conversation' (p. 100), but common in institutional talk, especially as a tool of interviewers who use them to accomplish a complex range of moves. Such moves include maintaining the interviewee's talk as the continuing topic of the interview and selectively confirming or elaborating elements of the interviewee's talk. Formulations are also claimed to be 'neutral' because they avoid assessments; however, it is notable that Fairclough (1989) finds that the selective formulation of prior talk can be used as a means of controlling the other participant (p. 136). Furthermore, the choice of words used to re-present the interviewee's prior talk will itself display some preference for aspects of that talk. This issue will be taken up in greater depth as part of the critical analysis of the findings in Chapter 7. Broadly speaking, the analysis will consider utterances in terms of their situational context and how the participants in the discourse orient to their understandings of the interaction.

The CA emphasis on the 'temporal organisation' of turns provides an appropriate framework within which to explore the implications of the mythology which concern the difference in communicative goals for the different roles represented in the interview (i.e. police officer and suspect). That is, the focus on how meaningfulness is built turn by turn will serve to highlight the differences between the participants' orientation to the discourse as each participant's utterances will be made in context of, as well as in contrast to, the other's.

Finally the understanding of 'rules' in CA provides an important distinction between what the analyst may impose over the discourse as an explanation for the interaction, and what the participants themselves invoke as a way of 'framing' the interaction. The latter conceptualisation is one that allows the participants to be aware of conversational rules and both to draw on such rules to help make sense of their interaction and incorporate the rules into the interaction. This is consistent with the notion of 'rules' for social activities proposed by Giddens (see above). When considered in relation to the analysis of the mythology of police interviewing proposed here, this approach permits us to discover the rules which govern the mythology by examining how such rules are created or invoked by participants in the discourse, as well as how they become part of the discourse. Since we are interested in the manner in which the mythology is both created and drawn upon by participants, this is a far more fruitful approach to the analysis than one where some set of rules said to govern the mythology is imposed during the analysis to explain the conduct of participants in theoretical terms but is not seen as available to the participants at the time of the interview.

2.2   Language and the law

We have observed that the legislative requirements relating to the interviewing of suspects by police officers have specific implications for the discursive construction of the interview. In this section, we will discuss the ways in which various researchers have addressed issues arising from the distinctive character of language in a legal setting. The body of research in this field can be roughly divided into two areas: that which results from the provision of evidence in a court case relating to questionable linguistic behaviour in a police interview; and that which investigates language use in legal settings as a theoretical exercise.

The presentation of expert linguistic opinions as evidence in Australian courts, and related research (e.g. Cooke 1996; Eades 1994; Gibbons 1996; Jensen 1995; Walsh 1994) has generally been concerned with describing exceptional cases of miscommunication in police interviews. However, these studies make certain assumptions about the features of a police interview in unexceptional circumstances and it is the nature of these assumptions that is relevant to the present research. It is important to note that this category of research, known as Forensic Linguistics, includes the application of linguistic analysis to address any type of legal dispute about language and language use, not just disputes arising from police interviewing techniques. Furthermore, while such a field of applied linguistics is identifiably 'forensic',[5] a broader definition of Forensic Linguistics includes any research which has as its focus the intersection of language use and the legal system, including the linguistic analysis of police interview data. However, it is useful to consider how this broader understanding of Forensic Linguistics has emerged from a narrower scope of research which mainly concerned itself with contributions by linguists to legal cases. Therefore this brief overview will begin with a description of the research carried out by those linguists employed as expert witnesses in court before moving on to discuss more general research into 'language and the law' in section 2.2.2. Both areas of study will then be considered in the context of similar, non-linguistic research, such as criminological and sociological investigations of police interviewing.

2.2.1   Forensic Linguistics

It is a feature of forensic linguistic research involving police interviews that it results from professional involvement of the researcher in specific legal cases, where the linguistic analysis of the interview data is used to construct a case, usually on behalf of the interviewee. Thus the data analysed are necessarily problematic to begin with – some exceptional circumstances must exist for the case to proceed otherwise there would be no legal challenge to be addressed by linguistic analysis. By logical extension, this means that in each of these cases, as mentioned earlier, there is also an assumption of 'standard procedure' – some ideal police interview where the interviewer and the interviewee understand each other with minimal communicative impediment and cultural and/or language differences are not a determining factor in the probity of the interview procedure. One of the purposes of this research project is to address such assumptions about 'standard procedure' by providing an analysis of data which result from interviews between native English-speaking participants where no breach of police procedure is known to have taken place.

Several published reviews of research in the field of Forensic Linguistics are available that provide an introduction to the issues faced by linguists working as expert witnesses, including Danet (1980), Eades (1990) and Levi (1994). Levi (1994) explains how various areas of research, such as phonetics, phonology and dialectology, morphology, syntax, semantics and pragmatics have been used to provide evidence in court, exemplifying each with case studies.

The description of linguists as expert witnesses provided by Levi (1994) includes a comprehensive introduction to the type of research that falls into the narrower category of Forensic Linguistics mentioned earlier. This includes such applications as identifying trademark and patent infringements (for example Genine and Shuy 1990), attributing authorship of texts (for example Woolls and Coulthard 1998 and Coulthard 2000), and analysing police interviews where there is some dispute over the suspect's ability to participate properly, usually because the interview is not conducted in the suspect's native language (see below). Sociolinguistic analysis has been used in numerous cases concerning intercultural communication, perhaps most notably by Labov (1982) in his landmark testimony regarding the recognition of Black English Vernacular in education.

Other forensic linguistic studies have analysed the validity of the transcription methods used by police both before and after the introduction of audiotaped interviews to record the statement of evidence. For example, Coulthard (1997) describes a case in which a handwritten police record of interview could be shown to have had lines added at a later stage.

Voice identification is sometimes identified separately as 'forensic phonetics' and involves phonetic or spectographic types of analysis to attribute speech to a given person. The reliability of such evidence has long been a point of controversy (see Hall and Collins 1980) and, although some researchers such as Milroy (1984) have introduced sociolinguistic analyses to assist with the task, the results are a differentiation of voices rather than a positive identification of the speaker.

In Australia, forensic linguistic studies have identified certain troublesome aspects of the police interview such as the use of a question and answer format (as opposed to a narrative format) in interviews with Aboriginal interviewees (Cooke 1996; Eades 1982, 1994), distortions in interviews with suspects of a non-English-speaking background (Gibbons 1996), and discrepancies between a tape-recorded interview with a non-native speaker of English and the police written record of the same interview (Jensen 1990).

In addition to those cases cited, there have been many other cases involving linguists as expert witnesses, either as part of an investigation of police interviewing techniques or in some other aspect of the case (see for instance the large number of case studies documented in *Forensic Linguistics: The International Journal of Speech, Language and the Law*). The brief overview presented above is intended to illustrate the types of applications for linguistics in court cases, and to make a distinction between those cases where the police evidentiary interview was under investigation (such as Cooke 1996; Coulthard 1997; Eades 1982; Gibbons 1996; Jensen 1990) and those where linguistic evidence was used for some other purpose (such as Coulthard 2000; Genine and Shuy 1990; Labov 1982).

However, while those studies involving police interview data may provide a precedent for the present study, they differ from it in one crucial factor: in each of the Australian cases, and in many of the other cases cited above, the interviewee and the police officer have different cultural and/or language backgrounds. Furthermore, these studies make various comparisons between what they see as divergent interview features, found in their data, and some set of features which comprise a 'normal' or 'standard' interview and assert that it is the application of procedures based on the features of the 'standard' interview which causes significant problems in interviews where the interviewee does not share the culture and/or language of the interviewer. For example, Eades (1982) finds that information seeking, such as might be normally undertaken by an Australian police interviewer, may cause communicative difficulties when applied to suspects from south-east Queensland Aboriginal society because of differences between standard Australian English information seeking and native south-east Queensland Aboriginal information seeking procedures. Findings from this and other studies involving non-English speaking suspects, suggest that it is unlikely that such communicative difficulties would be experienced by suspects who are native speakers of standard Australian English, since they would share information seeking procedures with the police interviewers. I suggest that such assumptions may be problematised by an analysis of miscommunication in interviews with native Australian English speakers and may therefore require some reconsideration. This is not to dismiss the findings of prior Forensic Linguistic research in the area. On the contrary, the present study emphasises the need to address issues concerning miscommunication in police interviews whatever the context.

2.2.2   Police power in institutional discourse

As mentioned earlier, a broader definition of 'Forensic Linguistics' includes linguistic studies that have been carried out independently of the legal system, creating a body of research that supports the professional Forensic Linguistic research mentioned above. This broader area of research provides background analyses of court language, police interviews, police statements and related aspects of the legal process, such as lawyer–client interviews, and serves to inform the more results-driven research carried out for particular cases. Furthermore, this research expands the boundaries of linguistic theory by applying analytic tools and theories to describe the peculiarities of legal discourse, in particular, courtroom discourse. This enrichment flows both ways, with specialists in particular analytic fields contributing work which is invaluable to forensic linguists, for instance Atkinson and Drew (1979), Atkinson (1992), Auburn, Drake and Willig (1995) and Thomas (1989).

Atkinson (1992), for example, uses Conversation Analysis to show how adjudicators in informal court settings design their feedback to maintain a neutral position relative to the utterances of other participants. Thomas (1989) examines the use of discoursal indicators by dominant participants in discourse to guide and manipulate conversations and includes police institutional discourse in her analysis, while Auburn et al. (1995) discuss the way in which a narrative is constructed in police interviews with police participants using language to influence the interviewee towards a 'preferred version' of the allegedly criminal events (that is, a version preferred by the police force).

Although a great deal of linguistic research has focused on courtroom language, such as Atkinson (1992), Atkinson and Drew (1979), Cotterill (1998, 2001), Drew (1985), Fisher and Todd (1986c), there are fewer studies available of police interview interactions, no doubt due to the relative difficulty of obtaining interview data. As the present research is concerned with issues of power in a police institutional setting, many of the findings related to courtroom language are not directly relevant. However, insofar as police interviews are institutional interactions that take place in a legal setting, some of the issues of power and discourse raised by courtroom-based research can be usefully drawn upon in the analysis of the data (see section 2.1.4).

Of particular relevance to the present research are studies that address those concerns about police behaviour which are indirectly expressed in the legislation and police regulations, as discussed earlier. For instance, a common theme in studies of police interview behaviour is the inclination of police officers to impose their own interpretation of events on the discourse while minimising the influence of the suspect's narrative (Linell and Jonsson 1991 and Auburn et al. 1995, see below). Concerns over police behaviour that may unduly influence the content of the evidence are expressed in several places by police regulations, such as the Victoria Police Standing Orders, which emphasise the importance of giving a suspect 'every opportunity to speak about events connected with the offence'(Section 8.6) and of being 'scrupulously fair in interviewing any person'. The following discussion draws together those studies that address concerns over the probity of the police interview procedure and police behaviour more generally.

Police regulations that stipulate 'the clearing of the innocent as well as establishing the guilt of the offender' (Victoria Police Standing Orders, Section 8.8) are clearly concerned with the presumption of guilt by police interviewers. This issue is the focus of research undertaken by

Auburn et al. (1995), mentioned above. Crucial to this study of accusations of violence in police evidentiary interviews is the finding that the police officer's primary objective in an interview is to gain a confession from the suspect 'and implicit in this purpose is the presumption that the suspect is guilty of the crime' (Auburn et al. 1995: 355). Their study examines the negotiation of the narrative by the participants and the way in which one particular version of events is favoured by the police participants, known as the 'preferred version', a label that reflects 'its status as a version which facilitates the functioning of the criminal justice system in disposing of suspects' (p. 357). That is, it is the version through which legal considerations are addressed (e.g. establishing that the crime occurred and there was criminal intention on behalf of the suspect) and the guilt of the suspect is constructed as an underlying assumption (p. 356). Auburn et al. (1995) find that in the preferred version, the suspect is attributed responsibility for acts of violence through the use of footing (Goffman 1981), by constructing the event as distinctively and noticeably violent, and by constructing the suspect as a person with a history of perpetrating violence. Importantly, the researchers note that the articulation of the preferred version through the course of the interview is a project that is achieved jointly insofar as 'displaying and agreeing on the preferred version requires a mutual adherence to a background assumption of intersubjectivity' (Auburn et al. 1995: 357). Thus the preferred version must be negotiated by the participants to maintain the 'basic assumption of social life' that any viewpoint is substitutable for any other (Billig 1991: 170). Viewpoints that are non-substitutable must be accounted for in some way, which is part of the process of establishing the precedence of the preferred version. This approach will contribute to the analysis in section 4.4 of the negotiation of competing version of events by participants in the police interviews.

This work of Auburn et al. (1995) can to an extent be seen as building on the findings of Linell and Jonsson (1991) who provide a comparison between police interviews and their accompanying written police reports based on a discourse analysis framework described as 'perspective setting'. The cases described all concern minor crimes committed by elderly citizens and the study finds that two perspectives in the tape-recorded interview are reduced to a single, police perspective in the written report. The primary difference between the interview and the report is the reduction or omission in the latter of the suspect's personal history and events leading up to the crime, aspects which serve to justify the criminal activity from the suspect's point of view.

The findings of Auburn et al. (1995) and Linell and Jonsson (1991) illustrate a point made by Settle (1990) which examines the use and abuse of power by police officers in Victoria in the 1970s and 1980s. Settle claims that police power can be abused by officers in pursuit of two distinct ends: personal and organisational (p. 13). It is the latter form of abuse that he claims is the most common amongst members of the Victorian police force and he provides many case studies and examples that support this claim.

In describing the abuse of power towards organisational ends, Settle notes that in the Victoria police force the pursuit of convictions is not the 'be all and end all' of police ambition, but that '[m]any abuses of police power in pursuit of organisational ends are...dictated by an assumption, accurate or inaccurate, that a suspect is guilty and by a fear of losing ratification of that by the criminal courts' (p. 19, cf. Auburn et al. 1995). In relation to interviewing practices, Settle claims that fabrication of evidence is relatively rare, but 'strengthening of evidence...is alarmingly common' (p. 19).

The examples given in Linell and Jonsson (1991) could perhaps be described in terms of 'abuse of power towards organisational ends' by such a 'strengthening of evidence'. Whilst the police officer has little, if anything, to gain personally by rewriting the suspect's story with an emphasis on the criminal activity, there are clear organisational benefits in having the court ratify the officer's assumption's regarding the guilt of the suspect. A police statement that concentrates on the criminal activity allegedly perpetrated by the suspect and does not indicate the circumstances surrounding the crime nor the suspect's reasons for (allegedly) committing the crime, is more likely to favour the prosecution when presented as evidence in court. Thus the police are seen to have been correct and justified in any actions they may have taken and any resources they may have expended to arrest the suspect and charge them with the crime.

Further to this discussion regarding the abuse of power in pursuit of organisational ends, Settle makes another important point about the conflict between law and order. To 'maintain law and order' has become so common as a way of describing the primary aim of a police force that it is easy to overlook the inherent paradox contained within that phrase. As Settle reminds us, to maintain order in society, we have handed over our right to coerce citizens (Weber's power; see Gerth and Wright Mills 1970: 180) to the police force. However, this 'right' is given to the police force in the form of Weber's authority: power exerted within a strict framework of law (Gerth and Wright

Mills 1970: 294). That is, without law, perfect order might be maintained, given that police officers would have limitless powers to exert their authority (Settle 1990: 4). That we consider this an unacceptable solution to the problem of maintaining order is implicit in a citizen's right to be considered innocent of a crime until proven guilty – a right which commits police officers to a due process of gathering evidence, including conducting interviews, themselves subject to certain regulations.

When seen in these terms, the motivation for abuse of power towards organisational ends becomes clear. Pressure is exerted on members of the police force to maintain order in our society. Yet the same society must place heavy restrictions on the manner in which order might be maintained or risk degrading the quality of life of its citizens. This conflict between the duty of the police officer to maintain order and the necessity to do so within a restrictive framework of laws occasionally produces questionable procedures such as those highlighted in some of the studies mentioned above (e.g. Auburn et al. 1995; Cooke 1996; Eades 1994; Gibbons 1990, 1996; Linell and Jonsson 1991; Walsh 1994). Where these procedures have been analysed and a clear abuse of power has been identified, then steps may be taken to redress the balance. For example, the distortion of evidence discussed in Linell and Jonsson's (1991) study (which is similar to distortions found in many other case studies cited above) might be avoided by using the original audio recording of the interview as evidence, rather than a written statement based on a transcription of the recording.

The above discussion demonstrates that the application of sociological research findings usefully informs our interpretation of linguistic analyses. We will continue to explore the benefits of a cross-disciplinary approach to the assessment of key concerns in language and the law in the following section, which assembles the evidence for a mythology in police interviewing behaviour.

2.2.3   Myths in institutional discourse

The notion of a mythology surrounding the discourse of a particular institution is discussed by Wodak (1996a) in her analysis of interactions in the outpatient ward of a hospital. Myths are identified by Wodak as beliefs about discourse held by participants to an interaction and underlying various types of institutional discourse. Such myths are said to distort interactions producing 'disorders of discourse' (Wodak 1996a). I will briefly describe the approach which Wodak takes to the analysis and the theoretical issues she identifies before exemplifying this notion of myths distorting the discourse of institutions through a description of one of Wodak's own case studies.

Wodak works within a framework of critical discourse analysis using a model which she calls 'discourse sociolinguistics' – 'a sociolinguistics which not only is explicitly dedicated to the study of the text in context, but also accords both [text and context] equal importance' (p. 3). She examines instances of miscommunication in institutional settings that occur both between members of the institution and lay participants, and between different members themselves. Wodak finds that in the outpatient ward, the complexity of the organisation together with constantly changing, unpredictable circumstances lead to certain contradictions arising, such as role conflicts among staff members. As a response to these contradictions, myths are created, presumably as a framework within which the staff believe they can best deal with the difficult circumstances of their situation.

Through her study of problematic institutional interactions, Wodak identifies myths as beliefs held by participants about the discourse practices of a given institution. She finds that myths, produced and reproduced through routine interactions between lay and professional participants, may produce social or communicative effects that are counterproductive to the aims of the institution. In other words, partici-pants may allow erroneous beliefs about an interaction to influence their judgement on how that interaction ought to be conducted. In doing so they risk producing a conflict between the intended outcome of the exchange and the unintended consequences of their actions. The potential for counterproductive behaviour in police interviewing will be explored in the next section through a review of research into police institutional discursive behaviour.

2.2.4 Institutional discourse and interviews

Three key features of institutional talk are proposed by Drew and Heritage (1992), which can be summarised as follows:

(1) At least one of the participants in an institutional interaction displays an orientation towards some core goal conventionally associated with the institution.
(2) There may be constraints on what one or all participants will treat as an allowable contribution to the interaction.
(3) Institutional talk may be produced within context-specific inferential frameworks.

(adapted from Drew and Heritage 1992: 22)

In keeping with the CA emphasis on identifying structures as they are oriented to by the participants in an interaction, Drew and Heritage (1992) and Drew and Sorjonen (1997) reject a definition of institutional discourse that relies on the setting of the interaction (Drew and Heritage 1992: 4). For instance, in Sarangi and Roberts (1999) and Fisher and Todd (1986c), the interactions being investigated are grouped according to their setting (e.g. medical, legal, educational or managerial) and these settings are considered central to the institutionality of the talk. Furthermore, whereas the pursuit of organisational goals is described by Drew and Heritage (1992) in terms of the orientations of the speakers (see above), Fisher and Todd (1986b) see the institution as providing a structure for the pursuit of goals. That is, rather than focusing on how speakers construct institutionality through talk that is oriented to the achievement of organisational goals, Fisher and Todd (1986b) find that 'the structure of the institution is organised so as to lend those in power the authority to pursue defined goals' (p. ix). Drew and Heritage (1992) and Drew and Sorjonen (1997) claim that talk can be institutional whenever the 'participants' institutional or professional identities are somehow made relevant to the work activities in which they are engaged' (Drew and Heritage 1992: 5). Thus, a police interview that takes place in a private home is still identifiable as belonging to the same category of institutional discourse as one that takes place in a police station as long as the interaction makes relevant the participants' identities as police officers and suspects/witnesses. Conversely, an interaction that takes place in a police station, even in an interviewing room, need not be classified as 'police institutional discourse' if the participants are engaged in an activity that does not make relevant their institutional identities, such as a casual chat (Drew and Sorjonen 1997: 92). Certainly there can be little question that a police interview displays all three of the features proposed by Drew and Heritage (1992), though the exact nature of the 'core goals', the 'constraints' and the 'inferential frameworks' will be examined through the analysis of police interview data in Chapters 4 and 5.

The police interview shares with other institutional interviews a basic turn-taking system consisting of sequences of questions and answers (Greatbatch 1988; Heritage 1985; Levinson 1992; Perakyla and Silverman 1991) as well as a turn pre-allocation system whereby questions are allocated to interviewers and responses to interviewees (Perakyla and Silverman 1991; Frankel 1990). More specifically, police interviews appear to share some key features with news interviews (Heritage 1985; Greatbatch 1988). For instance, in the case of both police interviews and news interviews, the talk is knowingly produced for a third party. In the case of a police interview, this third party may be one of a variety of members of the judicial system, whereas in the case of a news interview, the third party is an audience in the literal sense. As a consequence of this arrangement, news interviewers are found to exhibit particular behaviour that marks their talk as 'produced to be overheard'. Heritage (1985) and Greatbatch (1988) find that a prominent feature of news interviews is the withholding of a range of responses that would normally be expected of questioners in ordinary conversation. Following the supply of answers to their questions, news interviewers do not customarily produce 'third turn objects' such as news receipts (e.g. *oh*), newsmarks (e.g. *did she*) or assessments (e.g. *good*) (Heritage 1985: 98). The news interviewer behaviour is said to indicate that the interviewers are deliberately avoiding an alignment with a role of 'news-recipient', because news interviewers are elicitors of information that is already known to them but that is 'news' for the audience.

In this respect, police interviews appear to be quite similar to news interviews, as such third turn objects are rare in the data analysed here. Police interviews are classified by Shuy (1997) as 'an elicitation interview, not an information interview' (p. 178), emphasising that the interviewer in such an interaction is not asking questions for the purpose of self-illumination, but in order to 'elicit answers that they believe, know, or suspect to be true' (178–9). The use of third turn objects that align the questioner with a role of 'news recipient' would therefore be inappropriate in a police interview, just as it is in a news interview. However, police interviewers do not behave identically to news interviewers. Whereas Greatbatch (1988) and Heritage (1985) find that news interviewers routinely avoid turns which act as continuers, such as *mm hm*, this is not found to be the case in police interviews. In fact, the police interviewers featured in the present data are found to use overt continuers, such as *go on* and *continue on* as well as *mm hm* during long turns of narrative or reporting by the suspect. This difference may be an indication of the different interactional roles played by police interviewers and news interviewers.

A further finding that relates news interviews to police interviews is the requirement of interviewer neutrality. Greatbatch (1988), Heritage (1985) and Atkinson (1992) find that questioners in news interviews and courtroom proceedings maintain a neutral footing by avoiding responses that constitute assessments of interviewee turns. We would expect that the onus on a police officer to undertake 'the clearing of the innocent as well as establishing the guilt of the offender' (Victoria

Police Standing Orders, Section 8.8) would require a neutral footing to be maintained during questioning, although it is difficult to reconcile this expectation with the assertion that police interviews are designed to elicit 'known' information (Shuy 1997: 178–9). This apparent conflict of requirements will be explored further in Chapter 5, together with several other issues raised here, such as the nature of 'inferential frameworks' and speaker roles.

Participation frameworks (Goffman 1974, 1981) and Conversation Analysis (e.g. Sacks et al. 1974; Schegloff and Sacks 1973) are approaches to real language data that provide powerful resources when analysing institutional discourse. Although these analytic frameworks will be considered in detail in sections 2.1.3 and 2.1.4, it is salient to this discussion to note that the particular features of interviews, which are an extremely common form of institutional discourse, can be described by reference to both frames and participant alignments, and turn taking mechanisms. For example, Perakyla and Silverman (1991) note that the concept of 'pre-allocation', applied first to turns (Sacks et al. 1974) and later to turn-types (Atkinson and Drew 1979), is useful in describing the way that institutional interactions are organised so that specific types of turn can be pre-allotted to specific types of participant. Thus, in an interview, questions are pre-allocated to interviewers and responses are pre-allocated to interviewees. The recurrent alignment of participants to this turn-exchange system is described as a 'communication format' and different communication formats imply different alignments by participants to turn-type pre-allocations (Perakyla and Silverman 1991: 629). Within a speech exchange system, such as an interview, participants can be shown to display their alignment to the content of their utterances through an analysis of the participation frameworks (see section 2.1.3). Clayman (1992) finds that interviewers maintain a neutral alignment to utterances through shifts in footing and by distancing themselves from participant roles that imply responsibility for the content or phrasing of utterances, such as *principal* or *author* roles (Goffman 1981). Moreover, Roberts and Sarangi (1999) find that '[a]lthough, Goffman developed his concepts in everyday contexts, they apply superbly to institutional settings where deft footwork and face saving are the stuff of routine interactions' (p. 229).

The analysis of shifts in frames (Goffman 1974) provides a participant-based perspective on the negotiation and achievement of goals through the discourse. Frames can be described as schemas or structures that encode knowledge of the features of stereotyped situations or interactions together with knowledge of the roles played by participants. The notion of frames and knowledge schemas is drawn upon by Tannen (1993) in an investigation of the management of interactions between medical practitioners, child patients and their parents. The interactions are constructed using frame shifts that indicate sensitivity to different knowledge schemas of participants. Coupland, Robinson and Coupland (1994) also present a comprehensive analysis of the negotiation of frame changes in medical interviews and observe that frame transitions are achieved interactionally and negotiated within the context of an institutionally defined exchange. They find that shifts from a 'socio-relational' frame into a 'medical' frame are achieved through the use of a 'frame transitional utterance' (*how are you?*) that displays the speaker's alignment to their role as both a 'caring person' and a 'doctor'.

Clearly, the contributions to the study of 'institutionality' by CA have been significant, especially in the identification of specifically institutional interactional behaviour. However, this overview of literature concerning institutional discourse has also revealed that the concept of frames and participation frameworks can be usefully employed to describe the negotiation between different parts of an institutional encounter and this enables us to conceive of such an interaction as 'multifaceted'. This is an important consideration in the present study, which aims to provide a descriptive framework of the interviews and to differentiate the various phases of the interview on the basis of the discursive activities of the participants. Such analysis will be usefully informed by a notion of frames and participation frameworks as a feature of institutional talk. This will be discussed further in section 2.1.3. In the next section, we will consider the gathering and processing of police interview data for the present study.

2.3   Data gathering and processing

As discussed in the previous chapter, an examination of existing research into police institutional discourse raises a number of issues that have yet to be addressed. For instance, we have found that very little linguistic research has focused on issues of comprehension in police interviews between native English-speaking participants. Furthermore, much of the research in this area concerns itself with discrepancies between the spoken interview and the written record of the interview made by the police officers. Whilst there is no doubt that work on cross-cultural communication issues in interviews and the distortion of records is extremely valuable and has advanced the field of Forensic Linguistics greatly in the past ten or fifteen years, it seems timely to approach some of the more mundane data and provide general linguistic descriptions of behaviour in a police interview setting.

To this end, a methodology was selected to facilitate the collection of data that would best suit the purposes of this research. First and foremost I decided to collect actual tape recordings of interviews with suspects, as opposed to a written record of the interview. As I wished to analyse language use itself, rather than reported usage, I had also ruled out the possibility of conducting interviews or surveys with police officers and/or suspects about their behaviour in the interview.

Additionally, the selection criteria for the data were intended to minimise the likelihood of obtaining interviews which had as a feature some communicative conflict or dispute. This meant that, unlike many other researchers in this area, I would not be able to base my work on data that had been made available to me as part of a legal case where I was involved as a linguist. By definition, such interviews would involve language or communication issues (typically misunderstandings between native and non-native speakers of English). Thus the need to base my research on (apparently) linguistically unproblematic interviews further restricted access to data. Based on the assumption that the number of interviews available would be very limited, a method of analysis had to be selected which was capable of providing meaningful results from a small sample. It would not be appropriate to use a methodology that entailed a quantitative analysis across the range of interviews, for instance. Rather, analytic techniques were chosen which could reveal features of the language use which the participants themselves oriented to in their turn-by-turn construction of the interview. This way, the linguistic description resulting from the analysis was validated through the alignments and orientations displayed by the participants themselves rather than through quantitative analyses of predetermined features.

The police interviews collected for this study were conducted and recorded in accordance with police regulations and the requirements of the relevant criminal legislation at the time of their recording.[6] These requirements dictate the setting of the interview (i.e. in an interview room at a police station) and the tape recording of the entire interaction. The fact that a recording is made as part of the interview process, separate to any subsequent analysis which takes place, allows us access to data that are untouched by the researcher paradox, in the sense that the researcher cannot have any influence over the interaction. There remains, of course, the influence that the research requirements will have over the inclusion or exclusion of individual interviews for the study.

2.3.1   Interview selection

The selection of interviews took into consideration some practical concerns, such as ease of transcription and manageability of the data. The interviews selected therefore conformed to the following criteria:

- all the interviews were conducted at the same rural Victorian police station;
- the legal case to which each interview pertained was closed at the time of the interview's selection; and
- all the interviews pertain to minor crimes.

Notwithstanding the confidentiality ensured by the methodology chosen, the second criterion was stipulated to avoid any possible judicial ramifications of analysing material which comprises the evidence in a case still being contested in court.

The last of these criteria, that the interviews pertain to minor crimes, is intended to convey the sense that the crimes committed are reasonably common. I did not want to include interview data concerning a crime that is rare, unusually serious or involving some special circumstances which are unlikely to be replicated. Some valuable research has been done on 'celebrity' cases where a great deal of background information is available through the media (see Cotterill 1998, 2001 for an investigation of discursive aspects of the O. J. Simpson criminal trial); however, the results of the present research are intended to be as broadly applicable as possible. Interviews were therefore chosen that are more representative of the majority of police interviews. In total, thirteen interviews were used in the analysis, all recorded between 1993 and 2000.

All the names in the transcription extracts have been changed. This includes place-names, however, as frequent reference is made during the interviews to the town where the police station is located and a number of nearby areas, I decided to choose pseudonyms that reflected the relative size of each location. Although this means that the names sound rather artificial, it does enable the reader to recognise relationships between the locations. The name of the town where the recordings took place is therefore transcribed as Middletown. Middletown is not far from a major rural centre, which I have simply named Bigtown. The police station at Middletown services a number of outlying areas, and events in some interviews take place in one of the smaller towns near Middletown, which I have called Littlevillage. In several interviews, areas are mentioned which are in close proximity to Middletown, but which are considered distinct locales, and these have been named accordingly (e.g. Satellite River in Interview 2).

Of the thirteen interviews, all but one (Interview 8) are with male suspects and all but two (Interview 1 and Interview 12) are conducted by male primary interviewing officers. The suspects are charged with a variety of offences: Interviews 1, 2, 11 and 12 relate to assault charges; Interviews 3 and 7 relate to minor drug charges (possession and use of cannabis); Interview 9 is about possession of illegal firearms; Interview 10 concerns a charge of indecent exposure; and the remainder of the interviews relate to theft and/or burglary charges. Table 2.1 summarises these features and shows whether the interview was recorded at the police station (PS) or Criminal Investigation Branch (CIB).

2.3.2   Transcription methodology and extracts in the text

The transcription of talk and its attendant methodological theories are an important consideration in this study. The transcription conventions followed in this book are based on those found in Levinson (1983). As part of the analysis of these data employs the tools of Conversation Analysis, an appropriately narrow transcription is required, though as CA represents only one of several sources of analytic tools used, a set of transcription conventions has been selected which best serves the

Table 2.1   Main features of the interviews

Code	Location	Sex of participants				Charges
		Pio	Sio	Tio	SPT	
INT1	PS	F	M		M	Assault and criminal damage
INT2	PS	M	M		M	Assault
INT3	PS	M	M		M	Possession and use of cannabis
INT4	CIB	M	M		M	Burglary
INT5	PS	M	F		M	Car theft
INT6	CIB	M	M		M	Theft
INT7	PS	M	M		M	Possession and use of cannabis
INT8	PS	M	F	M	F	Burglary
INT9	CIB	M	M		M	Firearms
INT10	CIB	M	M		M	Indecent act
INT11	CIB	M	M		M	Assault
INT12	PS	F	M	M	M	Assault
INT13	CIB	M	M		M	Burglary

research aims of the book and does not necessarily conform to one particular system. A complete list of the transcription conventions and symbols used in the extracts can be found on page xi.

Except where pronunciation differs radically from standard Australian English as it sounds in normal rapid speech, standard English spelling has been used in the transcripts. The use of an 'eye-dialect' or an orthography that supposedly represents the sound of the speech accurately was generally avoided in favour of producing transcripts that are easy to read.

The extracts from the interview data (see Extract 2-2 below) are presented in a format which is not only consistent with the requirements of CA but which maintains the anonymity of the participants and facilitates the identification of the various parties by the reader. Each extract appears as three columns which contain (from left to right) the line number, the speaker identification and the transcribed utterances.

Extract 2-2 INT3

221. pio3   (0.8) all right (.) and <u>who</u> hung 'em up in the back shed↓
222. SPT3:   <u>I</u> did↓

Occasionally a column is added between the first and second columns for the inclusion of a right arrow (→) to indicate a particular line being discussed in the text.

Line numbers are consecutive but restarted for each interview, thus an extract cannot be identified by line number alone. Where extracts are not presented in full and in the table format, they will be identified by using the same information as the first two columns of the table, but in a compressed format separated by a forward slash and followed by a colon, then the extract, all in italics. For instance, an extract might appear as *212/SPT3: <u>I</u> did↓*. The identifying information will be omitted if the extract is already adequately identified.

Within extracts, identification is provided by the speaker codes, which are used in place of pseudonyms (as used in the transcribed talk), and these codes contain the interview number. Thus the primary interviewing officer in Interview 1 is assigned the code *pio1* and it is this code which appears in the second column of the transcript table whenever that speaker begins an utterance.

The secondary interviewing officer, the one sometimes referred to in the interviews as the *corroborating officer*, is assigned the code *sio* together with the number of the interview. In the single case of a third officer being present, this officer is identified with the code *tio*.

The suspect is in each case referred to as *SPT* together with the interview number. The use of upper case for the suspect and lower case for the police officers is another simple way to distinguish the codes at a glance.

Although the codes do not have the same 'flow' in the text as a name, I decided that these codes would be used instead of names or initials because that way there will never be any confusion for the reader about which interview is being discussed when referring to a participant.

There is, however, a slight complication to the identities of the participants: in some instances, the same person may participate in more than one interview. For example, the primary interviewing officer in Interview 2 (pio2), is the same person as the secondary interviewing officer in Interview 3 three years later (sio3) The coding system does not address this coincidence; however, it does allow the different roles played by an officer to be distinguished, which is more relevant to this study. That is, the fact that Officer Atkins asks several questions during Interview 3 is more important to this study because of his role as the secondary interviewing officer than because he also interviewed SPT2 three years later.

This section has discussed the collection and transcription of data used in the analysis of police-suspect interviews, which is the main focus of this book. However, in Chapter 5 a case study is presented which involves police training interviews with child witnesses. The method used to collect that data is unique to those interviews and will be described in Chapter 5.

3
An Analysis of the Interview Structure

3.1 Introduction

This chapter presents the initial phase of the analysis, which aims to provide a descriptive framework of the police interview structure. Using an analysis of participation frameworks and participant roles (Goffman 1974), it will be shown that there are three parts of the interview (Opening, Information Gathering, and Closing) and that each part can be meaningfully described and distinguished from the other parts by examining the language used by the participants. The analysis will demonstrate that the changing use of language in the different interview parts mirrors the changing goals of the police participants.

The goals of a police interview can be described in terms of institutional requirements. For example, we know that a voluntary confession from the suspect being interviewed will provide strong support to the prosecution or police case in court. Therefore, one of the goals of a police interview is to elicit a voluntary confession from the suspect. This is referred to as an institutionally defined goal. It is noted that institutionally defined goals of the interview relate to different functional parts of the interview and that there are three distinct functional parts of the interview in which different goals are prioritised and pursued by the police participants. If we can align these various institutionally defined goals (and their associated interview parts) with changes in the participation framework, then we can also provide a description of the parts of an interview which is based on a linguistic device (i.e. the invocation of participant roles) but which describes a parallel interview structure from the perspective of the goals of the police participants.

As a final part of this analysis, the discursive features which mark the shift from Opening to Information Gathering are examined to reveal the means by which the shift is achieved and to discuss how this relates to the functional, institutional requirements of the interview of ensuring that the suspect begins a voluntary confession with minimal police input.

Ultimately then, this chapter will provide a linguistic description of the police-suspect interview which is aligned with both the institutionally defined goals of the interview and the functional structure to which those goals relate. This will support the subsequent analysis in Chapter 4 of participants' discourse practices as they negotiate the institutional requirements of the interview.

3.2   Participation frameworks

To reiterate the key points discussed in 2.1.3 above, participation frameworks (Goffman 1974) are a way of describing spoken discourse in terms of the roles occupied by the speakers, and these roles (*principal, author, animator* and *figure*) are defined by the speaker's 'attitude' or orientation to the content of the utterances which comprise the discourse. Thus, the speaker is assigned the role of *author* if she or he has selected the words which express the sentiment of the utterance and arranged them appropriately, and she or he is also assigned the role of *principal* if she or he is responsible for the sentiments so expressed, and for any consequences arising from the expression of the sentiments.

3.2.1   Participant use of participation frameworks

The aspect of the participation framework approach which makes it eminently suitable for this research is that, even though the names for the roles are invented by analysts, the roles themselves are available to participants for use in composing utterances which invoke different participation frameworks. Participants display to each other in their language which role(s) they are occupying, as can be demonstrated in the following extract:

Extract 3-1 INT2

13.	pio2:	(1.2) I <u>intend</u> to interv' you in relation to: (.) an assault that occurred in <u>Bigtown</u>∧ (.)
14.		on ah New Year's Eve and the <u>early</u> hours of e:r New Year's Day↑
15.		(0.2) nineteen ninety-eight↑
16.	→	(0.3) .h <u>before</u> continuing I <u>must</u> inform you that you are <u>not</u> obliged to <u>say</u> or <u>do</u> anything∧
17.		(0.2) but anything you say or do may be given in <u>evidence</u>↑ do you under<u>stand</u> that↑
18.	SPT2:	(0.8) yes⇒

In line 16, marked with the right arrow, we see pio2 displaying to SPT2 that while he (pio2) occupies the role of *animator* for the 'caution' (*you are not obliged to say or do anything...*), he does not occupy the role of *author* or *principal*. This is expressed with the phrase *I must inform you that.* Anything which follows this phrase is uttered by pio2 because he is legally bound to utter certain words, not because he personally creates an utterance and decides to use it.

That the invocation of participant roles is available to the participants as a conversational resource has important consequences for the use of the results of this part of the analysis in section 3.6 as well as in Chapter 5 which focuses on the CA approach to the data. One of the key aims of the analysis of participant roles is to provide a basis for the proposed structure of the interviews upon which the subsequent analysis of discourse practices will be grounded. Were we to use a top-down approach to identifying the structural components of the interviews, this would be of limited value as a basis for focusing the detailed analysis on certain structural features, since CA takes most emphatically a bottom-up approach to the data.

3.2.2   Participation frameworks in an institutional setting

In Heydon (1997) it was argued that when, in a police interview, police officers make formal utterances (e.g. the identification of the participants or the acknowledgement of the time of the interview), they are ascribing the roles of *author* and *principal* to the police institution, and not to themselves. This was said to be due to the fact that the police officer as an individual has no influence over wording (*authorship*), nor any choice to make the statement or not, nor even any choice over the timing of the statement (all Formal Statements must be made at certain points in the interview). Additionally, the police officer as an individual does not take responsibility for the consequences of these types of utterances (*principalship*) as they are making such utterances only in their capacity as a representative of the police institution. Thus the only role which the police officer personally takes up is that of *animator*.

An investigation of whether these same claims can be made of the data in this study provides a useful starting point for our analysis of the participation frameworks of the interviews as a whole. This investigation is the focus of the next section.

3.3   Interview structure and participation frameworks: opening and closing

The opening and closing of the police interview can be defined with reference to the institutional goals of the interview fairly simply due to the known police regulatory requirements. Both the opening and closing sections of the interview are used to inform suspects of their rights and obligations and to carry out certain administrational tasks, such as obtaining the personal details of the suspect for official police records and laying formal charges. The goals of the opening and closing are therefore to carry out these tasks in such a way that all the institutional requirements are met, including legal requirements. This is absolutely critical for a successful interview, as far as the police are concerned, as their failure to comply with even one of the legal or institutional requirements will weaken the legitimacy of the interview as evidence in court. For instance, the Crimes Act 1958 states in Section 464A(3):

> Before any questioning (other than a request for the person's name and address) or investigation under sub-section (2) commences, an investigating official must inform the person in custody that he or she does not have to say or do anything but that anything the person does say or do may be given in evidence.

The precision of the opening and closing in institutional terms is safeguarded by providing police officers with training and interview aids, such as written forms that guide them through the requisite utterances and are filled out with the suspect's responses as appropriate.

3.3.1   Formulaic utterances in the opening and closing

In examining the data we can see that each interview, though separated by as much as seven years, contains a formulaic set of statements and requests at the beginning and end of the recording which are produced in a consistent format, in accordance with the governing legislation. We will first examine in detail the types of utterances produced by primary interviewing officers at the start of the interview as a way of demonstrating how such an analysis of institutional discourse might proceed. We will then look briefly at the discursive features of the end of the interview.

Table 3.1 presents a list of the various functions that formulaic utterances can perform at the start of the interviews. It is worth noting that individual utterances can be grouped together in clusters which reflect their similar content and function.

Having established the functions of utterances that officers produce, it is then useful to compare the presence or absence of these utterance types in each interview. Of the interviews analysed in this study, the

Table 3.1   Functions of utterances produced in opening of interviews

Utterance number	Utterance function
1.	Identify participants, location, date and agree time.
2.	Request name, address, age and date of birth of suspect.
3.	Confirm citizenship of suspect.
4.	Request occupation of suspect.
5.	State intention to interview and right to silence.
6.	State suspect's right to contact lawyer or friend.
7.	Confirm that suspect has spoken to one or both of these people and/or ask if suspect wants to exercise these rights now if they have not attempted contact with one or both of these people already.
8.	Confirm reason for suspension of interview or suspect's well-being and treatment whilst in custody during suspension of interview.
9.	Reiterate the time and place of the alleged criminal activity (and commence questioning).

differences between utterances produced in the beginning and end of the recordings can, in all but one case, be ascribed either to changes in the legislative requirements over time (see Chapter 2, note 6), or to the differing requirements of the individual case. In relation to the beginning of the interviews, this is made clear in Table 3.2 where it can be seen that there is a remarkable consistency in the types and functions of utterances produced in this part of the interview. It stands to reason that only some of the interviews required the use of the utterance types numbered 8, which are used when an interview is suspended.

The exception to this pattern of consistency is the request for the suspect's occupation (number 4), which appears in all but four of the interviews. There is no clear reason why it does not appear in all of the interviews – it may be an optional question – but is still clearly part of the institutional pattern of questions in this part of the interview.

Having established such a set of formulaic utterances, it is just as important to note that in each interview there are no utterances produced by the primary interviewing officers at the start of the interviews that do not form part of one of these required institutional functions. That is, each interviewing officer starts with the same statement and works through the same set of utterances until she or he is finished. Extract 3-2 below is indicative of how these functions are realised in INT1.

Table 3.2 Presence of formulaic utterances identified in Table 3.1 in each of the 13 interviews

Utterance number	_Presence of utterances in INT1–INT13_												
	INT 1	_INT 2_	_INT 3_	_INT 4_	_INT 5_	_INT 6_	_INT 7_	_INT 8_	_INT 9_	_INT 10_	_INT 11_	_INT 12_	_INT 13_
1.	✓	3	3	✓	✓	3	3	3	3	3	3	3	3
2.	✓	✓	✓	✓	✓	✓	✓	✓	✓	✓	✓	✓	✓
3.	✓	✓	✓	✓	✓	✓	✓	✓	✓	✓	✓	✓	✓
4.	✓			✓	✓	✓	✓			✓	✓	✓	✓
5.	✓	✓	✓	✓	✓	✓	✓	✓	✓	✓	✓	✓	✓
6.	✓	✓	✓	✓	✓	✓	✓	✓	✓	✓	✓	✓	✓
7.	✓	✓	✓	✓	✓	✓	✓	✓	✓	✓	✓	✓	✓
8.						✓		✓			✓		✓
9.	✓	✓	✓	✓	✓	✓	✓	✓	✓	✓	✓	✓	✓

Extract 3-2 INT3

8.	pio1:	→2	(0.6) Right could you <u>state</u> your full <u>name</u> please↓
9.	SPT1:		Jonathon Arthur <u>Young</u>↑
10.	pio1:	→2	(1.0) and your <u>address</u>↑
11.	SPT1:		(0.4) one hundred <u>Black</u> Street <u>Littlevillage</u>↓
12.	pio1:	→2	(1.2) your <u>date</u> of birth↑
13.	SPT1:		<u>fourteenth</u> of the <u>third</u> fifty-<u>four</u>↑
14.	pio1:	→2	(0.5) and how <u>old</u> are you↓
15.	SPT1:		(0.7) forty-<u>one</u>∧
16.	pio1:	→3	(1.0) r't you're an Aust<u>ralian</u> citizen↑
17.	SPT1:		<u>yes</u>↑ I <u>am</u>↑
18.	pio1:	→4	(1.6) and your occu<u>pation</u>↑
19.	SPT1:		(0.7) unem<u>ployed</u> at the <u>moment</u>⇒
20.			I'm (0.3) <u>on</u> a (0.6) <u>support</u> (0.4) <u>parents'</u> pension at the <u>moment</u>⇒

Pio1 divides statement 2 into four separate parts (indicated by →2), whereas statements 3 and 4 only occupy one question/answer sequence each (16/pio1–17/SPT1 and 18/pio1–20/SPT1 respectively). Nonetheless, the utterances are produced in a form that preserves the consecutive occurrence of the functional cluster. The same is true for all the interviews.

Given the remarkable consistency across all of these interviews, it would be difficult to argue that the police interviewers are producing the talk spontaneously. Obviously, they are reading from a type of script (possibly one they have memorised – see Chapter 1, note 1), and in fact some of the statements have as a feature reference to their own obligatory nature (e.g. pio2/16: *I must inform you that…*).

When the same kind of analysis is carried out on the closing stages of each interview, an identical pattern of institutional discourse emerges. As in the beginning, throughout the final part of the interviews the primary interviewing officers confine their talk to producing sets of formulaic utterances or related discourse, such as clarifications. We will now briefly consider the issue of clarifications and their role in the institutional discourse of the opening and closing parts of police interviews.

3.3.2   Clarifications and institutional discourse

It should be noted that throughout both the opening and closing of the interviews, whenever the suspects are being told of their rights or obligations (as opposed to being asked to say or do something), the

statement ends with a request for confirmation of comprehension.
Extract 3-3 below provides an example of this sort of sequence:

Extract 3-3 INT2

351.   pio2:   (1.0) OK Charles you going to be charged with an <u>assault</u>∧
352.   SPT2:   (0.2) mm hm↑=
353.   pio2:   =you're not obliged to say or do anything unless you wish
              to <u>do so</u>∧
354.   (0.6) but whatever you <u>say</u> or do may be given in <u>evidence</u>↑
355.   (.) do you <u>understand</u> this↑
356.   SPT2:   mm hm↑

Usually the suspect responds affirmatively; however, if the suspect indicates that she or he doesn't understand something, then the police
officer is obligated to repeat the information or explain it in simpler
language or point by point until the suspect indicates that she or he
does understand. This means that occasionally, additional utterances
are required following one of these types of statements in order to follow this procedure. Later in INT2, we see pio2 having to engage in this
sort of clarification, as illustrated in Extract 3-4 below:

Extract 3-4 INT2

367.   Pio2:   your <u>fingerprints</u>↓ (.) may be <u>used</u>↓ (.) in <u>evidence</u> in
              <u>court</u>↑
368.   (0.6) if you <u>refuse</u> to give your fingerprints <u>voluntarily</u>∧
369.   (0.2) a member of the police force⇒ may use <u>reasonable</u>
              force to <u>obtain</u> them↑
370.   (0.6) if you are <u>not</u> charged (.) with a relevant offence
              within <u>six</u> months∧
371.   (0.4) or if <u>so</u> charged⇒
372.   (0.2) but the charge is not <u>proceeded</u> with∧
373.   (0.8) or i- you are found not guilty of the <u>offence</u>⇒
374.   (.) or any other relevant <u>offence</u>⇒
375.   (.) before the end of that <u>period</u>∧
376.   (0.4) then the fingerprints <u>will</u> be destroyed↑
377.   (0.2) do you <u>understand</u> all this information↑
378.   SPT2:   (1.6) <u>not</u> the bit wif⇒ (0.8) proceeded with⇒ //(*)
379.   pio2:   right* if (0.2) you're ee-ah (.) <u>summonsed</u> for the ah (.)
              offence of ahm (.) <u>assault</u>∧
380.   (.)//but* if it's not <u>proceeded</u> with↑
381.   SPT2:   yeah∧*

382. pio2:   within six <u>months</u>∧
383.   (.) or if you're (.) <u>charged</u>⇒ (.) and it (.) and you're
               found not <u>guilty</u>⇒
384. SPT2:   (0.2) yeah↓
385. pio2:   well then the fingerprints <u>will</u> be <u>destroyed</u>↓
386. SPT2:   (0.4) yeah∧

In this clarification, we can see that pio2 is repeating the information given in his initial production of one of the formulaic utterances types in the closing which might be labelled *Rights and obligations regarding fingerprinting*. However, in the 'clarifying' version, some of the institutionality has been removed from the utterances. For instance, 371/pio2: *(0.4) or if <u>so</u> charged⇒* is rendered in the clarification as 383/pio2: *(.) or if you're (.) <u>charged</u>⇒*.

Despite these changes, the terminology used remains the same and there is not an attempt to define the terms used, such as *proceeded with*, that SPT2 has specifically identified as requiring clarification. This sequence, and others like it (see section 6.2) reinforces our view of the opening and closing as consisting of continuous sequences of formal, scripted police officer turns, interspersed with suspect responses.

3.3.3   Participant roles in the formal statements

We have identified that the utterances used by police officers at the beginning and end of the interviews are extremely similar across all the interviews and that they have features that overtly suggest scripting and lack of choice in the utterances (e.g. *I am obliged to inform you*). As mentioned earlier, Heydon (1997) finds that where police officers are using 'formal police discourse', they cannot be said to be responsible for 'writing' the utterance nor for the decision to produce it, or to produce it at a particular stage in the interview. Thus it can be argued that at such times, the participant role of the police officers themselves reflects their institutional role of acting only as representatives of the police force as a whole. That is, the participant roles (Goffman 1974) of *author* and *principal* are assigned to the police institution, rather than to the police officer as an individual. The role of *animator* is assigned to the police officer though, which would make him or her responsible for speech errors.

This arrangement seems to be true of the data for this study as well. The utterances identified conform to the definition of 'formal police discourse' in the sense that, as discussed, they are individually scripted, and their sequence largely predetermined, by the police institution.

Thus in this set of interview data, the participation framework of the Opening and Closing can be described as one in which the police officer is assigned the role of *animator* but the roles of *principal* and *author* are assigned to the police institution, and this framework is recognised by the participants and displayed in their discourse structure. This participant alignment to a particular footing, indicated by the participation framework, will be discussed more fully later in this chapter.

3.3.4   Achieving institutionally defined goals

The institutionally defined goals of the Opening and Closing can be defined as the things that the institution prioritises in these parts of the interview. Police regulations ensure that certain legislative requirements are met when police officers carry out interviews and the adherence to the regulations is therefore a priority for the institution if the legislative requirements are to be fulfilled. This has a large impact on language use in the Opening and Closing of police interviews because the regulations stipulate what must be said by the interviewing officer and in fact provide a script for the officer. Note too that the required script is not assigned to an individual, but to a role.

We have seen that the participation framework invoked in the Opening and Closing of the interviews, at least by the police officers, is one which assigns the roles of *author* and *principal* to the police institution and only the role of *animator* to the police officer. This distribution of roles will be assigned the code PI2R, which indicates that the Police Institution (PI) is assigned two roles (2R), namely *author* and *principal* (see p. xii for a list of abbreviations used in this study). We have noted that this is a participation framework recognised by the police participants and overtly expressed in various utterances which typically take the form of *I must inform you*. A brief analysis of data from the Closing segments demonstrated an unwillingness on the part of the police officers to deviate from the actual terminology provided by the institutional script when they had to explain a phrase or concept, although it was noted that some less formal or institutional structures were employed by officers in this situation. Further cases of this adherence to the institutionally scripted forms will be presented in Chapter 7 when we examine the relationship between institutional discourse and police power.

When we consider the institutional goal of achieving a high level of conformity to the regulation script, which is intended to ensure that the legislative requirements have been fulfilled, then we can appreciate that the participation framework that is invoked by police officers assists in the achievement of the institutionally defined goals. The individual officer who relegates to the institution the authorship of and responsibility (*principalship*) for the words she or he utters is reducing the possibility of deviating from the police regulations outlined in the Police Manual. On the other hand, if officers were to rely on their own judgement of which words best fulfilled the police regulations, they would run a great risk of getting it wrong. As interviews are tape recorded and used by the defence in court, the risk of any error being detected and the interview evidence being disregarded is very high. The use of a script, written or memorised, and the participation framework this invokes, is therefore more than a mere convenience: it provides interviewing officers with a reasonably reliable mechanism for producing interviews which adhere to the relevant parts of the Police Manual and the legislative requirements.

This section has found that not only can we identify that the participants display affiliation to an institutionally scripted type of discourse (through participation frameworks), but further that the invocation of this linguistic device by the police participants greatly assists, and may be instrumental to, the achievement of institutionally defined goals. Moreover, the institutionally defined goals are themselves responsible for the structure of the interview as having an Opening and a Closing, since it is by making certain utterances and initiating certain question–response sequences at these points of the interview that the relevant police regulatory requirements are fulfilled.

Thus, the requirements dictated by the institutionally defined goals which provide functional parameters of the Opening and the Closing are aligned with the language use in the same parts of the interview in such a way that the Opening and the Closing can be meaningfully referred to as discrete parts of the police interview's discursive structure.

In short, we can be comfortable about using the terms Opening and Closing to describe the first and last parts of the interview because they are parts that are marked by the participants in their language use and recognised by the institution for their functionality.

3.4   Interview structure and participation frameworks: information gathering

As we continue to establish the participation frameworks in terms of the structure of the interview, we may consider how the participant roles are assigned during the middle section or the remainder of the interview between the Opening and Closing. We may also need to consider whether the assignment of roles in the remainder of the interview suggests only one frame, such as an Information Gathering section in the middle, or several distinct frames or sections.

3.4.1   Participant roles in a voluntary confession

Firstly, it might be useful to consider an ideal situation, a participation framework that would conform to a police best-case scenario. We know that the most successful evidentiary interview with a suspect is one in which the suspect is shown to be guilty (Settle 1990) because ultimately in court this will support the police decision to use state resources in making the arrest. Further, we know that the best kind of revelation of guilt is a confession by the suspect (Shuy 1998) and that such a confession will be most effective, useful and believable if it is produced spontaneously by the suspect with no prompting or leading by the interviewers (Shuy 1998). We might imagine the perfect interview, from a police perspective, to consist of the formal police statements at the beginning and end, and a suspect-produced monologue forming a confession in the middle. Although this is obviously an oversimplified ideal, it serves to illustrate an important point: for any confession that may be embedded in a suspect's utterances to be used to convict the defendant in court, it must not be seen to be the product of police influence through suggestion or coercion in the interview (or outside it, for that matter). The effect this has on interview procedure is to produce an awareness in police officers that it is always going to be best if suspects tells their story in their own words. If the entire middle section of the interview consists of spontaneous talk by the suspect, then there is absolutely no danger of any confession contained therein being dismissed in court as 'forced' or illegitimately obtained.

We can therefore speculate that the ideal participation framework for the middle stage of an interview, would be one where the suspect is assigned the role of *animator, author* and *principal* – she or he is responsible for the production of the utterances (*animator*), the writing of the words spoken and their meaning (*author*) and the consequences of the utterances (*principal*). By contrast, the police interviewer would, ideally, be assigned none of these roles for the duration of the information gathering phase and furthermore the importance of maintaining this participation framework would be considered by the police officer to be paramount to obtaining a conviction in court when a confession from the defendant is a key piece of evidence.

An extract from INT13, which represents as close to an ideal interview as any police officer might hope for, overtly demonstrates that interviewing officers are aware of the importance of the suspect using their own words.

Extract 3-5 INT13

165.	pio13:		okay↓
166.			<u>Pete</u> on <u>Tuesday</u> the <u>fourth</u> of Oc<u>tob</u>er this <u>year</u>∧
167.			um a <u>burglary</u> occurred in Jones <u>Road</u>∧
168.			in <u>Smith's</u> Creek∧
169.			premises er owned by Mr <u>Johnson</u> and his family∧
170.			that's a du- white double story <u>premises</u>∧ on top of a hill↓
171.	SPT13:		yes↑
172.	pio13:		um I <u>believe</u> that ah you were in<u>volv</u>ed in that <u>burglary</u>↑
173.		→	would you <u>care</u> to tell me in your own <u>words</u>∧
174.			um <u>if</u> or what you <u>know</u> about that <u>burglary</u>↓

Pio13's utterance represented by line 173 above, marked with the right arrow, indicates that he actively promotes a participation framework where SPT13 will be the *author*, *principal* and *animator* of the evidence. In the following section, we will see that other aspects of the discourse – other discursive practices of the participants – further support this footing.

3.4.2　Representations of knowledge states in the information gathering

Extracts from the middle sections of the interviews can be used not only to demonstrate the participation frameworks invoked by the participants, but also to show how certain participation frameworks are preferred by the police participants. We are able to observe the police participants displaying their alignment to a certain participation framework through their display of knowledge. There are several instances in the data where the police participants are forced to negotiate the 'ownership' of information in an effort to maintain a certain participation framework. On these occasions, the requests for information made by the police participants are made not because the police do not know the answer to the question, but because they want the suspect to answer the question on record, as though the suspect is the owner of the 'new' information. However, in the cases examined, various complications cause the police participants to reveal to the other participants that they in fact are already in possession of this knowledge.

If we take the following extract as an example, we can see this process in operation:

Extract 3-6 INT1

209.   pio1:   can you just* <u>explain</u> to us who <u>Ian</u> is∧ (.) like⇒
210.   SPT1:   (0.4) I don't <u>know</u> him↓
((Ten lines of discussion of Ian's role at the shop omitted))
220.   pio1:   but he serves* at the <u>counter</u> and stuff <u>doesn't</u> he↓
221.   SPT1:   <u>yeah</u> just helps //<u>out</u> a *bit there
222.   pio1:   he <u>assists</u>:* the sales↓
223.   all <u>right</u> so it's <u>Ian</u> <u>Flemmings</u>↑
224.   SPT1:   (0.6) I- I don't <u>know</u> him∧
225.   I <u>honestly</u> don't know him∧
226.   pio1:   right↓
227.   SPT1:   I //don't know (where he comes from or)*
228.   pio1:   his <u>name's</u> Ian Flemmings* ⇒
229.   <u>you</u> only know him as <u>Ian</u>↓
230.   SPT1:   that's <u>it</u>⇒

This extract from INT1 demonstrates the way in which the participation framework proposed as an ideal in section 3.4.1 is treated by the interviewing officer as the preferred structure in the elicitation of information from the suspect. In this section, pio1 is establishing the identity of the person who has already been referred to by both SPT1 and pio1 as 'Ian'. As discussed above, this is a particularly interesting segment as far as participation frameworks are concerned because the way that knowledge is displayed does not correlate to the actual 'ownership' of information. For instance, all present in the interview know that Ian is the victim of the assault, and they are all aware that they all know this. They even display this in their use of language by introducing Ian as a known *figure* in lines 190 and 201: no explanation for his appearance in the narrative is offered by SPT1, who introduces him in line 190, or requested by pio1, who asks two questions in lines 201 and 203 about Ian's possible involvement in making the threatening phone call to SPT1 before she seeks to identify Ian more fully, or more formally. We see in line 209/ pio1: *can you just explain to us who Ian is∧ like⇒*, that in establishing the identity of Ian, the interviewing officer first attempts to elicit the information from SPT1. This proves a little fruitless as SPT1 claims not to know Ian, although it is fascinating what this segment tells us about how we define 'knowing somebody' – in practical terms for SPT1 at least

I don't know him↓ means perhaps that he is not a friend of SPT1's and he doesn't know his full name.[7] Clearly Ian is not a stranger to SPT1.

Following this, pio1 makes some suggestions to SPT1 about Betty's relationship to Ian (lines omitted from Extract 3-6) and about what Ian's role at the shop might be, which SPT1 comments on and revises to some extent. Finally in line 223 pio1 states: *all right so it's Ian Flemmings↑* to which SPT1 continues to respond that he doesn't *know him∧*.

What is so revealing about this segment is the fact that although pio1 had quite a store of knowledge about Ian, she only revealed this information when she failed to elicit it from SPT1. That is, the segment and the elicitation attempts had little to do with pio1's need to attain further knowledge about Ian, but were intended to provoke a display of this knowledge by SPT1. SPT1 was also an active participant in this struggle – his claim that he didn't know Ian stands in contrast to his ability to display quite a lot of information about him and, indeed, his spontaneous mention of Ian in the first place.

We can see then, that pio1 is keen to invoke a participation framework in this segment where the roles of *author* and *principal*, together with the role of *animator*, are assigned to SPT1 for the display of knowledge about Ian. She can only ask questions to which she is known to have the answer if she assumes only the role of *animator* herself and assigns the *principal* and *author* roles to the police institution. That is, as an individual, even as an individual police officer, she is known by the other participants to 'own' certain knowledge about Ian and it would not be appropriate for her to take *author-* and *principalship* of utterances which contradict her knowledge state – i.e. utterances which request information about Ian's identity. The police institution, on the other hand, may ask these questions in order that the information be supplied 'on record'. It might be helpful to imagine the participant role that is preferred by pio1 here as being one which allows her to ask questions 'on behalf of' the police institution, which she could not sensibly or logically ask herself.

Extract 3-7 from INT1 highlights another instance of this sort of behaviour by pio1.

Extract 3-7 INT1

299.	SPT1:	=°no↓° (0.6) <u>AFTER</u> THE SECOND ONE ⇒
300.		SO I'VE TURNED <u>AROUND</u> ⇒
301.		I was <u>gonna</u> walk out ⇒
302.		and I've // (seen him*)
303.	pio1:	sorry⇒* after the <u>second</u> one∧
304.		so you <u>hit</u> him a // <u>sec</u>*ond time∧

Line 297 contains a mention by SPT1 that he hit Ian a second time before he has actually arrived at this point in his chronological telling of the story. This is because SPT1 is responding to a query about the onset of bleeding to Ian's mouth (following the assault on him), which SPT1 claims began *AFTER THE SECOND ONE*. In line 298, SPT1 restarts his story, describing how, having hit Ian once, he then went to leave the store but hit Ian again before leaving, as we find out later in the interview. This is the 'second one' referred to in line 297. However, before SPT1 gets to the point in his story where he describes the second blow in chronological order, pio1 interrupts – *sorry⇒* – overlapping SPT1's speech, and then repeats SPT1's statement – *after the second one∧* – this time moving the emphasis from the timing (AFTER) to the number (second). The shift in emphasis clearly demonstrates pio1's area of interest in SPT1's statement as the number of blows SPT1 has described and she then requests confirmation from SPT1 that this is indeed what he is claiming. Further, the placement of pio1's turn indicates that this information is extremely important to her. She has interrupted SPT1 and acknowledges that she is speaking 'out of turn' by prefacing her turn with *sorry⇒*. Pio1's repetition of SPT1's exact words, with a shift in emphasis, indicates very clearly that it is something that SPT1 has mentioned which interests her, not something she has initiated, and the fact that she explicitly requests confirmation of what SPT1 has stated is a further indication to the participants that she requires clarification of the events as SPT1 describes them.

She gives no indication that this is information that she may already be aware of, or that the version of events that SPT1 describes is competing with a police version of events. Instead, as described, she gives every indication that SPT1's statement *AFTER THE SECOND ONE* has caused her to revise her current count of the number of blows inflicted on Ian by SPT1 from one to two.

Pio1's turn may seem ordinary and unremarkable: she is indicating that she had thought that SPT1 hit Ian once, but then she found, through an 'aside' by SPT1, that SPT1 hit Ian twice. In this sense, pio1 is maintaining her role as a 'story' recipient, tracking the development of the narrative by clarifying the 'newness' of the information that SPT1 presented in line 299 as 'given' information. However, this does not accurately reflect pio1's knowledge state. A short time after these turns, in line 333, pio1 says *it's also alleged that there was actually three hits ↓*. This turn clearly indicates that pio1 was aware of another version of events where SPT1 hit Ian three times. Note that her turn in lines 303 and 304 highlight not that SPT1 claims he hit Ian twice, but that he *hit him a second time*∧. This conflicts with the version of events which we know pio1 is aware of (though at this stage SPT1 may not), and her turn in lines 303 and 304 is not consistent with this knowledge state. Logically, if pio1 is aware that SPT1 is alleged to have hit Ian three times, then it follows that SPT1 has allegedly hit Ian a second time. This does not mean that either version of events is true or factual, but what we are concerned with is the representations being made by the participants, in particular pio1, regarding their knowledge of the various versions of events. And in lines 303 and 304, pio1 is making a representation to SPT1 that until that time (line 299, to be precise) she was unaware that pio1 may have hit Ian a second time. In light of pio1's turn in line 333, this is a false representation.

We have therefore revealed another instance of pio1 deliberately concealing her knowledge state that allows her to eschew the participant roles of *author* and *principal* for the telling of an important part of the evidence. We know how important this information is to pio1 because of the way she has prioritised its clarification as an interruption. In a similar way to that illustrated by Extract 3-7, pio1 requests information that she already has. In this instance this is not quite as clear as the instance concerning Ian's identity since in Extract 3-6 SPT1's version does not exactly match pio1's version of events as stated in line 331. However, only a single blow had been mentioned by SPT1 up until line 299 and if SPT1 is prepared to admit to two blows, this makes his story fit more closely with pio1's allegations in line 333 than if he had only admitted to the single blow.

Had pio1 revealed her knowledge about three blows before ensuring that SPT1 had taken up the *author* and *principal* roles in relation to his statement regarding a second blow, then the voluntary and spontaneous nature of SPT1's statement may have diminished. Thus the choice by pio1 to disguise her actual knowledge state helps ensure her successful invocation of the participation framework where the roles of *author* and *principal* are taken up by SPT1 in relation to pieces of information which comprise the evidence.

The above analysis of extracts from INT1 clearly demonstrates that the participation framework that was proposed above as an ideal for the elicitation of information from suspects is deliberately invoked by pio1 such that her preference for this framework is displayed.

Data from INT2 confirm that this behaviour is not unique to pio1. In the extract below, Extract 3-8, we can see that pio2 is involved in a similar negotiation with SPT2 over information pertaining to injuries caused to the assault victim, Leila.

Extract 3-8 INT2

230.   pio2:   all right↓* well when you had hold of her <u>bicep</u>⇒
231.   (.) which↓ (0.2) arm was that do you <u>remember</u>↑
232.   SPT2:   (0.4) yip↑
233.   pio2:   (0.4) which <u>one</u>↓
234.   SPT2:   (0.2) <u>right</u> one∧
235.   pio2:   (0.2) a::hm↓ at some <u>stage</u>⇒
236.   didja have ever have hold of 'er <u>other</u> arm↑
237.   (0.6) <u>bicep</u>∧
238.   SPT2:   (1.0) no∧ I↓ (0.4) no∧
239.   pio2:   <u>a::hm</u>⇒ (2.0) it's a::h⇒ (.) she's had (.) some <u>injuries</u> on
                  'er <u>arm</u>⇒
240.   (0.2) <u>bruising</u> to <u>bo:th</u> (.) biceps↓
241.   SPT2:   mm hm∧=
242.   Pio2:   =at some stage↓ (0.2) didju have hold of er <u>other</u> bicep↑
243.   (.) dragging her <u>outside</u>↑
244.   ((sound of door closing⇒ or seat moving))
245.   SPT2:   (1.4) not that I can <u>remember</u>⇒
246.   pio2:   so you can't explain⇒ how those⇒ (.) <u>marks</u> would've
                  got there↑
247.   SPT2:   (0.4) the one on the right (.) arm∧ would have been
                  from me⇒// *<u>grabbin</u> a∧ (.) but
248.   pio2:   right* (4.4) and⇒ OK⇒ u:m⇒
249.   (1.0) after the <u>second</u>⇒ (0.2) time you've (0.2) <u>grabbed</u>
                  a∧
250.   (0.6) you went back <u>inside</u>∧
251.   what happened <u>then</u>↓

Extract 3-8 highlights an instance of the negotiation of participation frameworks in the information gathering section of INT2. Here pio2 is seeking to establish the cause of bruising to Leila's upper arms. In a manner similar to the examples from INT1 above, pio2 first attempts to elicit the information he is seeking from SPT2 by requesting it in a way that minimises the exposure of SPT2's knowledge of the situation. Pio2 asks in line 231: *(.) which↓ (0.2) arm was that do you <u>remember</u>↑*. (It has been established earlier that SPT2 had hold of at least one of Leila's arms.) SPT2 states that he does remember and after a further prompt from pio2 in line 233 states that it was the *<u>right</u> one∧*. This leaves pio2 with an unresolved problem, as becomes immediately obvious in his next turn: he wanted to establish the cause of the injuries to both of Leila's arms but his wording of the initial request as 'which one?' has resulted in SPT2 producing the preferred response 'the right one'. That is, the question asked by pio2 contains an underlying assumption that only one arm was held by SPT2 so to respond 'both arms' would challenge this underlying assumption and thus be dispreferred (Bilmes 1988; Sacks 1987). Since SPT2 has no reason to admit spontaneously to causing more damage than pio2 is suggesting he might have caused, the request is hardly likely to result in an elicitation of SPT2's confession to causing injuries to both Leila's arms. Hence pio2's resulting dilemma: through the wording of his question he has now put himself in a position where the elicitation of a further confession will require SPT2 to contradict what he has just said. That is, pio2 now needs SPT2 to say that he held not just the right arm, but the left arm as well. It is extremely interesting to note what happens next. Pio2 moves to his next, less preferred, option for eliciting the confession: he reveals ownership of certain knowledge he has previously withheld (much as pio1 did in Extract 3-6 and Extract 3-7 above) in a bid to force SPT2 to confess to causing injury to Leila's left arm as well. He reveals that he knows of injuries to Leila's left arm and then asks SPT2 a question which would require him to revise his prior description of his actions: 242/pio2: *at some stage↓ (0.2) didju have hold of er <u>other</u> bicep↑*. SPT2, however, declines the invitation to contradict himself, even in the face of pio2's (fairly strong) evidence in favour of a revision of his earlier statement. That is, the suspect in this instance chooses to contradict the police officer, and the physical evidence pio2 brings to bear, in preference to contradicting his own story. Given the suspect's commitment to the consistency of his own version of events, the interviewing officer would have done well to phrase his original question more carefully.

What is so very interesting here is that the behaviour of SPT2 is not unique – there are several similar instances in the interviews where the suspects demonstrate that their priority is to produce a consistent narrative, irrespective of claims made or evidence produced by the interviewing officers. In fact, we have already seen an instance of this behaviour in Extract 3-6 above. When pio1 requests that SPT1 identify Ian, the victim of the assault, SPT1 avoids complying with the request by claiming not to know Ian.[8] SPT1 then continues to claim that he does not know Ian, even though he has already described seeking Ian out and blaming him for the threatening phone calls he received. This is similar behaviour in the sense that, having made a claim, SPT1 then ensures that he avoids contradicting this version of events, no matter how difficult that becomes. The same situation arises following the exchange in Extract 3-7 in that when pio1 alleges that SPT1 punched Ian, rather than 'backhanded'

him, SPT1 does not change his version of events to match this allegation, despite the production of physical evidence by pio1.

Furthermore, in all of these cases, this type of suspect behaviour results
in the interviewing officers having to reveal knowledge previously
withheld and thus align with a participation framework in which they
assume the roles of *animator, author* and *principal* in relation to their
utterances. It appears that this participation framework is invoked in
response to a conflict between the suspect's narrative and the evidence
already accumulated by the police, but it is not a participation framework which is preferred as a starting point to the elicitation of a
confession.

Extract 3-9 below indicates that even when eliciting seemingly minor
details from the suspect the police officer takes care to avoid the *author*
and *principal* roles.

Extract 3-9 INT2

63.   SPT2:   ah Oscar <u>Green</u>∧
64.   (0.2) and then⇒ (.) <u>later</u> that night⇒ (.) some⇒ <u>other</u>
              friends⇒ (0.6) from <u>Littlevillage</u>⇒
65.   (0.2) °which I didn't know were gonna be there°⇒ (.) <u>they</u>
              turned up⇒ um⇒
66.   (1.2) Larry <u>Smith</u>∧ (0.8) an his <u>girlfriend</u>⇒ (5.2) mh caie
              Rob <u>Long</u>∧
67.   (0.4) u::m⇒ (5.3) °who w's a else was there° (1.2)
68.   pio2:   if I <u>said</u> to you it was <u>someone</u> by the name of <u>Jacqui</u>↑
69.   SPT2:   yeah <u>Jacqui</u> was the:re⇒ // and her*
70.   pio2:   and <u>her</u>* las name↑
71.   SPT2:   (0.4) no I wouldn't 'ave a <u>clue</u> abou' her↓=
72.   pio2:   =right⇒=
73.   SPT2:   and um⇒ (.) <u>Adam</u> Brown⇒
74.   pio2:   right⇒ (1.0) OK∧ <u>u::m</u>⇒ (0.8) yeah∧ you're <u>at</u> the hotel∧

Prior to line 63, pio2 has requested the names of the people who were at
the pub with SPT2 before the assault. SPT2 obliges with three full names;
however, pio2 then seeks confirmation that *Jacqui* was there, though
Jacqui is evidently known by pio2 to have been present. The way that
pio2 tolerates very long pauses – 5.3 seconds in line 67 – in SPT2's turn
tends to indicate that he (pio2) was waiting for SPT2 to mention
information already known to pio2. Finally, when SPT2 offers a list of
names which does not match the police list, pio2 is forced to take over
the *animator, author* and *principal* roles in relation to the last name and,

in line 68, make it clear that he did indeed have access to knowledge about who was present at the pub.

Pio2's tolerance of the long pauses demonstrates his reluctance to take up the *author, animator* and *principal* roles at this point – he is prepared to wait far longer during SPT2's turn in lines 63–7 than he does after line 73, for instance, when SPT2 adds the name *Adam Brown*⇒ to the list. In pio2's next turn (line 74), he closes the list-making activity (*right*⇒ *(1.0)*) and, with several discourse markers (*OK*∧*u::m*⇒ *(0.8) yeah*∧), moves back to SPT2's narrative (*you're __at__ the hotel*∧). Between SPT2's turn in line 73 and pio2's turn in line 74 there is no more than a 0.2 second silence. Pio2 does not simply make a habit of allowing very long silences before making a response – in line 67 he is waiting for a specific name and is prepared to wait a very long time before having to take over the *author, animator* and *principal* roles from SPT2 to supply this piece of information himself.

This extract therefore supports the findings of the prior analysis that the preferred participation framework for the police participants is one where the suspects take up the role of *author, animator* and *principal* in relation to all parts of the evidence.

The analysis of extracts from the information gathering parts of these interviews has revealed that while our prediction of a particular participation framework (where the suspect occupies the roles of *animator, author* and *principal*) being preferred by police remains accurate, we can identify a second participation framework (where the interviewing officer occupies the roles of *animator, author* and *principal*) which is invoked when the responses of the suspect do not match the police knowledge or evidence of events. These two participation frameworks can be labelled S3R (suspect occupies the three roles of *animator, author* and *principal*) and P3R (police officer occupies the three roles of *animator, author* and *principal*) The analysis suggests that P3R is a dispreferred option for the police officer, not only because it is used when the alternative, S3R, fails, but because it does not necessarily result in agreement between the two versions. In fact, in two of the four extracts analysed so far, the alignment to P3R resulted in the interviewing officer having to abandon the line of questioning altogether and in doing so admit the extent of the police knowledge of that part of the narrative (the full name and role of Ian in INT1 and the bruising to Leila's arms in INT2). Clearly it is undermining the voluntary nature of the confession if parts of the narrative have to be supplied by the interviewing officer.

INT3 provides us with an interesting view of the invocation of participation frameworks, particularly with reference to the prior assertion that a given participation framework, S3R, is preferred by interviewing officers. This interview is quite different in circumstance to both INT1 and INT2 as it concerns allegations of a different type. The talk in INT3 revolves around establishing SPT3's possession and care or use of certain items (marijuana and unregistered guns), rather than the elicitation of a narrative leading to a confession. The police have conducted a raid on SPT3's house and other relevant premises and their subsequent discovery of the marijuana and related items, as well as the guns, is known to all the interview participants.

Thus, in Extract 3-10 below, pio3 readily identifies the contents of the film container *as marijuana (.) seeds*↑. Nonetheless, he then goes on to request SPT3's verification of this information in line 331, which emphasises pio3's desire to have even known information reconfirmed by the suspect – given that SPT3 has already offered an agreement token in line 330. New information – the ownership of the seeds – is then elicited via a direct question in line 333 and then the original information – the contents of the container – is elicited from SPT3 in the following way: 335/pio3: *(1.2) and (0.2) can you tell me (1.2) what they what they are*↑. This elicitation more clearly invokes the participation framework S3R; however, it should be kept in mind that when this request is made in line 335, the information has already been offered by pio3 and affirmed by SPT3, then a confirmation of its correctness requested by pio3, and delivered by SPT3, and now it is being elicited again.

Extract 3-10 INT3

327.   pio3:   (0.4) <u>film</u> container∧
328.   (0.6) ah (0.5) containing approximately half <u>full</u> of ah
329.   (1.3) <u>marijuana</u> (.) seeds↑
330.   SPT3:   yes⇒
331.   pio3:   is that <u>correct</u>↑
332.   SPT3:   yes⇒
333.   pio3:   whose are <u>they</u>↓
334.   SPT3:   mine⇒
335.   pio3:   (1.2) and (0.2) can you <u>tell</u> me (1.2) what they what they are↑
336.   SPT3:   (0.7) <u>marijuana</u>↑ le- seeds↓
337.   pio3:   seeds↑ all <u>right</u>↑ (.) <u>why</u> have you got them↓

Earlier we saw that P3R is used as an alternative to S3R, when the latter has failed to elicit the desired response. In this case, S3R is invoked after the request made in the P3R framework has already been successful in obtaining agreement. This seems quite illogical unless we consider that a response elicited within the P3R framework is not as strong as one elicited in the S3R framework. Hence the invocation of the S3R framework by pio3, even after the agreement offered by SPT3 earlier in response to the presentation of the same information.

As in Extract 3-9, Extract 3-11 below demonstrates that even details such as, in this case, the place where the cannabis plants had been growing, are elicited within the S3R framework wherever possible.

Extract 3-11 INT3

79.   pio3:   (0.4) ah (.) and where were <u>they</u>↓
80.   SPT3:   (0.5) in the <u>fernery</u>↓

Here this information is elicited from SPT3 and accordingly he aligns to the S3R framework. However, later turns by the interviewing officers indicate that they are both aware that the plants were grown in the fernery and are able to provide a description of that location. For instance, in Extract 3-12, pio3 demonstrates that he is familiar with the fernery and its main features, including those that contribute to its status as a secluded place for the cultivation of an illicit plant.

Extract 3-12 INT3

95.   pio3:   OK (0.3) now (0.6) this (.) <u>fernery</u>∧
96.   (0.3) would it be fair to say that
97.   that was (.) <u>enclosed</u> all around by <u>fence</u>⇒
98.   (0.4) and ah (.) <u>shade</u> cloth mesh↑

As found in the analysis of extracts from INT1 and INT2, a brief examination of Extract 3-11 and Extract 3-12 from INT3 finds the police officer asking questions which misrepresent his knowledge state for the purposes of having the suspect take up the *author, animator* and *principal* roles in relation to any part of the evidential statement. This strongly supports the proposal for a preferred S3R participation framework, and a dispreferred P3R framework.

Similarly in Extract 3-13, a short set of requests for information reveal the same preferences being displayed by pio12.

Extract 3-13 INT12

85.   pio12:   ((clears throat))
86.   do you remember what <u>time</u> you went up and went to
                 the <u>toilet</u>↓

87.   SPT12:   no∧
88.   pio12:   I put to <u>you</u> it was a<u>round</u> two thirty⇒
89.   would that be <u>right</u>↑
90.   SPT12:   don't <u>know</u>↑
91.   don't <u>look</u> at your watch when you go to the <u>toilet</u>⇒

Pio12 first attempts to elicit from SPT12 the time of his trip to the toilet and when this is unsuccessful she presents her version taking over the roles of *author, animator* and *principal* 4/pio12: *I put to <u>you</u> it was a<u>round</u> two thirty⇒*. In fact, this practice is extremely common in all of the interviews analysed here. One indication of how normalised this discursive practice has become in police institutional discourse is the fact that no matter how contrived the interviewing officer's pretence that she or he is in need of some piece of information, suspects in these interviews never display any surprise when it is revealed that the officer knew all along the answer to the question. Even suspects who clearly demonstrate their willingness to challenge police discursive behaviour at other times never ask, for example, why information is requested when it is clearly already known to all present.

3.4.3   Displaying a preference for S3R

In summary, these seven extracts from various interviews all support the assumption that the information gathering can be identified by the interviewing officer's preference for the S3R over the P3R participation framework. In each of the cases analysed, we were able to see that the police officers actively avoid aligning to the P3R framework by attempting to elicit the information from the suspect within an S3R framework. These discursive practices are found to be characterised by requests for information already known to the interviewing officer. However, such misrepresentations of knowledge states will be revealed both to the analyst and to the suspect if the suspect's continued claims of ignorance cause the police officer to present the concealed knowledge to further the narrative or challenge the suspect on some point. This whole process is captured schematically in Table 3.3.

This schema is only intended to represent those occasions when *x information* is known to the interviewing officer but not presented by the suspect and does not represent the occasions when the information requested is supplied by the suspect, or when the police officer does not know what *x information* is to be.

There are occasions in the data, for instance, when the interviewing officer requests information, the suspect responds that she or he does

Table 3.3 Participation frameworks and the presentation of previously concealed information

Speaker	Action	Participation framework alignments
pio:	Request x information	Attempt to invoke S3R relative to x information
SPT:	Fail to provide x information	Reject S3R relative to x information
pio:	Present knowledge of x information	Invoke P3R relative to x information
SPT:	Concede or deny x information	Maintain P3R relative to x information

not have the information and the request is abandoned without revealing whether the police officer was in fact in possession of the requested information in the first place. An example of this follows the lines reproduced in Extract 3-9, where Jacqui's surname is requested by pio2 but not known by SPT2. Given that Jacqui is known to pio2 it is possible that he (pio2) does know her surname, but for whatever reason does not reveal this knowledge. Alternatively, the information may be unknown to either party. Under these circumstances it is only possible to speculate what the knowledge state of the interviewing officer might be.

In those cases which do fit this schema, such as the extracts analysed above, it is clear that the interviewing officer is actively seeking to align with S3R participation framework and only invokes the P3R framework as a last resort. In other words, it is the failure of the interviewing officer to persuade the suspect to align with an S3R framework relative to the information requested that allows us to see how important this framework is to the police officers and how they systematically display their preference for it by avoiding utterances that align them with a P3R framework.

3.4.4 Achieving institutionally defined goals

The analysis in sections 3.4.1, 3.4.2 and 3.4.3 clearly demonstrates that in terms of the discursive structure and the participants' orientation to their version of events, there is a constant attempt by both parties to achieve the same alignment to information that they present. This alignment can be represented as the participation framework labelled S3R. Although it may not seem immediately apparent that this is always the case, we have found through analysis of the data that the behaviour of the police officers strongly supports their preference for a participation framework where the suspect takes up the roles of *author*, *animator* and *principal* of any part of the evidence. As for the suspects, they too display a strong preference for the S3R framework, but only relative to information that aligns with their version of events. We noted in relation to extracts from INT1 and INT2 that when the interviewing officer presented information which conflicted with their version of events, the suspects chose not to contradict their own story, despite strong physical evidence presented by the police officers.

Thus it can be said that both the suspect and the police officer are maintaining consistent preferences for participation frameworks throughout the Information Gathering.

If we consider the institutionally defined goals of the interview in this section we can see that there is an alignment between the consistency of the participation frameworks and the key institutional requirements. As discussed in section 3.4, the overriding police institutionally defined goal for the information gathering is to provide a forum in which the suspect will produce a voluntary confession. In terms of participation frameworks, this would mean maintaining an S3R framework throughout the information gathering, since any part of this section can form part of the suspect's confession, and should ideally be elicited within the S3R framework.

Therefore, the fact that we have found a consistency in the discourse of all participants in terms of their orientation to particular participation frameworks correlates directly with the key functional requirement of the Information Gathering: to achieve the goal of a voluntary confession.

It may appear that this goal does not take into account the behaviour of the suspect. However, if we consider that the key goal of the suspect is to put forward their version of events and not to be misrepresented, then we can find an alignment between this goal and the consistent preference for S3R, in relation to utterances which support the suspect's version of events. That is, the invocation of the S3R framework corresponds to the desire to produce a confession that accurately – from the suspect's point of view – represents the suspect's story. We know that this position is maintained throughout the information gathering because of the 'caution' in the Opening which warns suspects that *anything you say or do may be given in evidence*↑ (part of line 17/pio2). Thus, from the position of the suspect as well as the police participants, a consistency in the preference of participation frameworks aligns with the key functional requirement of the achievement of the goals relevant to the interview from the end of the Opening to the beginning of the Closing. It is therefore possible to consider the Information Gathering as a discrete part of the interview, having distinct linguistic features which not only delineate it from the surrounding talk, but which are aligned with the particular functional requirements of this section.

3.5   A discursive, goal-oriented structure of the police interview

The preceding analysis revealed an alignment between institutionally defined goals and participation frameworks invoked by participants in these police interviews. The importance of these findings is that it allows us to describe the structure of interviews in terms of the participants' language use, knowing that this discursive description reflects the functional requirements of the interview as prescribed by the institutions governing the interview (i.e. legislation and police regulations).

A structural framework can now be proposed which is both oriented to by participants, as evidenced in their invocation of particular participation frameworks, and valid in terms of the institutional goals. This framework can be represented as in Table 3.4.

Table 3.4 illustrates the relationship between the discourse structure of the interview, identified as participation frameworks, and the key institutionally defined goals of the participants. The resulting tri-partite framework (Opening, Information Gathering and Closing), can now provide a valid basis for further linguistic analysis of the participant negotiation of shifts between parts of the interview and participant achievement of interview goals. Most importantly, further analysis does

Table 3.4 Goals and participation frameworks in the tri-partite interview framework

Goal	Primary or target participation framework			Structural frame
	Author	*Principal*	*Animator*	
Adhere to legislative requirements	Police institution	Police institution	Primary Interviewing Officer	OPENING
Produce voluntary confession	Suspect	Suspect	Suspect	INFORMATION GATHERING
Adhere to legislative requirements	Police institution	Police institution	Primary Interviewing Officer	CLOSING

not have to take for granted a correlation between participant recognition of both discursive interview structure and institutionally defined goals. Both of these things are not only aligned with each other, but also oriented to by the speakers.

3.6   Achieving shift into S3R

The tri-partite interview framework described above provides a basis for the analysis in this section, which is concerned with the negotiation of the shift between the Opening and the Information Gathering parts of the interview. The analysis thus far has demonstrated that the participants must attempt a shift in the distribution of participant roles as they move into the Information Gathering if they are to fulfil the functional requirements of the interview. This shift from the Opening to the Information Gathering is described in participant role terms as a shift from a PI2R framework to an S3R framework, and in this section relevant parts of the interview data are examined with the aim of describing the negotiation of this shift in roles.

The analysis begins with a description of those turns that mark the point in each interview where the shift occurs. Thus in section 3.6.1 data extracts which contain the relevant turns are presented and the discursive activities of the participants are described in broad terms. In section 3.6.2 the interviews are compared to see the results of the different approaches to the shift as the interviews progress into the Information Gathering. Each interview is examined for an alignment with the S3R framework by the participants and how this is achieved on a turn-by-turn basis. Finally, in section 3.6.3 the turns which had been used by the police officers to prompt a shift (those featured in the extracts examined in section 3.6.1) to the S3R framework are analysed to see if a link can be made between the discursive behaviour of the police officers when prompting the shift and the immediate results of that shift – i.e. alignment with the S3R framework (or lack thereof) in the initial phases of the Information Gathering.

The intention of the analysis, therefore, is to describe how police discursive behaviour in the initiation of the shift to the Information Gathering may affect the uptake of the S3R framework by suspects.

Finally, a methodological note: the following sections present the analysis and findings relating to data from INT1, INT2 and INT3, as these three interviews present an interesting range of discursive behaviour during the transition from Opening to Information Gathering. The analysis of the remaining ten interviews revealed various patterns of behaviour, but in each case the transition could be mapped to one of these three interviews in terms of the approach of the police officers and the response of the suspect. In other words, the transitional phases of INT1, INT2 and INT3 appeared to represent three 'prototypes' of shift which were common to the other interviews. Given the small sample size, it is not being claimed that this finding could be generalised to all police interviews, only that none of the three patterns being discussed is completely unique – given similar circumstances, it is possible that police officers will display similar patterns of behaviour to those represented in INT1, INT2 and INT3.

3.6.1   Producing the turns which signal shift

Each of the interviews contains a turn that serves to mark the end of the Opening and the point after which the interviewing officers must negotiate the commencement of the Information Gathering. The extract below from INT1 shows how this 'transitional' turn is realised by pio1.

Extract 3-14 INT1

40.	pio1:	(0.5) r't↓ (2.2) .hh a- going back to <u>Friday night</u>∧
41.		hh the thirtieth of <u>June</u> ninety-<u>five</u>⇒
42.		(0.7) um an <u>incident</u> which <u>occurred</u> in <u>Littlevillage</u> ⇒
43.		(1.1) first of <u>all</u> we'll <u>start</u> um⇒
44.		(0.4) well the incident <u>occurred</u> at the <u>Littlevillage</u> takeaway <u>shop</u>↓
45.	SPT1:	(0.6) right↓=
46.	pio1:	=you know the <u>shop</u>↑
47.	SPT1:	yes⇒
48.	pio1:	what sort of <u>connection</u> do you have to the shop∧

Lines 40–2 are taken up with the reiteration of the time and place of the *incident* in fairly general terms. Line 43 is interesting for its overt recognition by pio1 that a frame shift is occurring: *first of all we'll start*. The interview has been underway for several minutes when this line is uttered, which indicates that pio1 sees this point as the beginning of a new phase, perhaps 'the interview proper'. Pio1 then finishes her turn by identifying the location of the *incident* more precisely using a formulation (Heritage and Watson 1979: see section 4.4) in line 44/pio1: *(0.4) well the incident <u>occurred</u> at the <u>Littlevillage</u> takeaway shop↓*. This does not elicit any narrative detail from SPT1 who offers only a confirmation second pair part in line 45/SPT1: *right↓*. Pio1's next turn in line 46 (*you know the <u>shop</u>↑*) can also be described as a formulation and this elicits

a further confirmation from SPT1 (*yes*⇒). Line 48 represents the prompt for the initial uptake of the S3R framework by SPT1. That is, the question 48/pio1: *what sort of connection do you have to the shop*∧ elicits a response from SPT1 in which he assumes the three roles of *principal*, *author* and *animator* for the first time.

Extract 3-15 below from INT2 demonstrates the turns used by pio2 and SPT2 as they negotiate the shift from Opening to Information Gathering.

Extract 3-15 INT2

27.   pio2:   (1.0) awrigh' <u>Charles</u> on um⇒
28.   (0.4) if y' c' jus tell me in your <u>own</u> words⇒
29.   there's an incident wuz: ah reported to me on New Year's <u>Day</u> this year∧
30.   SPT2:   °mm hm° ↑
31.   Pio2:   an assault that happened in <u>Bigtown</u>⇒ between <u>yourself</u> (0.6) and you:r: um⇒
32.   (0.4) girlfriend Leila Zovic↑
33.   SPT2:   °mm hm°
34.   pio2:   (0.2) <u>in</u> your own words tha' <u>evening</u> on New Year's <u>Eve</u>⇒
35.   can you just <u>tell</u> me um: (0.2) what happened over the course of the <u>evening</u>↓
36.   (0.4) from when you <u>left</u> ah⇒ was it <u>Littlevillage</u>∧ or Middletown↓
37.   you <u>left</u> from to go to <u>Bigtown</u>↓
38.   SPT2:   °Satellite River°⇒ (.) L- (.) Leila's place in Satellite <u>River</u>⇒=
39.   pio2:   =°right°

Pio2 also begins by reiterating the reason for the arrest and the time of the incident at this point. This occurs in lines 29, 31 and 32 where what is initially described as *an incident* in line 29 becomes *an assault* between SPT2 and his girlfriend in lines 31 and 32. However, pio2 prefaces his version of the transitional turn with a request for information to be made available by SPT2 within the S3R framework: 28/pio2: *(0.4) if y' c' jus tell me in your <u>own</u> words*⇒. This request is then repeated in lines 34 and 35, and a starting point for this requested narrative is proposed in the following lines. This proposal which starts from line 36/pio2: *(0.4) from when you <u>left</u> ah*⇒ and is completed in line 39/pio2: °*right*° includes a request for clarification in lines 36 and 37 of where SPT2 <u>*left from to go to Bigtown*</u>↓. Thus, pio2's production of the 'time and place' requirements becomes part of a broader, but overt, request for information to be volunteered by the suspect. Pio2 finishes with a request for clarification to which SPT2 responds by immediately volunteering further inform-ation than was requested SPT2/38: *°Satellite River°*⇒ *(.) L- (.) Leila's place in Satellite <u>River</u>*⇒.

Extract 3-16 from INT3 shows that initially, pio3's construction of the transitional turn is quite similar to the two examined above. He men-tions the focus of the interview in line 41/pio3: *in relation to ay a <u>search</u> <u>warrant</u>*↑ and the place and date of the search conducted. He also fin-ishes this utterance with a direct question in line 45/pio3: *(0.6) um (1.3) do you <u>live</u> there*↑, which is similar to pio1's question about SPT1's familiarity with the shop in line 46 of INT1 and pio2's request for confirmation of the starting point of SPT2's trip to Bigtown in lines 36 and 37 of INT2.

Extract 3-16 INT3

39.	pio3:	(0.3) a::h ((creaky voice)) right (3.7)
40.		w'l as I <u>said</u> wanna ask you some <u>questions</u>
41.		in relation to ay a <u>search warrant</u>↑
42.		(.) that was conducted a:h (.) .h at ah <u>your</u> address∧
43.		(0.2) that being fourteen <u>Abbot</u> Street in <u>Middletown</u>⇒
44.		(0.4) on the tw- twentieth of the second ninety-<u>five</u>↓
45.		(0.6) um (1.3) do you <u>live</u> there↑
46.	SPT3:	(0.4) yes⇒

However, whereas in INT1 and INT2 the suspects were willing to take up the S3R framework either in response to these questions which marked the end of the transitional turn, or in response to the following turn, SPT3 does not behave this way. The turns that occur between Extract 3-16 and Extract 3-17 are a series of question–answer adjacency pairs in which SPT3 responds only to the question asked and does not volunteer any additional information.

Extract 3-17 INT3

63.	pio3:	(1.2) ukay (1.0) .h (2.4) now the:
64.		(.) <u>search</u> warrant was <u>conducted</u> (.) a:h⇒ a' your <u>premises</u> a:h⇒
65.		(0.2) in <u>search</u> of a:h (0.6) <u>drugs</u>↓
66.		namey namely (.) a cannabis (.) <u>L</u>↓ (0.4) a::h (.) <u>plants</u> ∧
67.		(0.6) a::h (.) ca- (.) can you <u>tell</u> me anything about a:h
68.		(.) these ah (.) <u>plants</u> in <u>questions</u>
69.	SPT3:	(2.6) er waddaya // wanna <u>know</u>⇒*

70.   pio3   c'ya tell me* what t' (.) took <u>place</u> (.) a:h today↓
71.   (0.4) before the police <u>arrived</u>⇒
72.   (.) and a:h (.) and a:h (0.4) and <u>after</u>↓
73.   SPT3:   (0.4) jus' pulled em <u>out</u> and (.) took em <u>away</u>∧

Perhaps it is worth noting at this point that pio3's construction of the transitional turn was prefaced, not by a broad request for volunteered information, such as in INT2 (28/pio2: *(0.4) if y' c' jus tell me in your <u>own</u> words⇒*), but by an announcement of his (pio3's) intention to ask questions in line 40/pio3: *w'l as I <u>said</u> wanna ask you some <u>questions</u>*. This is exactly what he proceeds to do between lines 45 and 63. Having established the details of SPT3's living arrangements (the focus of these questions), pio3 then appears to be reproducing the transitional turn, although this time he provides greater detail of the search warrant, stating that it was 63/pio3: *(0.2) in <u>search</u> of a:h (0.6) <u>drugs</u>↓* and further that these drugs were 64/pio3: *namey namely (.) a cannabis (.) <u>L</u>↓ (0.4) a::h (.) <u>plants</u>∧*.

In line 67 pio3 produces an utterance which is quite similar to pio2's request for information mentioned above: 67–8/pio3: *(0.6) a::h (.) ca- (.) can you <u>tell</u> me anything about a:h. (.) these ah (.) <u>plants</u> in <u>questions</u>*. Following SPT3's request for clarification in line 69, pio3 specifies that he is requesting a description of the day's events 71–2/pio3: *(0.4) before the police <u>arrived</u>⇒ (.) and a:h (.) and a:h (0.4) and <u>after</u>⇓*. These turns comprise an insert sequence following which SPT3 responds to the original first pair part and provides a very brief summary of actions taken that day concerning the cannabis plants 73/SPT3: *(0.4) jus' pulled em <u>out</u> and (.) took em <u>away</u>∧*.

In the following section, SPT3's response and the responses of the other two suspects to similar requests by the interviewing officers for a version of events will be compared to see how the S3R participation framework is invoked by participants as they enter the Information Gathering part of the interview.

3.6.2   Uptake of the S3R participation framework by suspects

We saw at the close of section 3.6.1 above that SPT3 responds to pio3's request for a version of the day's events with a turn represented by line 73/SPT3: *(0.4) jus' pulled em <u>out</u> and (.) took em <u>away</u>∧*. This description is restricted to a very small portion of the day's events, which are later described more fully in the course of the interview. It also lacks any details about the actions that it does mention – even the agent is lacking and at this point the uninformed listener cannot say whether the actions were executed by the speaker or the police officers mentioned by pio3 in line 71. Given that the description of pulling the plants up and taking them away is substantive, new information (in the context of the interview) and results from an open question, it is clear that SPT3 is taking up the roles of *principal, author* and *animator* in relation to the content of his utterance. However, the S3R framework is not maintained by SPT3 – that is, he does not continue to offer new information or to expand on the information already given. Extract 3-18 below takes up INT3 from SPT3's line 73.

Extract 3-18 INT3

73.   SPT3:   (0.4) jus' pulled em <u>out</u> and (.) took em <u>away</u>∧
74.   pio3:   (1.0) OK (1.4) ah (0.4) when you say you pulled em <u>out</u>∧
75.   (0.2) ah do <u>agree</u> that a:h (0.2) you pulled out seventeen
               (0.4) ah⇒=
76.   SPT3:   =yes⇒=
77.   pio3:   =various sized (0.2) <u>marijuana</u> plants∧=
78.   SPT3:   =yes⇒
79.   pio3:   (0.4) ah (.) and where were <u>they</u>↓
80.   SPT3:   (0.5) in the <u>fernery</u>↓
81.   pio3:   (1.2) OK (0.6) and ah (.) <u>whose</u> were they↓

We see that a one second silence follows line 73, perhaps indicating that pio3 is awaiting further comment by SPT3, although it may be because pio3 is making notes. In any case, SPT3 does not choose to volunteer further information but rather waits for pio3 to take the next turn. In fact, in this part of the interview, SPT3 never takes up the opportunity to add further information when a silence develops between the speakers, as we can see in line 74, where a 1.4 second silence follows pio3's *OK* and in line 81 where a 1.2 second silence follows line 80/SPT3: *(0.5) in the <u>fernery</u>↓*. In both these cases, as in the one discussed above, it is pio3 who breaks the silence.

In Extract 3-18 we see SPT3 agreeing readily to information presented by pio3 in lines 75 to 78. SPT3 utters an affirmative *yes*⇒ twice in response to pio3's request for agreement. The first time he does not even wait for pio3 to complete the assertion to which he is agreeing but rather inserts his agreement into a very short silence in pio3's turn. This is indicated by the latching between the end of pio3's line 75 and SPT3's line 76 and then line 76 and pio3's line 77.

We can see, therefore, that while SPT3 has shown that he is unwilling to invoke the S3R framework, he is willing to *agree* to the validity of statements he has not authored or animated. We might propose that this constitutes a new framework where the police officer is *author* and *animator* of the utterance but the suspect agrees to take up the role of *principal* in relation to it. We can label this participation framework P2RA. This label indicates that the police officer (P) occupies the two roles (2R) of *author* and *animator* (A). The invocation of the P2RA framework indicates that the suspect, SPT3, is not unwilling to disclose his knowledge of certain events. In fact, the latching in lines 75 to 78 (see Extract 3-18 above) indicates that SPT3 is very prompt in his agreement to the allegations made by pio3. However, SPT3 continues to display an unwillingness to volunteer information in the form of a narrative, or to make statements about the events that are not in direct response to a question.

We might now compare this behaviour with that of SPT1 and SPT2. In section 3.6.1 above, we found that pio1 focused the final stages of her transitional utterances on the location of the *incident*. She mentioned the Littlevillage takeaway shop as the place where the incident occurred, and SPT1 responded with a confirmation 45/SPT1: *right↓*. Extract 3-19 below picks up INT1 at this point and we can see how the participants move towards the Information Gathering.

Extract 3-19 INT1

46.	pio1:	you know the <u>shop</u>↑
47.	SPT1:	yes⇒
48.	pio1:	what sort of <u>connection</u> do you have to the shop∧
49.	SPT1:	(1.7) nothin Betty and <u>I</u> we've
50.		(0.2) aw we've been together for nine <u>years</u> de facto relationship∧ // we-*
51.	pio1:	w'l who's* <u>Betty</u>↓
52.	SPT1:	(0.5) <u>Fisher</u>∧
53.	pio1:	(0.6) yeah∧
54.	SPT1:	and ⇒
55.	pio1:	what she <u>owns</u> the shop does she↑
56.	SPT1:	<u>no</u> her brother owns the <u>shop</u>∧ she only <u>runs</u> it∧

In the section of the interview immediately following the transitional utterances, pio1 asks for SPT1's confirmation that he knows the shop she has mentioned and then uses the shop as the focus of her first request for substantive information in line 48/pio1: *what sort of <u>connection</u> do you have to the shop∧*. Following an initial rejection of any connection (*nothin*), SPT1, without any further prompting, begins to describe his relationship to a pivotal character in the day's events, Betty, his ex-de facto wife. This swift uptake of the S3R framework by SPT1 is halted by pio1 who interrupts SPT1 to ask in line 51/pio1: *w'l who's* Betty↓*. He responds with Betty's surname and seems about to resume his narrative in line 54/SPT1 *and⇒*, when pio1 interrupts with a request for further clarification 55/pio1: *what she <u>owns</u> the shop does she↑*. Following this second interruption, SPT1 ceases to attempt to add information using the S3R framework. He responds to the clarification with an explanation of Betty's relationship to the shop but does not offer any further information about Betty or attempt to restart his narrative about their de facto relationship. SPT1 does eventually 'reinvoke' the S3R framework, however. After a number of turns in a question–answer framework – one we might describe as a P2RA framework (see above) – the following exchange takes place.

Extract 3-20 INT1

68.	pio1:	(0.5) right (1.9) w'l (0.8) y' how co- can you start <u>Friday</u>↓
69.		<u>what</u> di- (0.3) what <u>started</u> (0.4) on Friday↓
70.	SPT1:	well (0.3) what started <u>Friday</u> was Friday morning when I received a <u>phone</u> call↓
71.		(1.6) n that was around <u>ten</u>∧ (0.2) yeah (0.4) ten to ten thirty↓
72.		cause it was (0.4) not far after the <u>news</u>↓
73.		(1.3) so I <u>picked</u> it up answered and they said
74.		(0.3) Joh- ah Johnny⇒ <u>Johnny</u>↓
75.		(0.6) I said <u>yeah</u>↓ (0.5) <u>speaking</u>↓
76.		(1.2) they said right if you go anywhere near the <u>shop</u>↓
77.		(0.6) or any where near the <u>house</u>↓
78.		(0.8) you're going to get your <u>legs</u> broken↓
79.		(1.1) and that was <u>it</u>↓
80.		(0.2) just hanged <u>up</u>∧

By repeating pio1's question as the first part of his response 70/SPT1: *well (0.3) what started <u>Friday</u> was Friday morning* SPT1 frames his turn as directly relevant to pio1's request and presents himself as a co-operative respondent. However, SPT1's narrative detail stops a long way short of describing the incident about which he is being interviewed. So although SPT1 is willing to co-operate and provide new information in 'his own words' – that is, he is willing to invoke the S3R framework – he does so strictly with the boundaries of pio1's request. She asked him *what <u>started</u> (0.4) on Friday↓* in line 69 and he responded with a description of the first relevant event on Friday morning: a threatening phone call he received. His turn finished when he finished describing that event.

If we now compare this to a similar point in INT2, we can see a different approach being taken to the alignment with an S3R framework by the participants. Extract 3-21 picks up the interview where SPT2 is confirming the point of his departure of his trip to Bigtown. (We recall from section 3.6.1 above that pio2 had requested this confirmation as the last part of his transitional turn.)

Extract 3-21 INT1

38.	SPT2:	°Satellite River°⇒ (.) L- (.) Leila's place in Satellite <u>River</u>⇒=
39.	pio2:	=°right°
40.	SPT2:	(1.0) went to a f:::friend of <u>mine's</u>∧ in:: ⇒ (0.2) <u>Bigtown</u>∧
41.	pio2:	do you know the <u>address</u> of that <u>house</u>∧
42.	SPT2:	<u>Spray</u> Street⇒ // °I think°∧*
43.	pio2:	don't* know the <u>number</u>↑
44.	SPT2:	°no:: (0.2) it's <u>behind</u> 3ZX⁹°=
45.	pio2	=°rih°↓=
46.	SPT2	=that's (3.0) not sure if its↓ // there⇒ or u' hm↓*
47.	Pio2:	<u>yeh</u>⇒ no <u>that's</u> OK∧ <u>yep</u>↑*
48.	SPT2:	(0.8) um↓ got <u>there</u>⇒
49.		I'm not˙<u>sure</u> a' what <u>time</u> it was⇒ probably about⇒ (0.6) in between <u>eight</u> n' eight-<u>thirty</u>
50.		°'cause I <u>work</u> that day↓ n' I finished at <u>seven</u>°∧
51.		(1.2) um↓ (0.8) got <u>there</u>⇒ (0.6) had a few drinks with them⇒
52.		(0.4) him and <u>Leila</u>⇒ had a few (0.4) <u>smokes</u>∧
53.	pio2	(1.0) (h) ⇒m(h) ⇒

Like SPT1 in Extract 3-20 above, SPT2 seems willing to align with the S3R framework immediately and with no additional prompting in line 40 but does not get much further than one line of narrative before being interrupted for a clarification by the interviewing officer. The following six turns (lines 42 to 47) all concern the clarification of the address of SPT2's destination in Bigtown. However, in the case of INT2, this sequence of turns providing details inserted into the suspect's narrative does not cause any further delay to SPT2's reinvocation of the S3R framework. As soon as pio2 has indicated that SPT2 has given sufficient information (47/pio2: <u>yeh</u>⇒ no <u>that's</u> OK∧ <u>yep</u>↑*), SPT2 restarts his description of events. This is a detailed description compared to that offered by SPT3, for instance. Whereas SPT3 chose to reduce the events of the day to two, agentless actions – 73/SPT3: *(0.4) jus' pulled em <u>out</u> and (.) took em <u>away</u>∧* – SPT2 seems to do the opposite, expanding his description by inserting a mention that he worked that day and what time he finished to account for the time of his arrival in Bigtown. (It is interesting to note that SPT1 engages in the same activity in line 72, inserting a mention of the news programme to account for the time that he claims the phone call took place.) SPT2 even goes so far as to mention in line 52 that he and his friends *had a few (0.4) <u>smokes</u>∧*, which is most likely to mean that they smoked marijuana, given the immediately prior mention of a related activity (*had a few drinks with them*), the emphasis on *<u>smokes</u>*, the prior pause, the following silence and the response of pio2, which is a short outbreath and 'grunt', much like a snort of amusement and dismissal.[10]

Thus, not only is SPT2 willing to invoke the S3R framework and make a substantial voluntary confession within that framework, but he is also willing to reinvoke it when he is interrupted without any overt request to do so. This stands in marked contrast to the situation in INT3 where SPT3 invokes the S3R framework to convey a minimal amount of information and then responds only within a P2RA framework for most of the remainder of the interview. In INT1, the situation is slightly different again as SPT1 seemed willing to invoke the S3R framework at the earliest opportunity, but then changed his approach to respond within the P2RA framework before taking up his narrative again in a restricted S3R framework.

In the following section, we will return to the roots of the S3R invocations – the police officers' requests for information – and examine how this critical point in the interview may influence the subsequent uptake of S3R by the suspects.

3.6.3   Achieving frame shift

Through the analysis in section 3.6.1 of the use of the formulaic utterance in each of the three interviews in shifting from the Opening to the Information Gathering, and the analysis of the uptake of the S3R framework by participants in section 3.6.2, we have noted that there are certain consistencies in the discourse of the three interviews.

For instance, we can see that in each of the interviews there is an attempt by the primary interviewing officer to invoke an S3R framework. In INT2, this happens as part of the transitional turn when pio2 prefaces his mention of the time and place of the incident with the following request: *28/pio2: (0.4) if y' c' jus tell me in your <u>own</u> words⇒*. In INT3 there is also an overt request by pio3 for SPT3 to describe his version of events, taking up the roles of *author* and *principal* as well as *animator* in lines 67–68/pio3: *(0.6) a::h (.) ca- (.) can you tell me anything about a:h (.) these ah (.) plants in questions*. In INT1, pio1 does not make an overt request of this type, however she does ask SPT1 68–69/pio1: *right w'l. y' how co- can you start Friday↓ what di- what started. on Friday↓*, which SPT1 interprets as a request to describe the threatening phone call he received.

This consistency in the invocation of the S3R framework supports our earlier finding that, upon moving into the Information Gathering, the participants will be negotiating a shift in participation frameworks and that the S3R framework is one that facilitates a voluntary confession by the suspect.

Further similarities could be found in the pattern of question types used by police officers through this frame shifting process. In each interview, the attempts to invoke the S3R framework by the police officer were prefaced by at least one request for clarification first pair part, such as a formulation (Heritage and Watson 1979). These requests concerned background details such as locations and names of other people who feature in the events being described. SPT2, for instance, is asked to clarify the place he left to go to Bigtown. Pio2 makes this request as part of his broader request for SPT2 to describe the events in his own words in line 36 of INT2, as we can see in Extract 3-21 above. Having attained this information, pio2 does not make any further requests, or repeat his original request for a description of the evening's events, but waits through a one second silence in line 40 for SPT2 to begin the description.

After only one line from SPT2, pio2 again requests a clarification in line 41, though he does not interrupt SPT2 to make this request. The ensuing discussion of the address of the house contains some overlapping speech and further requests from pio2 such as in line 42/pio2: *don't* know the number↑* until in line 47, after the three second silence in line 46 where SPT2 has broken off his utterance, pio2 indicates that SPT2's response to the question is sufficient and he (SPT2) can continue his description of events. As we saw in Extract 3-21, SPT2 then describes getting to his friend's house and the following events, reinvoking the S3R framework without any discernible change in his alignment to the participation framework.

In INT3, there is a clearer distinction drawn between the clarification, or question/answer sequences and the police officer's request for the suspect's version of events. Whereas in INT2 we saw that pio2 requested SPT2's version of events as part of the transitional utterance and then engaged in clarification of details, pio3 does not ask for SPT3 to give his version of events until after he has completed the clarification sequences. Pio3 is explicit in saying as part of his transitional utterances that he intends to ask questions 40/pio3: *w'l as I said wanna ask you some questions* which he then proceeds to do in lines 45–61. When he has completed this task he attempts to elicit from SPT3 a description of the day's events, though at first all he elicits is a clarification sequence initiated by SPT3 in line 69/SPT3: *(2.6) er waddaya wanna know⇒*. Pio3's second attempt elicits only the rather brief description in line 73/SPT3: *(0.4) jus' pulled em out and (.) took em away∧*, as discussed above.

SPT3's utterance in line 69/SPT3: *(2.6) er waddaya wanna know⇒* is indicative of the approach taken by SPT3 to the remainder of the interview. As we noted above, all the information offered by him is in response to requests for confirmation or substantive information. He does not refuse the interviewing officers any information that they request, but they have to make the request. It was further noted that this behaviour could be described as showing a preference for a P2RA participation framework, where the police officer 'writes' the utterances and produces them for the suspect to confirm, responsibility for the utterances thereby resting with the suspect.

Given that pio3 moves directly into a question/answer phase from the transitional turn and does not attempt to elicit a narrative of any kind for a number of turns, and given that SPT3 complies with this arrangement and does not attempt to spontaneously invoke the S3R framework during this question/answer sequence, we cannot say whether SPT3 might have invoked the S3R framework had pio3 made such a request earlier. All we can say for certain is that SPT3 does not change his approach to the discourse but rather chooses to respond consistently within the P2RA framework throughout the interview.

INT1, despite having a similar discursive 'shape' to INT2 at this frame transitional point, differs significantly in the uptake of the S3R framework by SPT1 as the participants move into the Information Gathering. As noted above, the invocation of the S3R framework by the police officers in all three cases is prefaced by some requests for clarification. However, in the case of INT1, the suspect attempts to align with the roles of *author, principal* and *animator* but is interrupted by pio1 who makes the aforementioned requests for clarification and then has to re-invoke the S3R framework herself.

We saw in Extract 3-19 that SPT1 began his clarification of his connection to the shop with a description of his relationship to Betty, who works at the shop 49–50/SPT1: *nothin Betty and I we've (0.2) aw we've been together for nine years de facto relationship*∧ *we-*. However, his attempt to describe this relationship is halted by pio1's further requests for clarification in line 51/pio1: *w'l who's Betty*↓. Since Betty called the police following the assault, it seems highly unlikely that pio1 does not know to whom SPT1 is referring when he mentions Betty in line 49. Nonetheless, pio1, through her request for clarification, is ensuring that SPT1 take up the S3R framework in relation to the details of Betty's identity. On the face of it, this is remarkably similar to the situation in INT2 that we examined earlier where pio2 asked for details of the address of the house in Bigtown that SPT2 mentions in line 40. As SPT2 is referring to the house where the assault took place, it would be reasonable to assume that the police officer investigating the matter would be aware of these details. Thus, pio1 would appear to be engaging in the same activity at this point as pio2: ensuring the S3R framework is invoked for certain details relating to the incident.

However in the case of INT1, the interruption to SPT1's turn caused by pio1 engaging in this process of clarification changes the way in which the S3R framework is invoked thereafter. In fact, for several turns, from line 55 to 67, SPT1 displays a reluctance to realign with the S3R framework at all. Earlier, in lines 49 and 50, SPT1 delivers key information after only a rather oblique prompt from pio1 (i.e. 48/pio1: *what sort of connection do you have to the shop*∧), and, after giving Betty's surname in response to pio1's request for clarification, SPT1 appears to be about to restart his description in line 54/SPT1: *and* ⇒, but gets no further since pio1 requests further clarification of Betty's identity at that point. After this clarification has been delivered by SPT1, he shows no sign of restarting his description a third time. Instead, pio1 is obliged to take up the story in line 59/pio1: *yep*↑ *so you've been de facto for*⇒ and as soon as SPT2 has completed the statement he was presumably trying to make originally (62/SPT1: *and we separated about two months*∧ *ago*⇓), he stops talking and a lengthy silence ensues before pio1 asks another question about the identity of other shop staff. Again, SPT1 responds with only the relevant information, unlike in lines 49 and 50 where he departed from what he felt was the immediately relevant response to the question (*nothin*) and began to give other information, peripheral to the question but central to the interview.

As was noted in the previous section, when SPT1 does begin to describe in detail his version of the day's events in line 70, he does so within the parameters of pio1's request, even echoing the wording of her request utterance as the starting point of his response. We saw that SPT1's response describes only the events requested by pio1 – i.e. things that happened on the morning of the assault – and does not progress further with the narrative than pio1 has actually requested. This is a pattern that continues throughout the Information Gathering of INT1.

This analysis shows us that a clear change in the discursive behaviour of SPT1 takes place after pio1 interrupts him to request clarification about Betty's identity. This contrasts with the findings above concerning INT2 and INT3 where the discursive behaviour of the suspects and their alignment with the S3R participation framework, whilst different in both cases, does not change once the transitional utterances are completed and the Information Gathering has commenced.

If we now consider the way in which this frame transition was initiated by the police officers we find that INT2 and INT3 have in common a feature which is lacking in INT1: both of the primary interviewing officers in INT2 and INT3 clearly state their intentions with respect to their role in the ensuing discourse and they both do so as a way of initiating the frame transitional utterance. Extract 3-22 below takes up INT2 from the question/answer sequence prior to the transition out of the Opening.

Extract 3-22 INT2

25.	pio2:	do you wish to <u>exercise</u> any of these rights before the interview <u>proceeds</u>↓
26.	SPT2:	°no°↓
27.	pio2:	(1.0) awrigh' <u>Charles</u> on um⇒
28.		(0.4) if y' c' jus tell me in your <u>own</u> words⇒
29.		there's an incident wuz: ah reported to me on New Year's <u>Day</u> this year∧

In line 27 we can see that pio2 may have been about to begin the final request turn of the Opening with the institutionally required mention of the date and location of the incident 27/pio2: *(1.0) awrigh' Charles on um⇒*. But he does not complete this utterance, and instead produces an utterance in which he positions himself as the recipient of SPT2's own 'telling' 28/pio2: *(0.4) if y' c' jus tell me in your own words⇒* before proceeding with the institutional part of the turn.

Similarly, Extract 3-23 below demonstrates that after completion of the penultimate question/answer pair of the Opening in INT3 (lines 35–8), pio3 begins the final request turn with a clear indication of his intentions.

Extract 3-23 INT3

35.   pio3:   do you <u>agree</u> that a::h (0.5) you've a::h
36.   spoken to your ah <u>girlfriend</u> or <u>de facto</u>∧
37.   and that you've <u>also</u> spoken to a <u>solicitor</u>↑
38.   SPT3:   yes⇒
39.   pio3:   (0.3) a::h ((creaky voice)) right (3.7)
40.   w'l as I <u>said</u> wanna ask you some <u>questions</u>
41.   in relation to ay a <u>search warrant</u>↑

In line 40, pio3 unequivocally states 40/pio3: *w'l as I <u>said</u> wanna ask you some <u>questions</u>* before completing the institutional requirement of the formulaic utterance. In both cases, these intentions are realised: pio2 does indeed take up the role of 'telling-recipient', despite initiating several clarification sequences during SPT2's telling, and pio3, as we have noted, finds himself asking SPT3 questions or otherwise making requests for confirmation or information for the remainder of the interview.

By contrast, as noted above, pio1 does not make a clear statement regarding her intended role in the interview.

Extract 3-24 INT1

38.   pio1:   (0.4) r't do you wish to <u>exercise</u> any of these other <u>rights</u>∧
39.   SPT1:   no I <u>don't</u>↓
40.   pio1:   (0.5) r't↓ (2.2) .hh a- going back to <u>Friday night</u>∧
41.   hh the thirtieth of <u>June</u> ninety-<u>five</u>⇒
42.   (0.7) um an <u>incident</u> which <u>occurred</u> in <u>Littlevillage</u> ⇒
43.   (1.1) first of <u>all</u> we'll <u>start</u> um⇒
44.   (0.4) well the incident <u>occurred</u> at the <u>Littlevillage</u>
             takeaway <u>shop</u>↓

The extract above picks up INT1 at the same point as the previous two extracts – just prior to the final turn of the Opening. There are two places in pio1's formulation of the transitional utterance that give some indication of pio1's intentions. In line 40, the mention of *going back to Friday night*∧ may refer to 'casting one's mind back' prior to delivering a narrative and in line 43/pio1: *first of <u>all</u> we'll <u>start</u> um*⇒ there is an implication of starting a new phase of the interview.

The only mention by pio1 of her intentions in the interview is much earlier in line 21/pio1: *hm I'm <u>now</u> going to ask you some <u>questions</u> in rela-tion to an <u>incident</u>* which forms part of a previous question/answer pair. The same type of pair is realised in INT2 as 13/pio2: *(1.2) I <u>intend</u> to interv' you in relation to: (.) an assault that occurred in <u>Bigtown</u>∧ (.)* and in

INT3 as 20/pio3: *(0.6) Leigh I* intend *to interview: in relation to ah (0.4) some* drug *offences*∧. These earlier statements would appear to have much less bearing on the discursive behaviour of the suspects later in the interview since SPT2 and SPT3, who receive almost the same wording at this point, behave so differently following the shift into the Information Gathering. In any case, if pio1's statement in line 21 that she intended to ask questions to obtain information had an effect on SPT1's behaviour, it is not apparent in his response to pio1's first request for substantive information (line 48/pio1: *what sort of* connection *do you have to the shop*∧) where he almost immediately begins to produce an unprompted narrative. That is, SPT1 begins to behave in a way other than that of a 'respondent' – he begins to behave as an initiator of talk.

It is evident, therefore, that a part of the interview which is critical in determining the participant role alignment in the Information Gathering is the transitional police turn moving the interview out of the Opening and, specifically, the explication by the police officer of the two main participants' discursive roles in the Information Gathering. Where a clear statement of intention was made, the suspect's discursive behaviour in the Information Gathering matched the stated intentions of the police officer at that point. In INT1, where no clear indication was given by pio1 in the final Formal Statement of the Opening, the suspect began the Information Gathering by strongly aligning to the S3R framework, but then this alignment was weakened considerably following a series of clarification sequences inserted by pio1 into SPT1's description of events.

A similar disruption to SPT2's narrative caused no such change in his alignment to the S3R framework in the Information Gathering, though it should be noted that the clarification sequences initiated by pio1 constituted actual interruptions of SPT1's turns whereas pio2 chose transition relevance places to initiate his clarification sequences. However, these interruptions by pio1 do support the claim that pio1 does not adequately or clearly indicate her intended role in the Information Gathering. We established earlier that SPT1 appears to be beginning a narrative in the S3R framework in lines 49 and 50 (49–50/SPT1: *nothin Betty and* I *we've (0.2) aw we've been together for nine* years *de facto relationship*∧// *we-**) and it is this spontaneous invocation of the S3R framework that pio1 interrupts with her clarification sequence. This in itself may not demonstrate any confusion over roles – after all, pio2 also inserts a clarification sequence immediately after SPT2 has invoked the S3R framework but then proceeds smoothly into the Information Gathering with an S3R framework firmly in place shortly afterwards. A more obvious indication of pio1's uncertainty over role assignment is her second interruption of SPT2 in line 55 (55/pio1: *what she <u>owns</u> the shop does she↑*). This results in the clear change of footing as indicated by pio1's own attempt to restart the narrative in line 59 (59/pio1: *yep↑ so <u>you've</u> been de facto for⇒*) which is only minimally taken up by SPT1 and does not result in a further volunteering of information beyond that requested. Each of SPT1's framework orientations in the first three adjacency pair sequences are met with an orientation towards P2RA by pio1. Once SPT1 has moved towards P2RA himself, he appears reluctant to move back into a committed S3R framework thereafter despite pio1's invocation of S3R on two occasions in the segments examined.

3.6.4   Summary

This part of the analysis has found that each of the interviewers used a slightly different approach when producing the turn that initiates the shift into the Information Gathering. These slight differences could be seen to account for the various levels of commitment to the S3R framework displayed by the suspects as they began to respond to requests in the Information Gathering.

Broadly speaking, we found that SPT1 appears to move from a strong orientation to the S3R framework to a greatly weakened orientation towards S3R and a stronger orientation towards P2RA during the first few question–answer pairs of the Information Gathering.

We saw that SPT3, having moved (or been moved by pio3) into the P2RA framework as soon as the Information Gathering began did not ever commit to an S3R framework in the interview, despite attempts by pio3 to invoke S3R several turns into the Information Gathering. It should be recognised that SPT3's choice of frame may be a product of differing circumstances, in particular the much greater amount of incriminating evidence gathered by pio3 and sio3, which weakens SPT3's defensive position.

In contrast, SPT2 aligned with an S3R framework as soon as the Information Gathering began, following pio2's invocation of S3R at the point of transition from the Opening to the Information Gathering. Following this, pio2 had no difficulty at any time reinvoking the S3R framework after segments of P2RA turns.

The negotiation of frame transition will be considered in relation to a police mythology about interviewing in Chapter 6. However, before describing the features of the police mythology, it is necessary to provide a more complete picture of the interactional resources available to police interviewers as they elicit information from suspects in the Information Gathering. Points of conflict in the interview are of particular interest as they demonstrate the way that police officers draw on the interactional resources available to them to achieve institutional goals. A detailed examination of such discursive practices in the Information Gathering is presented in the following chapter.

3.7   Conclusion

This chapter began with the aim of providing a description of the interview structure which aligns the linguistic features of the discourse with the changing goals of the interview and shows that both are oriented to by participants in their turn-by-turn construction of the interview. Following the analysis presented in this chapter, it is proposed that the Opening and Closing can be considered discrete parts of the interviews as they consist entirely of formulaic police utterances which elicited suspect responses heavily constrained and classifiable as non-voluntary. The participation framework invoked by the police interviewers in these parts was unchanging and characterised by the assignment of *author* and *principal* roles to the police institution with only the role of *animator* assigned to the police participant.

This is consistent with the key functional requirements of the Opening and Closing, which are identified as maintaining adherence to the police regulatory requirements in order to ensure the validity of any confession elicited from the suspect in the remainder of the interview.

The lengthier analysis of extracts from the middle section of INT1, INT2 and INT3 reveals that despite the invocation of a number of different participation frameworks, it is still possible to see that the participants consistently oriented to one preferred framework. This is labelled S3R to reflect the assignment to the suspect of the three roles of *author, principal* and *animator.* Suspects align with the S3R framework only in relation to utterances which supported their version of events, whereas the police participants attempt to invoke an S3R framework for all utterances concerning the events in question. Nonetheless both approaches, or orientations, are consistent throughout the middle section of each interview and both reflected the key goals of the different participants. It is proposed that the Opening, the Information Gathering and the Closing can be identified as discrete parts of the interview oriented to by participants in their construction of the discourse, identifiable to analysts through their linguistic features and reflecting the key goals of the interview in each of the three parts.

The main findings of the analysis concerning the distribution of participant roles are outlined in Table 3.4 where they are presented in relation to the relevant parts of the interview structure: Opening, Information Gathering and Closing.

Finally, following an analysis of the negotiation of frame shift from the Opening to the Information Gathering it is concluded that the construction of the frame transitional utterance is critical to the successful invocation of an S3R framework. This finding provides the basis for an analysis in section 6.3 of the management of power underlying the discursive practices of each police officer in the negotiation of frame shift.

The next chapter presents an analysis of the turn-by-turn construction of the discourse in each part of the interview, taking a Conversation Analysis-based approach to the examination of utterance types and their distribution among the participants and across the interview parts.

4
The Institutional Embedding of Authority

4.1 Introduction

The establishment of a goal-oriented tri-partite framework for the police interviews in the previous chapter provides the starting point for a more detailed analysis of the construction and maintenance of the police institutional role in interviewing suspects, key features of this role and the implications of its construction and maintenance for the achievement of institutional goals in the interviews.

In this chapter, the first stage of analysis will examine the interactional resources of the police interview participants, paying particular attention to the turn-by-turn construction of the discourse. In section 4.2, the distribution of turn types, adjacency pairs (Schegloff and Sacks 1973: 295–6), and suspect-initiated utterances in the interview data will be discussed, facilitating a discussion of topic management by the participants in section 4.3.

The resulting descriptions of the participants' interactional resources will then be considered in relation to their role in the construction of a police version of events. It will be shown that interactional features of the police interview elevate the role of the primary interviewer to a position of authority over other participants and provide him or her with opportunities to construct a version of events which may compete with the suspect version. The negotiation of conflicting versions of events is the focus of the analysis in section 4.4.

4.2 Forms of turn taking

In order to best describe the forms of turn taking in the interviews it may be useful to consider the turn types that we would expect to find in this sort of data. As a form of institutional discourse, we would expect a police interview to feature 'restrictions on the kinds of contributions to the talk that are, or can be, made' (Drew and Heritage 1992: 25). Although his data were British news interviews, David Greatbatch (1988) notes that this institutional turn-taking system 'preallocates particular types of turns to speakers with specific institutional identities' (p. 404). As noted in section 2.2.4, news interviews and police interviews do in fact have some important features in common. For instance, both are produced with the knowledge that the interaction is being recorded and will be 'overheard' by a non-participating party – either an audience, in the case of the news interview, or the relevant legal or judicial authorities, in the case of the police interview. It may be pertinent, therefore, to note some ramifications of the pre-allocation of turn types in news interviews (summarised in Greatbatch 1988), and see how they may be applicable to police interview data following the analysis in the following sections. First and foremost, Greatbatch (1988) notes that interviewers and inter- viewees 'systemically confine themselves to producing turns that are at least minimally recognisable as questions and answers, respectively' (p. 404). If our data are to reflect the news interviews, we would expect that the interview would consist of mainly question–answer adjacency pairs and that the restrictions on participant contributions would allocate first pair parts of adjacency pairs to the police interviewer and second pair parts to suspects. Such a rule of turn allocation would imply that, in a police interview, utterances which initiate new sequences, such as topic shift, openings and closings, will be produced by the police interviewer and not the suspect. Indeed, Greatbatch (1988) specifically notes that 'interviews are overwhelmingly opened by IRs [interviewers]' and 'are customarily closed by IRs' (p. 404). A brief examination of some features of the Opening and Closing will enable us to consider how the turn taking structure in these sections of the interviews reflects the proposed rule of turn preallocation for news interviews.

Greatbatch (1988) also finds that the preallocation of turn types in news interviews is oriented to by participants and '[d]epartures from the stand- ard question–answer format are frequently attended to as accountable and are characteristically repaired' (p. 404). We will therefore investigate the data to see how this finding applies to the main, Information Gathering part of the interview, and examine suspect-initiated sequences, which appear to comprise such 'departures'.

The analysis in section 4.2.3 demonstrates the extent to which partici- pants in police interviews orient to an institutional interview structure in their turn-by-turn construction of the discourse. This analysis will inform the investigation of topic management in the following section. Finally, the implications of both the turn taking and topic management for the achievement of organisational goals in the interview will contribute to the discussion of the construction of an authoritative police voice.

4.2.1 Turn-taking in the Opening and Closing

We noted in the previous chapter that there is certain information which must be provided to suspects at specified times during the interview, and other information which must be provided 'on record' for the benefit of the tape-recording. It is the fulfilment of these institutional goals which shapes the participation framework (PI2R) invoked by the primary interviewing officer and the suspect in the Opening and the Closing. The primary interviewing officer is allocated the role of institutional questioner and 'information-provider' and the suspect is allocated the role of 'respondent'. That is, in each interview, the primary interviewing officer takes turns in order to ask questions or provide information on behalf of the institution and the suspect's turns are always response turns.

A noticeable feature of the Opening and the Closing is that they do not contain turns which report specific information about the events discussed in the remainder of the interview. All references to these events, such as the charging of the suspect in the Closing, are made by police participants using information available to them as members of the police institution (e.g. from official documents or police notes). Participants do not produce turns which introduce new information about the events or information which is available to them only by virtue of their having personally taken part in the events. In this way participants maintain a strong orientation to the institutionalised nature of the discourse in these parts of the interview and the PI2R participation framework.

A segment from INT1 that contains a possible deviation from the pattern described above is reproduced in the extract below.

Extract 4-1 INT1

500.	pio1:	and you're <u>also</u> going to be <u>charged</u> with the <u>damage</u> on the door↓
501.	SPT1:	(0.6) I'll <u>pay</u> for the door↑
502.	pio1:	yeah but you //under<u>stand</u>*
503.	SPT1:	I me Betty* <u>knows</u> I'll pay for <u>that</u>⇒
504.	pio1:	(0.5) but you //under<u>stand</u> * that there's <u>charges</u> pending as well⇒

505.   SPT1:   (1.0) I've already ( )* mm
506.   pio1:   (1.0)°ri° (2.1)you're not ob<u>lig</u>ed to say or do anything
                unless you wish to <u>do</u> so ↓

It appears that during the Closing of INT1, SPT1 produces utterances that report further information about the events as part of a response to pio1's question. However, closer examination reveals that these turns are the result of a misunderstanding of an institutional phrase on the part of SPT1. We can see that SPT1 has not perceived the use of the word *charged* in line 500 as a specific, police institutional term meaning that a criminal charge is to be laid. Rather, by responding with an offer to pay for damage caused, he recasts pio1's prior turn as a statement concerning a monetary charge. This helps to explain why SPT1 introduces event information at this stage in the interview – he has understood that pio1 is, for some reason, choosing to discuss the financial arrangements between him and the shop concerning the damaged door and he is responding appropriately, according to this belief. Pio1 uses a formulation sequence (Heritage and Watson 1979; see 4.4.4) in line 504 to try to re-establish the institutional understanding of her prior utterance, and SPT1 offers an agreement token *mm* in line 505.

The rephrasing of the question by pio1 indicates that pio1 is treating SPT1's production of event information utterances as inappropriate in this part of the interview. However, in seeking to address SPT1's inappropriate reference to event information, pio1 uses a phrase in line 504 which is more ambiguous than the one she used in line 500. In the original phrase pio1 stated that SPT1 would be *charged with the damage on the door* – the conjunction *with* indicating the institutional meaning of the verb *charge*. In her formulation in line 504, however, she uses the phrase *charges pending* which could refer to financial or criminal charges. Pio1 is demonstrating in her use of language that, at this stage of the interview, event information is no longer relevant – the talk is made meaningful by reference to its institutionality. Without this reference, she could not produce a phrase such as that in line 504 and intend it to be less ambiguous and more likely to clarify the participants' shared understanding of the prior turns.

This sequence demonstrates that the constraints on speakers to produce a narrow range of utterance types within a specific turn taking structure are actively upheld by the participants themselves, in particular the police participants. In this way, the police participants in their institutional role maintain access to and control over the entire Opening and Closing sequences. This supports the earlier proposal that interviewers will have exclusive access to utterances that initiate openings and closings of interactions.

4.2.2   The distribution and features of suspect-initiated sequences

Because this analysis examines the turn taking structure of the interviews by exception, here we will consider the use of utterances which appear to challenge the turn structure of an institutional interview and, as suggested by Greatbatch (1988), we will then be able to see whether or not departures from the turn pre-allocation are oriented to by participants. The first stage of this analysis is to identify the features that distinguish a suspect-initiated sequence. The analysis of the data revealed two main types of suspect-initiated sequences: repairs and clarifications.

It is inevitable that in any interaction misunderstandings, mishearings and similar communicative difficulties may arise. However, as Levinson (1983) notes, 'the tendency for an utterance to attend to those immediately prior to it provides, for both analysts and participants, a "proof procedure" for checking how those turns were understood' (p. 341). Upon perceiving some problem in an utterance, a repair may be initiated by the speaker who produced the problematic utterance – i.e. the repair may be 'self-initiated'. Alternatively, recipients of the utterance may initiate a repair sequence – i.e. the repair may be 'other-initiated'. In this section, we will primarily be examining 'other-initiated' repair sequences produced by suspects in response to a perceived problem in the police interviewer's prior turn.

An example of a suspect-initiated repair combined with a police initiated self-repair is found in the following extract from INT1.

Extract 4-2 INT9

163.	pio9:	and ah out of all those <u>photographs</u> ∧
164.		do you <u>agree</u> that I've got a photograph in my <u>hand</u> ∧
165.		(1.8) um of <u>this</u> for the purpose of the <u>tape</u> the photograph shows a ah
166.		(1.4) the ins the in the inside of an <u>amplifier</u> ∧
167.		is that <u>right</u> ↑
168.	SPT9:	aah <u>yes</u>
169.		it's a <u>speaker</u> box=
170.	pio9:	=a <u>speaker</u> box
171.		and there's a <u>sawn</u> off point two two calibre (.) ah <u>rifle</u> ↓
172.	SPT9:	yes ∧

In line 163, pio9 mistakenly identifies the place where the photographs were found as *an amplifier*, however SPT9, after first attending to the request for clarification by pio9, corrects this in line 169: *it's a speaker box*. As a repair sequence, this initiation does not provide an opportunity for SPT9 to take the floor beyond the repair initiation. Pio9 accepts the repair immediately (note the latching) and concludes his description of the photograph. As we would expect, the repair is treated as an insert or side sequence (see below) and the overall interview turn structure remains unchanged.

The only other kind of suspect-initiated sequences found in the data are requests by suspects for clarification. These initiations form first pair parts of insert sequences whose function is to clarify a police request and whose use does not disrupt the question–answer chain in the long term. The sequence involving a question that SPT8 produces is given in Extract 4-3 below.

Extract 4-3 INT8

58.	pio8:	<u>earlier</u> this afternoon we <u>attended</u> at your <u>premises</u> at
59.		two hundred and thirty <u>five</u> (0.5) <u>Smith</u> Street Middletown ∧
60.		(1.2) ah at that <u>time</u> ah we <u>spoke</u> to you at those <u>premises</u>
61.		(2.3) and ah you were subsequently <u>conveyed</u> by a <u>police</u> car
62.		back to the <u>Middletown</u> police station ↓
63.		is that <u>correct</u> ↑
64.	SPT8:	yeah ⇒
65.	pio8:	is there anything I've said you
66.		(0.3) that you <u>disagree</u> with ↑
67.	SPT8:	yes ⇒
68.	pio8:	what what do you <u>disagree</u> with
69.	SPT8:	what what do yo- what do you <u>mean</u> ↓
70.		what do you <u>mean</u> ∧
71.	pio8:	the police <u>attended</u> at your <u>place</u> earlier=
72.	SPT8:	=oh yeah no I <u>agree</u> ↓
73.	pio8:	we we <u>conveyed</u> you back to the <u>police</u> station ↓
74.		is that <u>right</u> ↑
75.	SPT8:	yes ∧

We see that in lines 58–63, pio8 is constructing a sequence of utterances which report on the events surrounding SPT8's arrest and he concludes this sequence with a form of request for agreement in lines 65–6. As

Table 4.1 Insert sequence embedded within a question–answer adjacency pair

	pio8:	Question 1
→	SPT8:	Question 2
	pio8:	Answer 2
	SPT8:	Answer 1

SPT8 offers a dispreferred response (Bilmes 1988), apparently indicating that she does not agree with pio8's summary of events, pio8 asks her to state what it is she disagrees with. SPT8 appears confused by the police officer's question and in lines 69–70 she initiates a clarification sequence. Pio8 responds with a new version of his summary and following this, SPT8 provides first a receipt marker *oh yeah*, and then her intended response to the original request in lines 65–6 *no I agree*. This pattern is consistent with an 'insert sequence' (Levinson 1983: 304–5) embedded within a question–answer adjacency pair. The extract above can be represented as in Table 4.1.

The right arrow indicates the turn representing SPT8's question 70/ SPT8: *what do you mean*. It is a feature of insert sequences that they do not as a rule disrupt the question–answer sequence into which they are inserted. It is for this reason that suspect-initiated questions which form part of insert sequences maintain the distribution of turn types which allocates first pair parts to police interviewers and second pair parts to suspects, despite being first pair parts themselves. All of the suspect-initiated requests for clarification found in the data conform to the pattern of an insert sequence, returning the floor to the interviewing officer at the conclusion of the clarification.

4.2.3 Summary of suspect-initiated sequences

The findings of this section have shown that in police interviews, participants orientate strongly to a structure where the first pair parts are allocated to the police interviewers and the second pair parts are allocated to suspects. The apparent exceptions to the turn allocation rule in these institutional interviews serve to demonstrate the strength of the participants' adherence to the rule. Suspect-initiated questions are found to be asked only within insert sequences, which automatically turn the floor back to the police interviewer at their conclusion. Furthermore, our findings support the observations made by Greatbatch (1988) regarding a pre-allocation of turn types in news interviews and demonstrate that the consequences for the discourse of such a system are also relevant to police interviews. Most importantly, questions and answers are allocated to interviewers and interviewees respectively and any deviations from this format are 'characteristically repaired', though this latter process occurs at a more subtle level than in news interviews, since the only 'departures from the standard question–answer format' are produced as insert or side sequences which have as a feature the return of the floor to the interviewer for the next question.[11]

It seems clear from this analysis that, just as the type of turns available to the participants is dependent on their role, participants' access to topic management tools may be similarly restricted. Thus, the next section will discuss the nature of topic management by the various participants.

4.3 Topic management

In ordinary conversation, changes in topic can be achieved in a number of ways (Jefferson 1984a, 1988); however, an institutional setting which pre-allocates turn types according to speaker roles will impose restrictions on the introduction or maintenance of topics by participants. If we consider the goals of the interview (particularly the Information Gathering) discussed in the previous chapter, we will recall that the elicitation of a voluntary confession is the overriding institutional concern. Constraints on the availability of topic management tools will necessarily restrict participants' access to the floor in order to provide new information voluntarily. Therefore, it is important that we have an understanding of the way that topic maintenance and shift is achieved in the interviews.

In this section, we will consider the initiation of topics by all interview participants, beginning with suspects, followed by primary interviewing officers and finally secondary/tertiary interviewing officers. This analysis will provide the basis for further analysis in the following section of topic management and the construction of an authoritative police voice.

4.3.1 Suspect topic initiation

When suspects wish to provide additional information that has not been specifically invited by the interviewing officer, they will construct a response to a police request in which this additional information is appended to a more direct response. These suspect topic initiations are described as 'multi-component answers' by Frankel (1990). This approach to topic initiation is demonstrated in the following extracts where the right arrows mark lines containing suspect-initiated utterances.

Extract 4-4 INT1

48.	pio1:		what sort of <u>connection</u> do you have to the shop∧
49.	SPT1:	→	(1.7) nothin Betty and <u>I</u> we've
50.	·	→	(0.2) aw we've been together for nine <u>years</u> de facto relationship∧//we-*
51.	pio1:		w'l who's* <u>Betty</u>↓
52.	SPT1:		(0.5) <u>Fisher</u>∧

Extract 4-5 INT2

41.	pio2:		do you know the <u>address</u> of that <u>house</u>∧
42.	SPT2:		<u>Spray</u> Street⇒ // °I think°∧*
43.	pio2:		don't* know the <u>number</u>↑
44.	SPT2:	→	°no:: (0.2) it's <u>behind</u> 3ZX°=
45.	pio2:		=°rih°↓=
46.	SPT2:	→	=that's (3.0) not sure if its↓ // there⇒ or u' hm↓*
47.	pio2:		<u>yeh</u>⇒ no <u>that's</u> OK∧ yep↑*

Extract 4-6 INT3

148.	pio3:		(0.4) was that set up (.) <u>predominantly</u> to (.) ah
149.			(0.3) to ah (0.6) to <u>water</u> these // (0.2) ah*
150.	SPT3:		mm*⇒ //no*↓
151.	pio3:		no*∧
152.	SPT3:	→	no↓ (0.4) there was going to be <u>ferns</u> and that in there↓
153.		→	(1.4) and I put <u>those</u> in there because we couldn't afford (0.3) <u>ferns</u>
154.		→	and (.) stuff like that (0.5) so↓

Each of these extracts contains suspect-initiated utterances that add information to a potentially complete response following a police question. That is, the first component of each response in the extracts above is a single word which could comprise a complete response: 49/SPT1: *(1.7) nothin*; 44/SPT2: *no::*; and 152/SPT3: *no↓*.[2] Appended to this is the suspect-initiated information that in each case expands upon the first word. This initial, potentially complete, response does not have to be a single word, and neither does it have to be a negative marker or denial of some prior police assertion. For example, in the following extract, SPT5 offers additional information in line 224 as a continuation of his answer begun in line 221.

Extract 4-7 INT5

220.	pio5	what did she <u>say</u> to you this <u>lady</u> ↓
221.	SPT5	she said what are <u>you</u> doing here
222.		and we <u>said</u> we come up to see a <u>mate</u> Hamish <u>Campbell</u> ↓
223.		(2.0) and that we're just waiting <u>around</u> for him ∧
224.		(1.2) cause I haven't seen him since I've been in Queensland ⇒
225.		it's the <u>first</u> opportunity I've <u>had</u> ⇒
226.		//really⇒*
227.	pio5	all <u>right</u>*
228.		what <u>else</u> did she say↓

Initiations can be much lengthier when they comprise part of the report being provided by the suspect concerning the events being discussed. An example is given in the following extract from INT1.

Extract 4-8 INT1

87.	pio1:		so <u>wadcha</u> do then↓
88.	SPT1:		(0.5) w'l (1.1) <u>made</u> meself another cup of <u>coffee</u>⇒
89.			and I just <u>thought</u> about it∧
90.			and I said what's going <u>on</u>⇒
91.			this can't be <u>right</u>↑
92.			(1.0) s- Betty and I are getting on <u>all right</u>∧
93.		(→)	I don't go anywhere near their <u>house</u> unless I <u>phone</u>∧
94.			(1.8) I <u>ring</u> her I say can I go and get <u>this</u> and go and get <u>that</u>∧
95.			she says <u>yep</u>∧ no <u>worries</u>∧
96.			and a (0.2) few times she said you don't have to <u>phone</u> to go <u>around</u> ere⇒
97.			you just go around and get what you∧ <u>want</u>⇒
98.		→	(1.8) and (0.4) I go to the <u>shop</u> there a couple aw
99.		→	(0.3) every second <u>day</u> or <u>third</u> day
100.		→	(0.8) and get milk <u>bread</u> and a few <u>vegies</u> and that that I <u>need</u>∧
101.		→	(1.1) and <u>smokes</u>∧
102.			and we get on <u>all right</u> just as <u>friends</u> ⇒
103.			like we bump into each other in the <u>street</u>⇒
104.			(0.5) //<u>best</u> of* <u>friends</u>∧

SPT1's long turn of talk (lines 88–104) moves through several topics, including his relationship with his ex-de facto, their arrangements for seeing each other, how often he goes to the shop and the items he usually purchases there. All of this information is provided following pio1's question 87/pio1: *so wadcha do then*↓. It is difficult to identify the exact point at which the suspect-initiated utterances commence, but the arrow in parentheses gives an approximate starting point for the initiations. In describing 'what he did then', SPT1 has begun with a direct response – that he made *another cup of coffee*⇒ and *just thought about it*∧ – and then he begins to report his internal monologue 90–1/SPT1: *and I said what's going on*⇒ this can't be *right*↑. From here, he is able to move into a description of his relationship with Betty, and the other topics mentioned above, as part of the set of things he is thinking about, although it seems unlikely that as part of his musings at the time he would actually have made a mental list of items he buys at the shop. The utterances in lines 98–101 in particular seem to be reporting not what SPT1 was actually thinking about, but background information that he wishes to present to the police officers in order that they better understand the circumstances of the assault. That is, instead of the topic of his turn being predominantly 'actions on the day of the assault', it is 'the state of affairs in the months leading up to the day of the assault'.

As a device for providing unsolicited background information, SPT1's 'what I was thinking about' approach is effective, since it allows him to shift away from a direct response to the question in order to initiate utterances, and yet he can still maintain the relevance of his utterances in relation to pio1's question.

In this way, the information he wishes to append is included in his response such that it remains relevant, albeit indirectly, to the topic initiated by pio1 in line 87. Thus, SPT1 is able to provide a great deal of background information without clearly shifting the topic of his talk beyond the parameters of 'what he did then'. Furthermore, the inner monologue device provides a mechanism for initiating topic shift so that the utterances produced comprise a kind of topical 'aside'. It is not a true 'side sequence', as no other speaker is involved, but it is the nature of the device that when talk on the topic is completed, the prior topic will be revived automatically. That is, when SPT1 has finished describing what he was thinking about at that time, the 'what happened next' topic will reassert itself as relevant. Thus, the inner monologue device is not even a true topic shift, as it has built into it a device for returning to the prior topic. This is demonstrated in a similar example from INT10 when SPT10 uses the device in lines 149–50 to describe why he decided to expose himself to his girlfriend's daughter:

Extract 4-9 INT10

146.   pio10:   and what happened <u>then</u> ⇒
147.   SPT10:   and she <u>said</u>
148.   well what's the <u>difference</u> ∧
149.   and I've just thought oh <u>well</u> she's seen me most of
               the <u>time</u> ⇒
150.   half the time she <u>walked</u> in on me and everything
               <u>else</u> ⇒
151.   and that's when I just <u>showed</u> her ↓
152.   and that was <u>it</u> ∧

A different device is employed by SPT1 later in that interview, as demonstrated in Extract 4-10. Here, SPT1 wishes to append a description of his feelings about the damage he caused Ian in the assault, but as this information has not been requested, he uses the multi-component answer format to present his views.

Extract 4-10 INT1

281.   pio1:   yeah↓(0.2) so the <u>two</u> (0.2) lacerations on your <u>hand</u> are
               actually from his <u>mouth</u>
282.   are they∧
283.   SPT1:   that's //<u>right</u>⇒*
284.   pio1:   from* his <u>teeth</u>↓
285.   SPT1:   (1.1) yep⇒ now I didn't <u>mean</u> to break his teeth ⇒
286.   I didn't <u>know</u> I did that⇒
287.   (0.8) I'm sorry I <u>did</u> that ⇒
288.   but I didn't know I was <u>doing</u> it↓
289.   pio1:   well you've <u>hit</u> him on the-
290.   (.) with <u>your</u> right <u>ha:nd</u> ⇒
291.   to almost the right side of his <u>face</u>⇒
292.   (0.9) pretty much at the <u>front</u> ⇒
293.   at the right <u>side</u>⇒ //and* you've

Following pio1's request for confirmation in lines 281–2 and 284, SPT1 provides a confirmation response and then he picks up the topic of Ian's teeth being struck by his (SPT1's) hand in line 285 in the context of the unintentional nature of the act. From this position, he is able to make relevant his ignorance of the amount of damage caused and his subsequent regret that Ian's teeth sustained such damage. Appending information to form a multi-component answer provides an opportunity for a topic shift that can be achieved within the constraints of the interviewee role.

Regarding the multi-component answer approach to suspect initiations, we should note that Frankel (1990) describes this approach as one which not only 'provides an option as to which portion of the information will be retrieved in the next turn' (p. 238) but one which minimally obligates the interviewer to produce a response to the new information at all. The data reveal that this observation appears to hold true in police interviews as well. The extract below from INT1 contains one example of a police response to new information introduced by SPT1 in the multi-component answer format.

Extract 4-11 INT1

380.	pio1:	do you know <u>why</u> she would have gone out the back room↑
381.		(0.4) li' would she have been <u>scared</u> or↓
382.	SPT1:	maybe she <u>was</u> ⇒
383.		but m' <u>Betty's</u> never ev <u>seen</u> me like that↓
384.		I've never <u>been</u> like that before↓
385.		(0.4) Betty <u>knows</u> I would not <u>hurt</u> <u>her</u> or <u>hurt</u> anyone↓
386.		(1.1) and she must have <u>known</u> something <u>really</u> sparked him off↓
387.		to get me <u>goin</u> like that ↓
388.		something had to be <u>goin</u>↓
389.		hh //something* had to ∧
390.	pio1:	w'l what* happened then-↓
391.	SPT1:	(1.1) get me going to <u>do</u> something like that↓
392.	pio1:	you've <u>hit</u> him a coupla <u>times</u>⇒
393.		he's um (.) <u>holding</u> his mouth or <u>bleeding</u> ⇒

In the above extract, SPT1 is responding to a question from pio1 about Betty's reaction to the assault on Ian. He begins by offering a partial agreement in line 382/SPT1: *maybe she <u>was</u>* ⇒ and then he extends his answer, explaining that the assault was very unusual behaviour for him and that Betty would know, in his opinion, that his actions were the result of extreme provocation. In lines 388 and 389, he initiates a self-repair which causes some repetition in his turn and perhaps it is this repetition which prompts pio1 to attempt to take the floor at this point, even though SPT1 has not reached a transition relevant place (TRP)

(Sacks et al. 1974). In any case, her utterance in line 390 does not retrieve any of the information that SPT1 has provided in his turn, but instead attempts to elicit further reports of the incident. However, SPT1 does not respond to this elicitation, which has partially overlapped with his repair of his prior utterance and instead he pauses for 1.1 seconds and then proceeds to complete the utterance that he had begun in line 389 and which pio1 interrupted. At the end of line 391 is the first TRP, which offers pio1 the opportunity to retake the floor without interruption. Despite SPT1's determination to complete his turn and provide information about his character, pio1 does not take up this topic in line 392, but rather, she continues the elicitation begun in line 390.

Many other cases exist in the data of interviewing officers ignoring new information provided by the suspect, and taking the floor to ask an unrelated question; however, this example best demonstrates the phenomenon because of the overt display by SPT1 that he considers the information important. SPT1 is making a considerable effort to complete his turn when he is interrupted by a topically disjunctive question put to him by pio1. However, SPT1's turn is subsequently ignored by pio1, which underlines the weakness of the obligation on the interviewer to take up new information provided by the interviewee in this format.

At other times the new information introduced by suspects is not ignored, but in retrieving it, a side sequence or insert sequence may result which enables the interviewing officer to 'initiate a query or series of queries regarding the additional information, at the completion of which he [sic] will return to his or her original line of questioning' (Frankel 1990: 238). An example of this phenomenon is given in the extract from INT4 below.

Extract 4-12 INT4

144.   pio4:   did you see any <u>sex</u> aids on the <u>floor</u> or // around* the
                 place ↑
145.   SPT4:   tuhh*
146.   yeah I seen a <u>dildo</u> there ⇒
147.   //but* sort of I didn't (0.8) <u>bother</u> picking that up ↓
148.   pio4:   right↓*
149.   right ⇒
150.   SPT4:   and I the only thing I <u>got</u> was a c<u>d</u> ⇒
151.   and um (0.5) a <u>roast</u> in the <u>fridge</u> (.h h)
152.   pio4:   right why'd you take the <u>roast</u> in the <u>fridge</u> ∧

153.   SPT4:   I was <u>hungry</u> ∧
154.   pio4:   all right ↓
155.   did you <u>take</u> a metallica <u>tape</u> ∧
156.   from um (.) the <u>bedroom</u> ↑
157.   SPT4:   yeah ↓

Here, SPT4 supports his assertion that he did not steal any *sex aids* during a burgulary by listing the items that he did take. Pio4 asks a clarification question about one of the items – *the roast* – and SPT4 answers straight-forwardly. Pio4 then uses a discourse marker *all right* to indicate a shift of footing back to the original line of questioning which is realised as line 155, *did you take a metallica tape*. Pio4's response to SPT4's initiations in lines 150–1 forms a side sequence in lines 152 and 153, following which he is able to resume the role of questioner in line 154, thus preserving the pre-allocated turn structure of the institutional interview.

There is evidence in the interview data that participants in police interviews maintain a structure where topics are initiated by police interviewers and not by suspects. Suspect orientations towards topic shift as outside their role can be demonstrated by examining extracts such as the following from INT2.

Extract 4-13 INT2

290.   pio2:   (2.0) so there was⇒ (0.6) absolutely no <u>reason</u>↓
291.   (.) <u>why</u> you should have <u>treated</u> 'er in that manner↓
292.   SPT2:   (1.0) nup↓
293.   (12.6) ((soft intermittent paper shuffling sounds during silence))
294.   pio2:   was there anything <u>else</u> that (.) a:h↓ you wish to <u>add</u> to (0.2) what's <u>happened</u>∧
295.   SPT2:   (2.8) no:oh jus (2.0) if you wanna (h)know what (h)<u>happened</u>∧ y'know⇒
296.   (.) we- (0.8) we went back to <u>Littlevillage</u>∧
297.   (2.0) I didn't have my <u>ke:ys</u>↑ hh
298.   (0.4) um⇒ (0.4) to get in⇒ (0.8) to the⇒ (.) <u>hotel</u>∧
299.   so↓ (0.6) we went back to u:m⇒ (0.6) <u>her</u> place in Satellite River∧
300.   (2.6) <u>talked</u> until↓ (1.8) five 'clock in the <u>morning</u>∧
301.   pio2:   (0.6) were⇒ at this <u>stage</u> (.) were y- (.) were you still <u>aggressive</u> towards her↑
302.   SPT2:   (0.6) no↑

303.   pio2:   (0.8) u::m⇒ (.) it's <u>alleged</u> that a::h⇒
304.   (0.8) she asked you to <u>leave</u> the house numerous times
                 you <u>refused</u>∧

At this stage in the interview, the information reported by SPT2 has covered actions and events up to the point when he and his girlfriend left their friend's house in Bigtown (where the assault took place). Pio2 has then produced a number of requests for confirmation of SPT2's reasons for the assault. The last of these appears in the extract above as lines 290–1. SPT2 produces a confirmation and there is a long silence (12.6 seconds) during which it is possible that pio2 is making some notes, given the sounds of paper being moved about. Pio2 ends the silence by asking SPT2 294/pio2: *was there anything <u>else</u> that (.) a:h↓ you wish to <u>add</u> to (0.2) what's <u>happened</u>∧*.

This turn (line 294) can be described as a 'topic initial elicitor' that follows closing components and 'makes a contrast between prior talk and talk that may proceed from their [pio2's, in this case] news enquiry' (Button and Casey 1984: 171). It functions to offer an opportunity for the recipient, SPT2, to offer new topical material, simultaneously avoiding an immediate move into the Closing.

At first, in line 295, SPT2 seems unwilling to take up the offer, as his first response to the request is to decline the offer to add information. Button and Casey (1984) describe such a response as a 'no-news report' and note that 'following the exercise of this option, and within this turn, newsworthy-event-reports can be made' (p. 180). Indeed, SPT2 does proceed to a 'newsworthy-event-report' within the same turn (lines 295–300). By prefacing the report with a 'no-news report' and a component (*jus* [just]) which marks the report as 'elicited and not immediately available for reporting' (p. 179), SPT2 downgrades the 'newsworthiness' of the report. In other words, he presents new information, but he also displays his opinion that this information may not be appropriately relevant to the interview.

Eventually in line 301 pio2 takes the floor and produces a 'topicalizer', or utterance which serves to 'both upgrade the newsworthiness of the previously downgraded reported event, and operate to transform a possible topic initial into an item for talking to' (Button and Casey 1984: 179). However, it is worth noting that there are several TRPs in SPT2's turn where long pauses occur and pio2 does not take the floor to offer any kind of topicalizer. According to Button and Casey (1984), 'the production of a topic provide[s] for topicalization as a preferred response' (p. 184). We would therefore expect that topicalization would be noticeably absent if it were not offered, and the dispreferred response – that the topic has not been taken up by the pio2 – would be inferred from pio2's failure to offer a topicalizer. The fact that SPT2 is not deterred from continuing his report despite an absence of a topicalizer in several TRPs in the above segment, would appear either to problematise the preference organisation for topicalizers in police interviews or to suggest that pio2 was engaged in some non-verbal activity, such as nodding his head, which might equally serve as a topicalizer.

When pio2 does produce an utterance which takes up the topic initiated by SPT2 (301/pio2: *(0.6) were*⇒ at this <u>stage</u> (.) were y- (.) were you still <u>aggressive</u> towards her↑), it is clearly oriented towards an issue that he is concerned with, rather than arising directly from something SPT2 has said. This is confirmed in lines 303–4 where pio2 indicates that he already had some knowledge of the events SPT2 is reporting by presenting an allegation concerning SPT2's behaviour at that time.

The topic that SPT2 initiates is clearly important to the case. For SPT2, the report presented supports his version that there was a reconciliation between him and his girlfriend, Leila, which may serve to minimise the impact of the assault. On the other hand, the presentation of the report gives pio2 an opportunity to produce allegations of SPT2's continued aggression towards Leila which challenge SPT2's version. It is clear that the topic provides important opportunities for both parties to support their version of events. Therefore, the fact that SPT2 uses a 'no-news' response and downgrades the newsworthiness of the eventual report which would otherwise have been excluded from the interview (we noted earlier that pio2 was preparing to move into the Closing) serves to underline the suspect's orientation to a structure where topic shift is initiated by police participants. Similarly in the following extract, SPT1 offers a 'no-news' report prior to a report of regret in response to a topic initial elicitor offered by pio1 in the Closing of INT1.

Extract 4-14 INT9

411.	pio9:	do you wish to make a further <u>statement</u> in <u>relation</u> to the matter ↓
412.	SPT9:	only that I haven't got the <u>gun</u> any more ∧
413.		(0.9) it's totally <u>destroyed</u> ∧
414.		yet I can't <u>prove</u> that ⇒
415.		(0.6) um e- that's about <u>all</u> ⇒

In Extract 4-14, SPT9 uses the downgrading components *only* and *that's about all* to reduce both the newsworthiness of his report and the obligation on pio9 to take up the new topic. In fact, in all cases of an 'anything else' question being asked prior to the initiation of a closing sequence, the suspect offers a response that downgrades the newsworthiness of the report. This is achieved either by prefacing the report with a no-news report or by introducing it with components such as *well* or *just* and hesitations that indicate that the report has been searched for and produced for want of something more obviously newsworthy. In other words, new topics, even when available to the suspect and elicited by the police interviewer, are not oriented to as newsworthy by the suspect, despite the importance they may have to the suspect's version of events.

4.3.2   Primary interviewing officer topic initiation

We have established that one of the differences between ordinary talk and a police interview is the fact that talk by participants in an institutional interview will display an orientation to a question–answer structure which constrains the distribution of turn types to speakers. Another way in which police institutional interviews differ from ordinary conversation is the availability of discursive resources to police interviewers when shifting from a current topic to a new topic. In a paper which focuses on the conversational resources accessed by participants to shift out of troubles-talk, Jefferson (1984a) cites Harvey Sacks's discussion of the use of a 'stepwise transition' to achieve topic shift. In particular, the following turn construction is described by Sacks as a general feature of the topical organisation in conversation:

> movement from topic to topic, not by a topic-close followed by a topic beginning, but by a stepwise move, which involves linking up whatever is being introduced to what has just been talked about, such that, as far as anybody knows, a new topic has not been started, though we're far from wherever we began. (Sacks, Lecture 5, spring 1972, pp. 15–16, cited in Jefferson 1984a)

This is the type of topic shift which we have already seen being used by suspects to introduce new topics. However, analysis of the police interview data reveal that for the professional participant, the police interviewer, this 'general feature of the topical organisation in conversation' observed by Sacks does not apply. To demonstrate this point, we can examine this extract from INT7.

Extract 4-15 INT7

289.	pio7:	how <u>often</u> do you <u>smoke</u> at this stage ∧
290.	SPT7:	(2.0) well I'm <u>trying</u> to cut it <u>down</u>=
291.		=I usually have a <u>smoke</u> usually every <u>night</u>
292.		if I ca-
293.		if I can get <u>hold</u> of one∧
294.	pio7:	mm hm ⇒
295.	SPT7:	but often you <u>can't</u> so I have it you know↓
296.		I ge- I get by <u>without</u> it∧
297.		I'm <u>not</u> like a
298.	pio7:	mm
299.	SPT7:	I don't <u>think</u> I'm a addict∧
300.		I met a good <u>friend</u> of mine while I was down in <u>Melbourne</u> the other <u>day</u>
301.		he used to smoke <u>a lot</u>∧
302.		and he just gave it up just like <u>that</u> ((clicks fingers))
303.	pio7:	mm
304.	SPT7:	cause his <u>wife</u> used to keep tipping it <u>out</u> ∧ hh hh ⇒
305.	pio7:	um what's your source of <u>income</u> at the <u>moment</u> ∧

It is interesting to contrast the approach taken to topic shift by SPT7 with that used by pio7. As discussed above in relation to similar extracts from INT1, it is difficult to identify the exact point at which SPT7 has begun to introduce new information on to the floor which was not requested by the police officer – pio7's original prompt for this part of SPT7's report was in line 289/pio7: *how often do you smoke at this stage*. If we examine the extract line by line, we can see that there is a gradual divergence from the topic of the request. This is achieved through 'step-wise transitions' from the topic of SPT7's drug habit, to a point where SPT7 is talking about a friend's ability to quit smoking marijuana. By the time he reaches this topic in lines 302 and 304, his utterances are relatively remote, topically, from the events being investigated in the interview. However, SPT7's use of stepwise transitions ensures that the utterances are not topically disjunctive.

By comparison, pio7 produces a request in line 305 which is not only topically disjunctive relative to SPT7's prior turn, but which is offered in response to a humorous anecdote in SPT7's prior utterance of which he might expect some acknowledgement.

Topically disjunctive police questions by primary interviewing officers are common in all of the interviews and on several occasions these questions interrupt the suspect's turn. Sometimes the police officer returns to the topic of the suspect's prior turn after several exchanges and other times the topic shift is permanent. In either case, it is evident that primary interviewing officers have more effective topic shifting devices available to them for use at almost any time.

In addition to devices for shifting topic, primary police officers also have available to them two devices for constraining available topics over the course of the interview. Firstly, the utterance that describes the police officer's intention to interview the suspect in the Opening specifically relates the interview to the alleged crime for which the suspect has been arrested. An example from INT10 is given below.

Extract 4-16 INT10

22.	pio10:	right ↓
23.		(1.4) I'm <u>going</u> to interview you in relation to (0.3) an indecent <u>act</u> ⇒
24.		that (.) <u>allegedly</u> happened in <u>January</u> of this <u>year</u> ↓
25.		(0.9) before I <u>do</u> I must <u>inform</u> you that you are not obliged to say or <u>do</u> anything
26.		but anything you say or do <u>may</u> be given in evidence ⇒
27.		do you under<u>stand</u> that ↓
28.	SPT10:	yes ⇒

The same basic phrasing is used by all the interviewing officers in the Opening of the interviews, though there are some variations, as discussed in section 3.6.

The second device available to police interviewers to constrain the topics of the ensuing talk is the discoursal indicator (Thomas 1989; see Chapter 5) produced by police interviewers as they shift into the Information Gathering which includes a description of the alleged criminal activity as the relevant 'macro' topic of the subsequent interview. An example from INT2 is given below.

Extract 4-17 INT9

65.	pio9:	right ↓
66.		um <u>since</u> you've been back at the <u>police</u> station here ah <u>Sam</u> ⇒
67.		we've <u>gone</u> through a heap of <u>photographs</u> ∧
68.		(1.1) um can you just ah <u>tell</u> us what all these photo-graphs <u>were</u> ∧
69.		um <u>roughly</u> that we've <u>gone</u> through ↑
70.	SPT9:	um (2.1) pictures of <u>guns</u> ⇒

| 71. | and some pictures of <u>me</u> and a few <u>friends</u> with <u>guns</u> and ⇒ |
| 72. | (1.2) pictures of <u>other</u> people that I haven't <u>seen</u> before ⇒ |

We noted earlier in Chapter 4 that the police interviewers provide descriptions of their role as 'questioners' or recipients of a report in the turns mentioned above. Here we can see that these turns are also a device for constraining the available topics over the course of the interview.

4.3.3   Secondary interviewing officer topic initiation

The role of the secondary interviewing officer (sio) or tertiary interviewing officer in the data is generally fairly limited and does not greatly enhance our understanding of police institutional discourse. For the sake of brevity, this discussion will be confined to an analysis of INT3. This interview has been chosen because it so happens that sio3 is the same person as pio2, a coincidence which provides us with an opportunity for comparisons between the discursive behaviour of primary and secondary interviewing officers.

The extract below demonstrates that there is a difference in the way that primary and secondary interviewing officers introduce information to the floor and shift or maintain topics. We have already seen that primary interviewing officers can introduce topics disjunctively and reintroduce prior topics for further elaboration. In this extract, we see the way that sio3 reintroduces a prior topic in line 246.

Extract 4-18 INT3

235.	pio3:	(1.2) <u>put</u> it to you that Sergeant Lassiter (0.6) <u>attended</u> that <u>address</u>⇒
236.		(0.5) and ah you were <u>arrested</u>∧
237.		(0.2) and ah taken back to (0.4) your <u>residence</u> at fourteen Abbot Street ⇒
238.		is that <u>right</u>↑
239.	SPT3:	yes⇒
240.	pio3:	(0.4) um (0.2) at that (0.8) ah (0.6) at that <u>location</u>∧
241.		(.) is (0.5) is that where y- (0.7) yooah (0.4) you met (0.4) myself
242.		and Senior Constable <u>Atkins</u>
243.		who were still <u>searching</u> the premises (0.2) at fourteen Abbot Street↑
244.	SPT3:	yes⇒

245.   pio3:   (0.4) OK↓ (0.6) now I'll go (0.4) on with <u>items</u> that were
ah // (0.3) ah *
246.   sio3:   just* on ah (.) just on the house at thirty-four (.)
<u>Crown</u> Road∧
247.   (0.4) that (.) shed (.) was that a <u>lockable</u> shed↑
248.   SPT3:   (0.6) yes⇒
249.   sio3:   <u>who</u> had the key to that shed↓
250.   SPT3:   Sybil↓
251.   sio3:   (0.3) did <u>you</u> have a key at <u>all</u>↑
252.   SPT3:   no↓
253.   sio3:   (0.3) she was the only one who had <u>access</u> to that <u>shed</u>↑
254.   SPT3:   yes⇒
255.   sio3:   (0.5) that shed was <u>locked</u>∧ // with*
256.   SPT3:   yes*⇒
257.   sio3:   with the <u>plants</u> inside↑
258.   SPT3:   yes⇒
259.   sio3:   r't↓
260.   pio3:   (1.4) that was locked with a <u>padlock</u> was it↑
261.   SPT3:   yes⇒
262.   pio3:   (1.0) OK↓ (1.0) now (0.6) do you have any <u>knowledge</u> of th-
263.   (.) what happened to the plants (0.2) <u>after</u> you left that
location↑
264.   SPT3:   (1.5) I do <u>now</u>∧ yes↓

The house that sio3 mentions in line 246 is the house being referred to
by pio3 in line 235. Sio3's utterance concerning this location is produced
at a point in the interview where it becomes clear that pio3 is moving
away from the topic of 'thirty-four Crown Road' and on to the topic of
'fourteen Abbot Street'. In order to maintain the topic of 'thirty-four
Crown Road', sio3 interrupts pio3, in line 245. Sio3 uses the phrase *just*
on ah (.) just on the house at thirty-four (.) <u>Crown</u> Road∧, which minimises
the imposition of his interruption by indicating that the interruption
will be limited to the topic of 'thirty-four Crown Road'. Sio3 marks the
end of the series of question – answer pairs he has initiated with the
discourse marker *r't*↓ ('right') and the next turn is passed unproblemat-
ically to pio3, despite the occurrence of a 1.4 second pause before pio3's
turn during which any participant could have taken the floor.

Sio3's turn in Extract 4-18 demonstrates that the two police officers
are not equally eligible to initiate new topics at any time. There is an
orderliness in the distribution of access to topic initiation and this is
displayed and maintained in the police participants' use of language.

Sio3 displays to pio3 that he is minimising the imposition of his topic initiation, recognising the restricted access to this facility that his role allows. Thus the institutionally endowed roles of primary and secondary interviewing officer are maintained at the level of topic management within the structure of the interview discourse. Finally, Extract 4-18 supports the findings of the previous section that the floor defaults to the primary interviewing officer at the conclusion of any recognisably complete sequence.

4.3.4   Question–answer chains and the deference structure

Within a Conversation Analysis framework, this analysis has thus far progressed through a consideration of the distribution of turn types to an examination of initiations and topic management tools. The analysis has revealed that participants in police interview discourse are able to appeal to their institutionally endowed discursive role in order to make utterances relevant. Thus, the primary interviewing officers are able to make relevant any request for information about the alleged crime by reference to their role as police officer and 'information gatherer'. Similarly, suspects are able to make relevant any utterance which provides information about the alleged crime by reference to their role as alleged criminal and 'information provider'. However, suspects do not have access to a role that will allow them to place information on to the floor without invitation – any information provided by the suspect can only be provided in response to police request.

The result of this allocation of speaker roles is that the range of topics available to the police interviewer when producing utterances is much broader than those available to the suspect, since the suspect's utterances must be topically relevant to the police request for information when responding to those requests. The way in which topic shift is managed by the primary interviewing officers reveals that there is no need for these officers to display the relevance of a topically disjunctive utterance. Their role as police interviewer makes relevant, as mentioned, a broad range of topics at all times, even during suspect turns. On the other hand, if a suspect wishes to provide information which is not directly related to the topic of the request made by the interviewer, he will be required to provide some link to the topic of the request in order to display its relevance.

It is interesting that the secondary interviewing officer role does not appear to have the power to make relevant disjunctive topic initiations in the same way as the role of primary interviewing officer. When sio3 wishes to reopen a topic which pio3 has just closed, he overtly refers to the fact that he is reopening this topic.

The interactional resources available to the participants all contribute to the construction of the interview as an oriented-to chain of adjacency pairs. Each turn of the interview participants is constructed to maintain this structure, even when the nature of the turn would normally cause some change in the chaining sequence. Suspect-initiated utterances and topic shift are produced only within exchange structures or turn types that facilitate the return of the floor to the police participant at their conclusion. In other words, there is an inflexible 'chain rule' (Sacks 1992a) governing turn allocation which operates in police interviews so that recurring sets of adjacency pairs obligate the suspect to respond to first-pair parts and return the floor to the police interviewer. It is not being suggested that participants have an opportunity to construct the discourse using different turn sequences. On the contrary, the behaviour of the participants in orienting to the chain rule underlines that there is no other sequential arrangement available in this institutional situation.

This arrangement is referred to by Frankel (1990) in the context of medical interviews as a 'deference structure' (p. 235), where 'the obligation to respond, insofar as it characterises and constrains the speaking opportunities of one member of a dyad and not the other, may be treated as a type of sequential deference' (Frankel 1990: 258). Clearly the orientation of the participants to an inflexible allocation of turn types which places a recurrent obligation upon the suspect to respond to first pair parts demonstrates that the participants actively maintain a sequential deference structure in their construction of the discourse.

Thus, the structure of the turn taking mechanism of the police interview ensures that primary interviewing officers are endowed with an 'authoritative voice' by virtue of their institutional role. An authoritative police voice is embedded in the turn-by-turn construction of the discourse, which is regulated by the police institution and oriented to by the interview participants.

The following section will explore the active construction and maintenance of a police version of events by the officers in interviews and the centrality to this process of an authoritative voice.

4.4   Constructing a police version

In order to identify the discursive practices of the police interviewers that invoke or maintain the S3R framework, this section will draw upon the notion of a police preferred version of events (Auburn et al. 1995) which is produced as an alternative to the suspect version. This analysis is concerned primarily with the discursive practices that construct a police version of events and the role of interactional resources such as accusation–denial/acceptance adjacency pair types (4.4.1), evidence and 'my side' tellings (4.4.2), topic management tools (4.4.2) and formulations (4.4.4).

4.4.1   Accusations in the construction of a police version

Making accusations is a way of presenting the speaker's version of events as a first pair part, to which the second pair part is a denial or acceptance (Atkinson and Drew 1979). Bilmes (1988) finds that accusations can be treated as a sub-category of a broader classification, identified as 'attribution' first pair parts, whereby 'some action or thought or attitude' is attributed to the recipient (p. 167). In terms of participation frameworks in police interviews, accusations or attributions are not turn types that permit voluntary invocation of the S3R framework by the suspect because the content of the accusation, the thing being alleged, is produced by the interviewing officer within the P3R framework. The second pair part produced by the suspect will either invoke the P2RA framework if she or he accepts the allegation (i.e. the suspect takes up the role of *principal* only), or maintain the P3R framework if she or he denies the allegation.

Several extracts from the data are analysed below to see how accusations and attributions are produced and responded to in police interviews.

Extract 4-19 INT12

750.	pio12:	I <u>put</u> it to you that you actually went into the <u>kitchen</u> ∧
751.		and <u>helped</u> drag in Wayne <u>Gibson</u> ↓
752.		one of the <u>bouncers</u> ↓
753.	SPT12:	(3) no <u>way</u> ∧
754.	pio12:	(2.5) can you <u>elaborate</u> on that ↑
755.	SPT12:	(3.5) wasn't in the
756.		anywhere <u>near</u> a kitchen ↓
757.	pio12:	(2.0) do you remember throwing a <u>coffee</u> cup ↓

In Extract 4-19 from INT12, the suspect is accused of dragging a bouncer into a fight which has broken out at a nightclub. Throughout this very long interview (over 80 minutes), the suspect continues to deny his involvement in the fight, at least to the extent alleged by pio12. Following the accustion in lines 750–2, SPT12 offers a firm denial *no way*, which pio12 asks him to *elaborate*. He offers an explanation relating to his distance from the kitchen and pio12 immediately turns to another topic. Pio12 makes a number of attempts to approach the issue of the suspect's involvement from different angles, and eventually introduces a witness statement, as we can see in Extract 4-20.

Extract 4-20 INT12

835.	pio12:	he'd <u>recognise</u> you ∧
836.	SPT12:	mm
837.	pio12:	at any given <u>time</u> ∧
838.		why would he <u>say</u> in his <u>statement</u> ⇒
839.		<u>specifically</u>
840.		Dave <u>Fielding</u> (0.8) <u>did</u> something ↓
841.		(1.2) and you're saying you <u>didn't</u> ↓
842.	SPT12:	(3.0) I don't <u>know</u> ∧
843.		I don't know <u>that's</u> why I don't n-
844.		why he come up and <u>blame</u> me for doing something
845.		he <u>hit</u> me (.) that night ↓
846.	pio12:	(8.5) I'll read a <u>section</u> (0.5) of his <u>statement</u> ⇒

Regardless of the quantity or strength of the evidence against the suspect's story, SPT12 maintains his position and does not agree with the accusations made by pio12. The police version of events is not ratified by SPT12 at any stage – at most he states that he does not know why the witness has made an allegation against him. In the following extract from INT1, the suspect goes further, claiming that the witness must be lying.

Extract 4-21 INT1

314.	pio1:	<u>he</u> states that it was a <u>closed</u> fist ↓
315.		that you //<u>punched</u>* him in the //<u>mouth</u>↓*
316.	SPT1:	nah↓* caw⇒*
317.	pio1:	(0.6) what do you say to that↓
318.	SPT1:	(0.6) that's a <u>lie</u>⇒

In Extract 4-21, pio1 is constructing the police version of events by repeating an allegation by the victim, Ian – 314/pio1: *he states that it was a <u>closed</u> fist↓*. In this way, pio1 attributes to SPT1 the action of striking Ian with a closed fist *in the //<u>mouth</u>↓*. This attribution contradicts the version of events that SPT1 has described just prior to line 314. According to SPT1, he struck Ian twice with the back of his hand, whereas pio1 is attempting to construct a different version in which SPT1 punched Ian.

Pio1's version is based on allegations made by the victim and offers a stronger case for the charge of assault, with which SPT1 is to be charged. Pio1 is therefore motivated to obtain SPT1's ratification of this version of events, which she attempts to do through the initiation of accusation/attribution adjacency pairs. However, SPT1 does not offer second pair parts which would provide for his uptake of the *principal* role in relation to pio1's version of events, e.g. agreement tokens. Instead, he offers a denial *nah↓** at the earliest TRP, which occurs at the end of line 314, although pio1 has self-selected and continued to talk so that SPT1's attempt to offer an explanation *caw⇒** (understandable on the recording as a truncation of "cause' or 'because') overlaps with the continuation of pio1's turn in line 315. Pio1 completes her turn by directly requesting a response from SPT1 in line 317/pio1: *(0.6) what do you say to that↓*. In this way, the reporting of an allegation made by a third party is transformed into a first pair part which requires a corresponding second pair part – that is, a second pair part which will account for the basis of the allegation. The strenuous denial of the accusation that SPT1 offers as a second pair part in line 318/SPT1: *(0.6) that's a lie⇒*, and the subsequent counter-argument he produces in defence of his own version of events are utterances designed to address the allegation by claiming that Ian was lying when he produced it. Given the nature of the relationship between SPT1 and Ian, it is not unreasonable for SPT1 to believe that Ian would lie about the details of the assault to increase the chances of a conviction being made against SPT1.

Whether or not pio1 believes SPT1's assertion that Ian lied about this aspect of the assault, she does not request any further information about Ian's allegation. Instead she allows a long silence to develop (4.2 seconds) and then discusses the injuries to SPT1's hand, claiming that these indicate that SPT1 punched Ian. This sequence was discussed in section 4.3.1 in relation to suspect-initiated questions. Here it is sufficient to note that although pio1 is seeking to support her version, represented by the accusation in the extract above, she does not repeat the accusation or explore SPT1's account (that Ian was lying). Rather she initiates a new topic concerning physical evidence. Once again, SPT1 provides an account for this evidence in lines 331–2/SPT1: *(1.4) na cus the way I go that they come up⇒ (0.7) I didn't get them straight out*. Following a 1.3 second silence, pio1 again initiates a new topic, this time concerning the number of times Ian was struck. The extract below takes up the interview at this point.

Extract 4-22 INT1

333. pio1:   (1.3) it's <u>also</u> alleged that there was actually <u>three</u> hits↓
334. SPT1:   (0.5) no=
335. pio1:   =<u>two</u> punches ⇒
336.   and then //a* <u>backhander</u> ⇒ before you <u>left</u>↓
337. SPT1:   w'l*
338.   (0.7) w'l I tell y what if I gave out <u>three</u> ⇒
339.   they must have been <u>quick</u>↓
340. pio1   (1.6) but you <u>a.dmit</u> to (0.4) to <u>hitting</u> him∧

Again, SPT1 takes up his turn at the earliest TRP to deny the accusation
(line 334) and begins his version, or at least a statement which casts
some doubt over the version pio1 has produced, in overlap with the
second part of pio1's turn. Following SPT1's turn, pio1 does not make
any attempt to reiterate the allegation of *three hits*↓. As in the previous
instances of accusation/denial pairs, pio1's next turn is prefaced by
a silence (1.6 seconds) and initiates a new sequence that is not based on
the original accusation. Furthermore, in subsequent talk, pio1 does not
attempt to reintroduce any of this evidence (that Ian alleges SPT1
punched him, that the lacerations on SPT1's hand support this, and
that SPT1 hit Ian three times) to support her version of events. Despite
being supported by rather insubstantial accounts or evidence, SPT1's
version of events prevails to the extent that he does not agree to ratify
the police version by taking up the role of *principal* in relation to it.

The extract below from INT3 demonstrates that accusations and
denials are treated similarly by pio3 and SPT3. Here, pio3 begins by
asking questions about the way that SPT3 stored the marijuana plants
in a shed.

Extract 4-23 INT3

223. pio3:   (0.6) <u>how</u> did you do that⇒
224. SPT3:   (0.6) tied em up with a <u>rope</u>∧
225. pio3:   (0.4) and <u>why</u> did you do that↓
226. SPT3:   (0.9) so that wouldn't <u>go</u> everywhere↓
227. pio3:   (0.6) so they <u>wouldn't</u>∧
228. SPT3:   <u>go</u> everywhere↑
229. pio3:   (0.4) oh <u>right</u>↓ (0.6) I'll <u>put</u> it to you that you <u>put</u> em
                there to <u>dry</u> out∧
230.   (0.8) for <u>later</u> use↓
231. SPT3:   (1.1) no (0.2) just (0.2) to (0.4) get out of the <u>way</u>∧

232.   pio3:   right⇒ (2.3) OK and then <u>explain</u> to me what <u>happened</u>
233.   <u>after</u> you got <u>there</u> then↓

Pio3 initiates a question–answer pair (225/pio3: *(0.4) and <u>why</u> did you do that↓*) in order to elicit from SPT3 a possible reason for his actions (226/SPT3: *(0.9) so that wouldn't <u>go</u> everywhere↓*). Pio3 repeats the first part of SPT3's response with a low rise intonation to initiate a clarification sequence in line 227/pio3: *(0.6) so they <u>wouldn't</u>∧*.

In his next turn, pio3 receipts SPT3's clarification as 'new' information by using the 'change of state' token *oh*, a phenomenon described by Heritage (1984) as follows:

> in sum, it is proposed that 'oh' specifically functions as an information receipt that is regularly used as a means of proposing that the talk to which it responds is, or has been, informative to the recipient. Such a proposal is not accomplished by objects such as 'yes' or 'mm hm,' which avoid or defer treating prior talk as informative. (p. 307)

Atkinson (1992) also notes the lack of 'oh' in data derived from small claims arbitration hearings and claims that its avoidance denotes neutrality on the part of the arbitrator. Additionally, Heritage (1984) mentions that in news interviews, 'oh' receipt is avoided not only due to a similar requirement of interviewer neutrality but also to 'maintain the interview as an event in which the "overhearing" audience, rather than the interviewer, is the target of the informing and in which the interviewer's role is restricted to eliciting such informings' (p. 339). These various observations are highly applicable to the police interview, where the interviewer is required to maintain neutrality and the interview is being recorded for the benefit of one or several third parties (i.e. various members of the legal system, possibly including the courtroom participants).

Correspondingly, 'oh' receipt is rare in the police interview data which makes its use in this case all the more noticeable. The police interviewer apparently wishes to draw attention to the fact that SPT3's explanation has been 'informative' to him and if we examine the rest of his turn, we see that he is proposing that SPT3 *<u>put</u> em there to <u>dry</u> out∧ (0.8) for <u>later</u> use↓*. Given that he has treated SPT3's explanation as 'news', it is possible to see that pio3 is presenting his own explanation as the one he had been expecting from SPT3. In this way, pio3 constructs an accusation about SPT3's intentions when he hung the marijuana plants in the shed. In response to this accusation, SPT3 offers a denial and reiterates his earlier account, thus confirming his version of events and rejecting the version proposed by pio3. As in the examples from INT12 and INT1 above, the police interviewer initiates a new topic in the following turn and does not attempt to reassert the police version.

This can be contrasted with a situation in INT1 where an accusation receiving an acceptance second pair part is followed by a reiteration of the police version.

Extract 4-24 INT1

252.	pio1:	so you∧*
253.		you've actually come around to the <u>service</u> side of the <u>counter</u>∧=
254.	SPT1:	=yeah well I normally <u>do</u> go around to have a cup of coffee↓
255.	pio1:	so instead of where the people <u>were</u> ⇒
256.		(0.3) where the (0.7) the actual <u>customers</u> go ∧
257.		you went around t' the <u>service</u> side where the <u>cash</u> register is⇒
258.	SPT1:	yeah↓

The formulation produced by pio1 in lines 252–3 attributes to SPT1 the action of moving into a part of the shop normally reserved for staff. SPT1 is comfortable with this accusation and explains that this is normal behaviour for him. Immediately following this acceptance, or agreement, pio1 restates the accusation, without any change to the basis of the content. This contrasts with the cases of accusation–denial pairs examined above, where any subsequent form of the accusation would be reconstructed as having some other basis than that first proposed. For instance, following a denial, an accusation initially based on third-party allegations may be reproduced as being based on physical evidence, as in the case concerning the punching and 'backhanding' of Ian in INT1. Alternatively, the interviewing officer would initiate a new topic following the denial of an accusation by the suspect. This case of an accusation–acceptance adjacency pair demonstrates that constraints that may exist for the type of interviewer turn following a denial do not apply to turns following an acceptance. The use of evidence to negotiate competing versions of events will be revisited in section 4.4.2 below.

Finally, it would be useful to consider sequences in which an accusation or attribution does not receive any direct response. There are no cases in the data of the suspects entirely failing to respond to a first pair part, which is an indication of how strongly suspects are constrained to respond to police initiations. INT8 contains mainly *no comment* responses, but these appear to be treated as denials in the context of an accusation or attribution adjacency pair, as demonstrated in Extract 4-25.

Extract 4-25 INT8

351.   pio8:   Bronwyn <u>did</u> you commit the burglary↑
352.   SPT8:   no <u>comment</u> ∧
353.   pio8:   do you know who committed the <u>burglary</u> ↓
354.   SPT8:   no <u>comment</u> ∧
355.   tio8:   Bronwyn ⇒
356.   pio8:   do you know a <u>person</u> called <u>Arnold Haywood</u> ↑
357.   SPT8:   no <u>comment</u> ∧
358.   pio8:   in fact <u>Arnold Haywood</u> is here in <u>custody</u> (.) at the
               present time ↓
359.   do you agree with <u>that</u> ↑
360.   SPT8:   no comment ↓

However, the following extract from INT1 contains an example of a response which does not directly address the attribution produced by pio1 and as such gives an insight into the way that a non-response is treated by police interviewers.

Extract 4-26 INT1

433.   pio1:   uh you <u>saw</u> the glass shatter to the ground∧
434.   SPT1:   (0.4) I just kept <u>walking</u>↓
435.   (0.2) I just got in the <u>car</u> ⇒
436.   and <u>Rob</u> (0.6) me <u>friend</u> said what the hell's going <u>on</u>∧
437.   (0.4) whadcha <u>do</u>∧
438.   pio1:   (1.2) so you didn't bother <u>saying</u> anything to them↓
439.   that the <u>glass</u> was <u>broken</u>∧ or↓

In response to pio1's attribution of seeing the glass shatter, SPT1 claims that he *just kept <u>walking</u>↓*. This is not an overt contradiction or acceptance of the attribution. He may have seen the glass shatter before he *kept walking↓*, or he may not have. SPT2 seems to be making an entirely different point to that which pio1 is pursuing and which she articulates in lines 438–9. Regardless of the point SPT1 may have been making though, pio1 has assumed that SPT1 accepts her attribution of seeing the glass shatter and being aware that it has shattered, as we can see in her next turn 438/pio1: *(1.2) so you didn't bother <u>saying</u> anything to them↓ that the <u>glass</u> was <u>broken</u>∧ or↓*. Logically, for SPT1 to alert the shopkeepers to the broken glass, he must be aware of it, having seen it or being otherwise aware of it. Thus there is evidence in this extract that a lack of a contradiction following an attribution is treated by the interviewer as an implicit acceptance by the suspect of that attribution.

Within the adjacency pair structure of the interview, accusations and attributions produced as first pair parts by the police interviewers function as a way of presenting their version of events in a format which requires a response from the suspect. Allegations – attributions made by non-present third parties – are particularly valuable resources as they provide an opportunity for the police to present views which support their version of events but which are not themselves based on police knowledge. In the following turn, the suspect must produce a second pair part which contains a corresponding account for the allegation. In this way, suspects whose version of events differs from the version supported by the allegation are interactionally constrained to producing a defence of their version of events and providing some explanation for any discrepancy between the two versions.

Most importantly, the analysis demonstrated that accusations and attributions which are not immediately or straightforwardly contradicted may be understood either to be accepted as valid by the suspect or to be sufficiently unresolved as to allow the police interviewer to continue to treat them as possibly valid. That is, even if a response to an accusation is not present, the lack of response will be interpreted by the interviewer as an acceptance or agreement. This situation was contrasted with one where the accusation or attribution is clearly denied. In such cases it could be seen that the denial was accepted and a new approach required if the issue was to be pursued. Further evidence might be produced, for instance, which supported the police version and required a separate corresponding account from the suspect.

4.4.2   Using evidence to challenge a version of events

In section 3.4 the analysis of the preferred participation framework in the Information Gathering revealed that police officers in the interviews requested information already known to them in order to maintain the S3R framework and avoid the P3R framework. If the information was not subsequently elicited from the suspect, the police officer would then reveal his or her own knowledge of this information and attempt to elicit a confirmation of its veracity from the suspect. Several examples of this behaviour were analysed to substantiate the preference for the S3R framework by police officers.

This section investigates the way in which the interview participants negotiate different and competing versions of the events being discussed in the interview. In particular, this section focuses on the use of evidence by participants to support their own version. Therefore, the analysis of extracts in section 3.4 is again of interest as it demonstrates one aspect of the use of evidence to negotiate competing versions. Some of the extracts analysed in Chapter 3 will be reconsidered here to describe in interactional terms the discourse practices of participants as they request or present evidence to resolve the conflict between suspect and police versions of the narrative.

A clear example of the discursive practice described in section 3.4 can be found in the extract below. As discussed in the analysis of this extract earlier, we can see that pio2 has withheld his knowledge about bruising to both of Leila's biceps until it becomes clear that he is not going to elicit a voluntary confession to causing injuries to both arms from SPT2.

Extract 4-27 INT2

230.	pio2:	all right↓* well when you had hold of her <u>bicep</u>⇒
231.		(.) which↓ (0.2) arm was that do you <u>remember</u>↑
232.	SPT2:	(0.4) yip↑
233.	pio2:	(0.4) which <u>one</u>↓
234.	SPT2:	(0.2) <u>right</u> one∧
235.	pio2:	(0.2) a::hm↓ at some <u>stage</u>⇒
236.		didja have ever have hold of 'er <u>other</u> arm↑
237.		(0.6) <u>bicep</u>∧
238.	SPT2:	(1.0) no∧ I↓ (0.4) no∧
239.	pio2:	<u>a::hm</u>⇒ (2.0) it's a::h⇒ (.) she's had (.) some <u>injuries</u> on 'er <u>arm</u>⇒
240.		(0.2) <u>bruising</u> to <u>bo:th</u> (.) biceps↓
241.	SPT2:	mm hm∧=
242.	Pio2:	=at some stage↓ (0.2) didju have hold of 'er <u>other</u> bicep↑
243.		(.) dragging her <u>outside</u>↑
244.		((sound of door closing⇒ or seat moving))
245.	SPT2:	(1.4) not that I can <u>remember</u>⇒
246.	pio2:	so you can't explain⇒ how those⇒ (.) <u>marks</u> would 'ave got there↑
247.	SPT2:	(0.4) the one on the right (.) arm∧ would have been from me⇒// *<u>grabbin</u> a∧ (.) but
248.	pio2:	right* (4.4) and⇒ OK⇒ u:m⇒

249.   (1.0) after the <u>second</u>⇒ (0.2) time you've (0.2) <u>grabbed</u> a∧
250.   (0.6) you went back <u>inside</u>∧
251.   what happened <u>then</u>↓

In SPT2's version of events, he caused injuries to Leila's right arm only. The police version of events, however, is that injuries were caused by SPT2 to both of Leila's arms. This conflict between the police version and the suspect version of events needs to be resolved if the interview is to produce a consistent confession that will support the basis of the arrest of SPT2 and result in a court conviction.

In lines 230–4, it is established through two question–answer sequences that SPT2 admits causing injury to Leila's right arm. The conflict is exposed in the following sequence (lines 235–8) when pio2 asks about injuries to Leila's left arm and SPT2 denies causing any further injuries. The attempt at a resolution of the conflict, which takes place in lines 239 to 247 begins when pio2 presents the physical evidence of Leila's bruising to both biceps 239–40/pio2: <u>*a::hm*</u>⇒ (2.0) it's a::h⇒ (.) she's had (.) some <u>injuries</u> on 'er <u>arm</u>⇒ (0.2) <u>bruising</u> to <u>bo:th</u> (.) biceps↓.

According to Pomerantz (1980), this use of evidence by pio2 could be described as a 'fishing device' in that it consists of the presentation of pio2's personal experience (or 'my side' telling; Pomerantz 1980: 190) as evidence of some state of affairs. The state of affairs evidenced by pio2's 'my side' telling in lines 239–40 is that bruising was caused to both of Leila's arms. The 'my side' telling invites a response from the recipient, SPT2, in which he may provide an account for the state of affairs evidenced, such as a description of an event corresponding to the state of affairs. Bergmann (1992) describes the process in relation to psychiatric interviews as the use of 'prior information as an economical and efficient means for the elicitation of authoritative descriptions' (pp. 144–5). In this case such a corresponding event or authoritative description might be that SPT2 grasped Leila by the left arm. 'My side' tellings are designed to present the speaker's knowledge or experience as 'limited or less than best access relative to the recipient's access' (Pomerantz 1980: 190). In this case, pio2 has presented his experience as being limited to knowledge of the injuries that Leila sustained to her arms. It might be said that 'my side' tellings provide a gap in the information being assembled which is to be filled by the recipient. However, because the 'my side' telling is designed to avoid specifying exactly the information that is sought, it does not strongly obligate the recipient to provide a corresponding event.

Consequently in line 241, SPT2 is able to respond only with a token which acts as a continuer (*mm hm∧*). On failing to elicit a corresponding event, pio2 immediately abandons the indirect approach provided by the 'fishing device' and asks SPT2 directly 242/pio2: *at some stage↓ (0.2) didju have hold of 'er other bicep↑*. This too is met with a denial from SPT2. In the following turn pio2 provides a formulation of SPT2's responses as a failure to provide an explanation of his (pio2's) evidence: 246/pio2: *so you can't explain⇒ how those⇒ (.) marks would 'ave got there↑*. He is displaying through this statement that the expected response to his presentation of evidence is an account that will explain that evidence. The use of *so* in the turn-initial position reflects a backward-looking, summarising function of the utterance indicating the lack of any account thus far, while the high rise terminal *got there↑* functions to elicit a further response. In this way, pio2 not only orients to the function of his 'my side' telling as a 'fishing device', but he increases the obligation inherent in the device for SPT2 to respond with an account by reformulating SPT2's responses as noticeably 'account-less'. SPT2 responds to this by reiterating his earlier explanation of the bruising to Leila's right arm and in doing so provides a partial account for *how those⇒ (.) marks would 'ave got there*, but he specifically avoids confessing to causing the injuries to her left arm. This lack of explanation (247/SPT2: *(0.4) the one on the right (.) arm∧ would have been from me⇒// *grabbin a∧ (.) but↓*) is finally accepted by pio2, and although he pauses for 4.4 seconds before he moves to continue the interview 248/pio2: *right* (4.4) and⇒ OK⇒ u:m⇒*, SPT2 does not take the opportunity to complete his attempt to explain the injuries.

To summarise the findings of this analysis, the version of events provided by the suspect through the question and answer phase in lines 230–4 is challenged by pio2. The challenge is made indirectly at first, using a 'my side' telling as a 'fishing device', but this approach is swiftly abandoned for a series of more direct challenges. This sequence of turn types reflects the observations noted by Pomerantz (1980: 198) regarding the elicitation of specific information, that 'early attempts [at such elicitation] display the participant's orientation to propriety ("fishing"), whereas successive attempts may have that orientation relaxed and take the form of direct requests' (p. 198). Furthermore, the alacrity with which pio2 proceeds to the second, more direct phase of questioning and his persistence in displaying SPT2's responses as inadequate demonstrate the weakness of the obligation that a 'my side' telling places on the recipient to provide an account for the state of affairs evidenced by the speaker. Further analysis of the data will seek to confirm this pattern of turn types in the discursive practices of police officers when negotiating conflicting versions of events.

Extract 4-28 demonstrates one of the instances in INT3 where two competing versions are being negotiated by the participants. Here, pio3 asks if the micro-sprinkler system that SPT3 has described in a prior turn was mainly to be used to water the marijuana plants. SPT3 claims that it was originally set up for the purpose of watering ferns, but the ferns were never purchased by SPT3 owing to a shortage of funds and instead he planted cannabis.

Extract 4-28 INT3

148.   pio3:   (0.4) was that set up (.) <u>predominantly</u> to (.) ah
149.   (0.3) to ah (0.6) to <u>water</u> these // (0.2) ah*
150.   SPT3:   mm*⇒ //no*↓
151.   pio3:   no*∧
152.   SPT3:   no↓ (0.4) there was going to be <u>ferns</u> and that in there↓
153.   (1.4) and I put <u>those</u> in there because we couldn't afford
                 (0.3) <u>ferns</u>
154.   and (.) stuff like that (0.5) so↓
155.   pio3:   (1.0) but you ah can <u>afford</u> to (.) grow (1.0) the marijuana
                 plants⇒
156.   SPT3:   doesn't <u>cost</u> anything↓
157.   pio3:   (0.4) right⇒ (0.9) now (0.7) do you use any <u>fertilisers</u>
158.   (.) or anything in // the <u>soil</u>* at all∧
159.   SPT3:   nah* (1.0) nup

Here pio3 is engaged in a series of questions designed to elicit information about how much effort SPT3 has put into growing the marijuana plants. SPT3 gives responses that are intended to show that he has put the minimal amount of effort into the exercise. As in the previous example, the sequence in the extract above begins with the establishment of some fact through a question–answer pair. Pio3 begins by asking about the purpose of the sprinkler system mentioned in a prior turn. A conflict of versions becomes apparent in line 150 when SPT3 rejects the suggestion that the sprinkler system was set up primarily for the benefit of the marijuana plants.

Pio3 offers a continuer by repeating SPT3's response with a questioning, upward intonation 151/pio3: *no*∧. This response actually overlaps SPT3's turn, indicating that pio3 was anticipating SPT3's utterance, perhaps because SPT3 conveyed his disagreement with the filler *mm* or with an accompanying headshake or facial expression as he began the turn. In any case, pio3's turn in line 151 serves to challenge SPT3's version and SPT3 responds to this challenge by repeating his disagreement and then offering an account of why he is disagreeing. SPT3's behaviour is consistent with the observation made by Pomerantz (1984b) that '[u]pon being challenged, people seem to recall as a reportable event the circumstance of establishing that information, i.e. the basis or source' (p. 615). Thus, in response to pio3's challenge, SPT3 reports the circumstances that provided the basis for his assertion that the sprinkler system was not set up to water the marijuana plants, that it had been his original intention to plant ferns, not marijuana plants. Following this account, SPT3 produces a further account which appears to provide a corresponding event to an anticipated police observation that no ferns were found in the fernery. That is, SPT3 extends his account to pre-empt any further challenges based on the non-existence of the aforementioned ferns by explaining that 153/SPT3: *I put <u>those</u> in there because we couldn't afford (0.3) <u>ferns</u>.*

In the following turn, pio3 makes another attempt to resolve the conflict between SPT3's version of events and his own by challenging the account provided by SPT3. He produces a 'my side' telling in which he observes that SPT3 could afford to grow marijuana plants. As it is placed adjacently to SPT3's description of not being able to afford ferns, pio3's 'my side' telling is intended to expose the inconsistency of being unable to afford to grow ferns and being able to afford to grow marijuana. He is therefore 'fishing' for an account that will resolve this inconsistency. SPT3 obliges by supplying an account in which he claims that marijuana costs nothing to grow. Pio3 then desists in his attempt to resolve the conflict between the two versions of events and moves on to the next question.

The analysis of this extract demonstrates that a similar approach to the negotiations is taken by the participants in INT2 and INT3. In the extract above, pio3's initial challenge in line 151 to SPT3's version clearly demonstrates an 'orientation to propriety'. The upward intonation both challenges SPT3's denial and invites an account in response, thus acting as a 'fishing device' without presenting a counter-argument or even a 'my side' telling. As such, it constitutes a comparatively weak obligation on the recipient to provide an account, since there is no evidence requiring a corresponding event. His second challenge in line 155 is more direct, involving a 'my side' telling and thus increasing the obligation for SPT3 to provide an account for the inconsistency the telling has implied. Pio3 does not progress to a more direct line of questioning, and if we compare this situation with the sequence from INT2 it is notable that pio2 moved to a direct challenge when he failed to obtain an account from SPT2. As pio3 has obtained an account, a direct request for another account would need to be made on the basis of some further evidence, which pio3 does not appear to have.

A similar approach is taken to the presentation of evidence as a 'fishing device' by pio1 during negotiations over the closing of the shop door, represented in the extract below.

Extract 4-29 INT1

487.	pio1:	<u>all</u> our witnesses say that ↓
488.		you <u>slammed</u> it the second time again↓
489.	SPT1:	°aw well (0.3) i that's what they <u>say</u> //( )*°
490.	pio1:	(0.6) you've got nothing * to say to that∧
491.	SPT1:	<u>nup</u>∧
492.	pio1:	(1.1) so then you- you've just <u>left</u> ↓

In lines 487–8 we see pio1 presenting knowledge previously concealed to support the police version of events – in the several minutes of argument over SPT1's actions this is the first time that pio1 mentions that she obtained witness statements. Pio1's turn is designed to elicit an account from SPT1 in which a corresponding event can be found to match the state of affairs evidenced by her report. However, as his account does not provide such an event, pio1 moves to a more direct approach, requesting confirmation from SPT1 that he has *nothing * to say to that∧*. This is very similar to the final turn produced by pio2 in the negotiation sequence from INT2 analysed above. That is, following a failure to elicit an adequate account, the police officer produces a formulation of the suspect's prior turn(s) as lacking an account and uses an upward intonation to request confirmation of this before abandoning the elicitation attempt altogether.

In Chapter 6 we will consider how these discourse practices relate to a myth about police powers of persuasion in the interview. Prior to the discussion of a mythology about police interviewing, however, the following analysis will demonstrate that differences between the police and suspect versions of events can be attributed to the police officer's discursive practices in the negotiation of competing versions of events.

4.4.3   Topic management in constructing a police version

In section 4.3 an analysis of topic management tools in the data revealed that topic shift is predominantly initiated by the primary interviewing officers and that police participants have available to them a wider range of resources through which topic shift may be achieved. For instance, it was found that whereas a suspect may only initiate topic shift using a 'stepwise transition' which minimises the impact of the topic shift on the interaction, a primary interviewing officer may initiate new topics disjunctively and even interruptively. Furthermore, topic initiation resources accessible to suspects were found to be less likely to obligate the recipients to respond to the topic. The interactional resources available to participants in police interviews are allocated in such a way as to endow the primary interviewing officer with an 'interactional authority' over the other participants, and especially over the suspect. This section will examine the way that this authority may be used by police interviewers as a tool in the construction of the police version of events.

The interactional resource commonly used by police officers in this process is a 'formulation', which is a term coined by CA researchers to describe utterances that summarise, gloss or develop the gist of the recipient's earlier contributions (Heritage 1985; Heritage and Watson 1979). Formulations are the focus of the analysis presented in the next section; however, as they are used to a degree in topic management it is useful to review their key properties here. Importantly, Fairclough (1989) notes that formulations have a 'controlling' function and provide 'a way of leading participants into accepting one's own version of what has transpired, and so limiting their options for future contributions' (p. 136). The use of formulations in news interviews is examined (less critically) by Heritage (1985) who finds that in institutional contexts where formulations are most common, they are generally undertaken by questioners and 'are more directly addressed to the overhearing audience than are the majority of questions and answers that make up a news interview' (pp. 100–1). In a police interview the members of the legal system who have access to the recording can be considered an overhearing audience.

The extract below from INT1 contains an example of a disjunctive topic shift discussed in the previous chapter.

Extract 4-30 INT1

87.   pio1:   so <u>wadc</u>ha do then↓
88.   SPT1:   (0.5) w'l (1.1) <u>made</u> meself another cup of <u>coffee</u>⇒
89.   and I just <u>thought</u> about it∧
90.   and I said what's going <u>on</u>⇒
((11 lines omitted – SPT1 describes relationship with Betty))
102.   and we get on <u>all right</u> just as <u>friends</u> ⇒
103.   like we bump into each other in the <u>street</u>⇒

104.		(0.5) //<u>best</u> of* <u>friends</u>∧
105.	pio1:	thi-* this <u>phone</u> call happened at ten-thirty in the morning↓
106.	SPT1:	(0.4) bout <u>ten</u> ten-thirty in the morning↓
107.	pio1:	right so what you <u>thought</u> about it all day <u>long</u>⇒
108.	SPT1:	and I thought about it <u>all</u> day long⇒
109.	pio1:	(0.3) yep <u>then</u> //what happened*↓
110.	SPT1:	I* <u>come</u> to Middletown⇒

We have seen previously that SPT1 uses a series of stepwise transitions to shift from the topic initiated by pio1 in line 87/pio1: *so <u>wadcha</u> do then↓* to the topic of his relationship with Betty. Just as SPT1 reaches the description of his friendship with Betty, pio1 takes up the TRP at the end of line 103 and initiates a disjunctive topic shift, requesting confirmation that 105/pio1: *thi-* this <u>phone</u> call happened at ten-thirty in the morning↓*. Although SPT1 had not intended to finish his turn at the TRP at the end of line 103 and his next utterance occurs in overlap with pio1's false start *thi-*, SPT1 does not attempt to hold the floor beyond the end of his utterance in line 104/SPT1: *(0.5) //<u>best</u> of* <u>friends</u>∧* and instead passes the floor to pio1 so that she can restart her request for confirmation in line 105, which she has produced as a formulation.

As the formulation is a first pair part, SPT1 offers a second pair part response in line 106/SPT1: *(0.4) bout <u>ten</u> ten-thirty in the morning↓*, but he does not attempt to hold the floor and continue his narrative. Instead, he passes the floor back to pio1 who uses a formulation-confirmation pair in lines 107–8 to summarise SPT1's narrative turn prior to reinitiating the topic of *<u>then</u> //what happened*↓*. However, the topic actually indicated by the formulation in line 107/pio1: *right so what you <u>thought</u> about it all day <u>long</u>⇒*, is not the same topic as the final utterances of SPT1's prior narrative turn, which concerned his friendship with Betty. In fact, the topic pio1 has initiated is more closely related to the one which appears near the beginning of SPT1's narrative turn, in line 89/SPT1: *and I just <u>thought</u> about it∧*, and the subsequent utterances which develop the theme of his good relationship with Betty are effectively ignored by pio1's formulation.

Thus the version of the narrative which is 'ratified' by the participants is based only on the earlier, police-initiated topic of what SPT1 'did next' – 87/pio1: *so <u>wadcha</u> do then↓* – and not on the topics introduced by SPT1 in stepwise transitions, which concern his efforts to act responsibly and maintain a friendship with Betty. These latter observations are important to SPT1's version because they support his assertion that the threatening phone call he received warning him not to approach Betty was both unprovoked and upsetting, and that his subsequent actions were as a result of his distress at what he saw as an unwarranted attempt to curtail his friendship with his ex-partner.

The extract above demonstrates that pio1 is able to employ her access to a wider range of topic management tools in order to present a summary of SPT1's narrative without including information supporting his version of events. In fact, throughout this interview, pio1 systematically and consistently fails to take up the topics which SPT1 initiates by stepwise transitions to provide background information supporting his version. One further example illustrating this finding is given in the extract below.

Extract 4-31 INT1

285.	SPT1:	(1.1) yep⇒ now I didn't <u>mean</u> to break his teeth ⇒
286.		I didn't <u>know</u> I did that⇒
287.		(0.8) I'm sorry I <u>did</u> that ⇒
288.		but I didn't know I was <u>doing</u> it↓
289.	pio1:	well you've <u>hit</u> him on the-
290.		(.) with <u>your</u> right <u>ha:nd</u> ⇒
291.		to almost the right side of his <u>face</u>⇒
292.		(0.9) pretty much at the <u>front</u> ⇒
293.		at the right <u>side</u>⇒ //and* you've
294.	SPT1:	right⇒*
295.	pio1:	<u>smashed</u> his front tooth <u>out</u> com<u>ple</u>tely⇒
296.	SPT1:	(0.6) <u>right</u>↓ //°I didn't know th-°*
297.	pio1:	was it <u>bleeding</u>* there an then ↑

Here we see that in lines 285–8 SPT1 uses stepwise transitions to initiate topics that support his version that the damage to Ian's teeth was unintentional and regrettable. These topics are not taken up by pio1 who instead, in lines 289–93 and line 295 presents a version which describes SPT1's actions using terms of violence such as *hit* and *smashed* without any recognition or response to SPT1's claims about the accidental nature of the injuries he caused. In the following line 296 SPT1 makes one further attempt to reintroduce his topic of 'accidental injury' *°I didn't know th-°**, though this is softly spoken and overlaps with pio1's next turn 297/pio1: *was it <u>bleeding</u>* there an then ↑*. Once again, the topic management tools available to pio1 permit her to initiate topics which promote the police version of events while ignoring topics initiated by SPT1 in support of his version of events.

Similarly, pio2 initiates topics about blame and responsibility, but ignores SPT2's initiations about remorse and his attempts to seek professional help, and downplays the possible provocation of the assault. These observations are demonstrated in the following analysis of extracts from INT2.

Extract 4-32 INT2

276.   pio2:   (0.6) um↓ (.) was there any reason why you had to e::rm↓
                (.) <u>treat</u> 'a this way at all↓
277.   SPT2:   (1.2) it was a <u>combination</u> of things (.) y' know∧
278.   I↓ (0.4) didn't like the <u>fact</u> that↓ (0.4) y' know↑
279.   (0.6) here <u>I</u> am goin' out with a girl⇒
280.   and she⇒ (0.6) jumps into <u>bed</u> with (0.2) one of my⇒
                so-called <u>mates</u>∧
281.   pio2:   (0.4) OK well regardless of that may have been the <u>case</u>∧
282.   SPT2:   auh-↓
283.   pio2   um⇒ (0.6) not to say whether that the case or <u>not</u>∧
284.   but regardless of that <u>might've</u> been the case⇒
285.   (0.4) do you agree⇒ that that ah⇒ (.) <u>warranted</u> your
                actions↑
286.   (0.4) by <u>draggin'</u> 'er out by the arm⇒
287.   (.) <u>pullin'</u> 'er by the hair⇒
288.   (0.8) // <u>forcibly</u>* removing 'er from the <u>house</u>∧
289.   SPT2:   nuo-* (1.0) nup∧

Towards the end of INT2, and following a discussion of SPT2's possible use of force against his girlfriend, SPT2 is asked by pio2 if there was *any reason why you had to e::rm↓ (.) treat 'a this way at all↓*. The use of the extreme case in phrases like *any reason … at all* implies that reasons for this sort of behaviour are unlikely to exist, however SPT2 is able to supply a fairly straightforward explanation – Leila's apparent infidelity – which, while it does not excuse his behaviour, certainly provides a reason for it. It is interesting, therefore, that pio2's next turn functions to deny the relevance of SPT2's contribution by overtly excluding his explanation from the set of things which might warrant SPT2's actions 281/pio2: *(0.4) OK well regardless of that may have been the case∧*. SPT2 then produces a response marker – 282/SPT2: *auh-↓* – which is hearable on the recording as a preface to an objection to pio2's prior utterance. Pio2 immediately qualifies his prior turn, making it explicit that he is not questioning the veracity of SPT2's explanation, only its relevance as a reason for his behaviour – 283/pio2: *um⇒ (0.6) not to say whether that the case or not*∧. Having discarded SPT2's version of 'reasons why he assaulted Leila', pio2 then formulates his version that *there was⇒ (0.6) absolutely no reason↓* for SPT2's behaviour and presents it for confirmation by SPT2, as demonstrated in the following extract.

Extract 4-33 INT2

290.   Pio2:   (2.0) so there was⇒ (0.6) absolutely no <u>reason</u>↓
291.   (.) <u>why</u> you should have <u>treated</u> 'er in that manner↓
292.   SPT2:   (1.0) nup↓

We have seen that in this sequence, pio2 elicits one version from SPT2, where SPT2 gives a reason for his actions, and then uses his role as interviewer to overtly set aside SPT2's version – *regardless of that may have been the <u>case</u>*∧ – and replace it with his own version in which there can be found *absolutely no <u>reason</u>↓* for SPT2's actions.

In the cases we have examined so far, it seems clear that the police officers are able to utilise the topic management resources available to them as interviewers in order to construct their own version of events. They are greatly assisted in this activity by the restricted topic management tools available to the suspects and, in particular, by the fact that the available tools minimise the obligation on police interviewers to respond to topics initiated by suspects. Thus, a police interviewer is able to ignore topic initiations that contribute to the suspect's version of events. A suspect, on the other hand, is often in a position of having to respond to police topic initiations because they are produced as first pair parts, such as formulations or requests for confirmation, which obligate the recipient to produce a topically↓ relevant response. As a result, the police version of events can be not only constructed, but favoured as the agreed-to version. The example from INT2 involving SPT2's reasons for assaulting his girlfriend demonstrated the extent to which a police interviewer can dismiss the suspect's contributions in favour of the police version and then present the police version as a formulation of everything that has been said on the topic. In the case mentioned, this resulted in the agreement by the suspect with a police version that did not represent the suspect's original version of events at all. In the next section, we will draw on these observations and consider the discursive practices of police interviewers in the negotiation of two competing versions of events.

4.4.4   Formulating the suspect's version

We have seen in the prior analyses that the police versions being constructed by pio1 and pio2 differ in certain recognisable respects from the suspect versions. For instance, in both interviews, the police interviewers omit sections of the suspects' versions. In the extracts from INT1 examined in section 4.4.2, pio1 produces a summary of SPT1's prior turn that does not include SPT1's description of his friendship with Betty, his ex-de facto partner. By including this information in his version, SPT1 had provided the listener with a possible reason for his behaviour. SPT1 conveys the closeness of his friendship with Betty and this can then be drawn upon to explain why he is so upset by the threatening phone call and why he feels compelled to respond to the call with violence. Conversely, by excluding this information in her version of events, pio1 diminishes the impact of the threatening phone call on SPT1's state of mind, facilitating the interpretation of SPT1's assault of Ian as unmitigated and irrational.

Similarly, in the extracts from INT2, we saw that when pio2 constructs his version of 'reasons for the assault', he overtly excludes SPT2's explanation that his girlfriend *jumps into <u>bed</u> with (0.2) one of my⇒ so-called <u>mates</u>∧*. Instead, pio2 presents a version where there was *absolutely no <u>reason</u>↓* for SPT2's actions. Again, the information omitted by the police interviewer when summarising the suspect's utterances is contextual information that serves to explain the suspect's behaviour.

This approach by the police interviewers in these two interviews can be compared with the findings of Swedish researchers that 'written police reports of interviews with suspects…emphasised the actions of the suspects which pointed to their guilt compared with the original version offered by the suspect which contained much contextual material designed to explain and excuse the offence' (cited in Auburn et al. 1995: 355–6).

In addition to constructing a police version of events which omits contextual information provided by the suspect, the police interviewers also use formulations to include aspects of the narrative which were not mentioned by the suspect. These types of interactions are present in INT1 and INT3 where actions are mentioned by the police interviewers that are specifically not undertaken by the suspects. For instance, during the discussion of the damage to the shop door in INT1, pio1 makes the following observation:

Extract 4-34 INT1

438.   pio1:   (1.2) so you didn't bother <u>saying</u> anything to them↓
439.   that the <u>glass</u> was <u>broken</u>∧or↓
440.   SPT1:   (1.0) °to <u>who</u>⇒°
441.   pio1:   (0.3) to <u>Betty</u> (1.3) in at the <u>store</u>↓

Here, pio1 formulates SPT1's prior turns about walking directly to his car after the glass door broke as demonstrating that *he didn't bother saying anything to them↓*. In this way, pio1 constructs a version of events where SPT1 is remiss firstly in evading the suggested course of action by leaving the scene, and secondly in failing even to consider that such a course of action may have been appropriate. In subsequent turns, SPT1 explains that a warning to the shop attendants was unnecessary as they could plainly see that the glass in the door had broken.

A similar interaction is found in INT3 when the participants are discussing the firearms belonging to the suspect.

Extract 4-35 INT3

384.	SPT3:	(0.5) um (0.3) they're off∧ (0.6) me uncle's <u>farm</u> in New South <u>Wales</u>↓
385.		(1.3) and they don't <u>work</u>⇒
386.	pio3:	(3.0) how do you know that they <u>don't</u> work↓
387.	SPT3:	(0.6) cause I been <u>told</u> that they don't work↓
388.	pio3:	have you tested them in any <u>way</u>∧
389.		(.) to know that they <u>don't</u> work↑
390.	SPT3:	no↓
391.	pio3:	(0.8) so for all you <u>know</u> they could <u>work</u>↓
392.	SPT3:	(1.0) well (0.3) the shotgun apparently has got a bent <u>pin</u>∧
393.		(1.2) and the other one's got a (0.5) <u>shaving</u> in the (.) barrel ↓
394.		or something like <u>that</u> I don't //know*⇒
395.	pio3:	have* they been <u>tested</u> // (.) ah*⇒
396.	SPT3:	no*⇒
397.	pio3:	by yourself or anyone to <u>prove</u> that they don't <u>work</u>↑
398.	SPT3:	no (1.0) I don- I don't want me <u>head</u> blown off⇒

Whereas SPT3 has included in his version only the statement that the guns *don't <u>work</u>⇒*, pio3 pursues a line of questioning which is designed to highlight the absence of a particular course of action – the testing of the guns – from SPT3's version. In line 391, pio3 formulates SPT3's version (*so for all you <u>know</u> they could <u>work</u>↓*) to illustrate that the status of the guns as inoperable cannot be assumed by SPT3, which undermines his version. Another effect of the formulation is to demonstrate that SPT3 has been remiss both in failing to have the guns tested and in failing to consider that this might be an appropriate measure. Just as SPT1 subsequently provided an account for this apparent shortcoming, SPT3 eventually explains that 392/SPT3: *the shotgun apparently has got a bent* *pin*∧ *(1.2) and the other one's got a (0.5) shaving in the (.) barrel* ↓ *and,* when pressed by pio3 for a reason why he did not test the guns himself he adds that 398/SPT3: *I don't want me head blown off*⇒.

In both of the cases examined, the police interviewers produced formulations that highlighted some perceived deficiency in the suspect's version of events. In both cases, the suspects were able to provide accounts for their chosen course of action; however, this discursive practice of the police places the suspects in the position of having to account both for what they did and for what they chose not to do. It remains possible for the police interviewers to maintain their version that certain actions that they deemed appropriate had not been carried out by the suspects, irrespective of how irrelevant or unnecessary the suspects considered these actions to be.

Finally, there is a tendency for primary interviewing officers to produce formulations of the suspects' turns that display a shift towards words and phrases which are more explicitly violent or otherwise socially undesirable than the descriptions used in the original version. For instance, in INT1, SPT1 describes his assault of Ian as comprising two 'backhanders'. The first he describes in line 266–267/SPT1: *I just*⇒*(0.6) opened me hand and just gave him a backhander*↓ and the second in line 311/SPT1: *(0.6) and I just (0.5) gave him another one*⇒. SPT1 uses expressions such as *just*⇒*(0.6) opened* and *just gave him* when describing the first part of the assault, and repeats the phrase *just (0.5) gave him* to describe the second blow. The use of *just* before each verb minimises the intentionality and violence of his actions, and the choice of the verb *give* in the utterances *gave him a backhander*↓ and *gave him another one*⇒ to describe the action of striking Ian carries no implications of force. Pio1 responds to the mention of the first 'backhander' with some further questions and then formulates SPT1's version of events as follows.

Extract 4-36 INT1

289.	pio1:	well you've <u>hit</u> him on the-
290.		(.) with <u>your</u> right <u>ha:nd</u> ⇒
291.		to almost the right side of his <u>face</u>⇒
292.		(0.9) pretty much at the <u>front</u> ⇒
293.		at the right <u>side</u>⇒ //and* you've
294.	SPT1:	right⇒*
295.	pio1:	<u>smashed</u> his front tooth <u>out</u> <u>completely</u>⇒

We can see that pio1 replaces SPT1's verb *give* with the more overtly violent <u>*hit*</u> in line 289 and <u>*smashed*</u> in line 295. Furthermore, she does not use the modifier 'just' in her formulation and she adds the adverb *completely* to her description of the damage SPT1 has caused to Ian's front tooth.

When SPT1 describes the second part of the assault in line 311, pio1 produces another formulation, this time so that it latches on to SPT1's description, as we can see in this extract.

Extract 4-37 INT1

311.   SPT1:   (0.6) and I just (0.5) <u>gave</u> him <u>another</u> one⇒=
312.   pio1:   =<u>whacked</u> him again↓ hh
313.   SPT1:   and then I walked <u>out</u>∧

In this second instance of formulation in particular it is difficult to see any purpose for pio1's turn other than the reconstruction of SPT1's version of events as a police version using phrases favoured by pio1.

One of the most contested aspects of INT1 is the allegation of criminal damage to the door of the shop where the incident took place. In the latter part of the interview, there is a lengthy discussion about the manner in which SPT1 closed the door as he left the shop, following the assault. When describing his actions the first time, SPT1 says that he closed the door hard as he left and the glass in the door cracked. As his jacket had caught in the door, he reopened the door to free the jacket and then closed it, at which point the glass shattered and fell to the ground. Rather than present for analysis the entire description and subsequent discussion, as it runs to over eighty lines, it is sufficient to note SPT1's choice of words to describe the events. SPT1 says 408/SPT1: *as I <u>closed</u> the <u>door</u> I admit I <u>closed</u> it a little bit too <u>ha:rd</u>⇒* to describe the initial closing of the door, which he claims was the moment that the glass cracked. He then describes the second part of the incident as 419–21/ SPT1: *and <u>closed</u> it again ⇒ that's when the whole <u>sho</u>- (0.2) the whole <u>glass</u> just <u>shattered</u>⇒*. The following extract picks up the interview at the point where SPT1 has completed this description and pio1 begins her response to his account.

Extract 4-38 INT1

422.   pio1:   so you pretty much <u>slammed</u> it the first time∧
423.   SPT1:   yeah↓
424.   pio1:   (0.3) very <u>hard</u> ↓
425.   and it's (0.3) <u>cracked</u> all the gra- all the glass⇒
426.   SPT1:   <u>yeah</u> that's //<u>right</u>*

427.   pio1:   you've* <u>re</u>opened it∧
428.   to get your //jacket* out⇒
429.   SPT1:   ja-* yeah ⇒
430.   pio1:   and you've <u>slammed</u> it shut again↓
431.   causing all the <u>glass</u> to shatter to the ground↓
432.   SPT1:   that's <u>right</u>⇒
433.   pio1:   uh you <u>saw</u> the glass shatter to the ground∧
434.   SPT1:   (0.4) I just kept <u>walking</u>↓
435.   (0.2) I just got in the <u>car</u> ⇒
436.   and <u>Rob</u> (0.6) me <u>friend</u> said what the hell's going <u>on</u>∧
437.   (0.4) whadcha <u>do</u>∧
438.   pio1:   (1.2) so you didn't bother <u>saying</u> anything to them↓
439.   that the <u>glass</u> was <u>broken</u>∧ or↓

It is important to recognise that pio1 is intending to charge SPT1 with criminal damage, which means that SPT1 is believed by the police to have intentionally caused the damage to the door. In the segment presented above, we can see that pio1 embarks on a process moving the shared understanding of the incident from one represented by SPT1's description (e.g. *as I <u>closed</u> the <u>door</u> I admit I <u>closed</u> it a little bit too <u>ha:rd</u>⇒ . . . and <u>closed</u> it again ⇒*) to one represented by pio1's formulation (e.g. *so you pretty much <u>slammed</u> it the first time*∧ *. . . and you've <u>slammed</u> it shut again*↓). It is interesting that pio1 prefaces the term *slammed* with the phrase *pretty much* which links her version to SPT1's version by 'roughly' equating one with the other. The device *so*, common to formulations ((Heritage and Watson 1979); see line 391 in Extract 4-35 for example), explicitly displays her construction as a restating of SPT1's utterances, rather than a separate version of events.

Apart from the term *slammed* introduced by pio1 in lines 422 and 430, several other elements are added to the formulation of events in her turns of which the most critical as far as the resolution of conflicting versions is concerned is her introduction of causality. Whereas SPT1 has said only that he closed the door *and* the glass broke, pio1 describes this so that SPT1's action is formulated as 431/pio1: *causing all the <u>glass</u> to shatter to the ground*↓. She follows this in her next turn with the formulation 433/pio1: *uh you <u>saw</u> the glass shatter to the ground*∧.

By altering the verb used from *closed* to *slammed* in both instances of the action taking place, she increases the degree of violence in SPT1's actions. Combined with her assertion of causality between these actions and breaking of the glass, this makes for a much stronger case of intentionality as regards the damage.

This demonstrates the power of formulations as a tool in the construction of a police version of events. Formulations are commonly used to provide a 'summary' of prior talk for the purposes of clarification and necessarily contain different words and phrases from the original as a demonstration of comprehension by the producer of the formulation (Heritage and Watson 1979). In the cases being discussed in this section, formulations are used to create the illusion that the police version is really only a summary of the suspect's version with some changes that may be required for clarification by the police interviewer. However, the changes that are made to the suspect version systematically introduce terms of violence and intentionality that were not present in the original utterances. As mentioned above, pio1's subsequent turn in lines 436 and 437 alters SPT1's description of returning to the car after the door broke to a description of a failure on the part of SPT1 to inform the 'others' (Betty and Ian) of the damage and she is thus able to associate with SPT1's actions an allegation of deliberate negligence – that SPT1 *didn't bother saying anything to them*↓. In a broader sense, pio1 is taking an approach to the negotiations at this point that is based around the association of violent or anti-social acts with the suspect's version of events. Her shift from the verb *close* to *slam* gives SPT1's actions a violence that his version does not contain and this enables her to introduce causality more plausibly in the following turn. By recasting SPT1's action of leaving the shop as an act of negligence, she is further able to support a version of events where SPT1 has wilfully and knowingly engaged in a destructive activity.

Incidentally, the fact that SPT1 offers agreement tokens to pio1's assertions does not adequately represent the suspect's response to these assertions. He later reiterates his original version of *closing* the door, and, although he eventually concedes that he did *slam* the door the first time, he continues to defend the view that the damage was accidental.

In INT11, the suspect attends to the police interviewer's use of language when they are discussing the way that the suspect invited another man, Bob, back to a friend's house where Bob was assaulted. The contentious issue in this interview is the extent to which the suspect was an accomplice in the assault, which, according to SPT11, was perpetrated by his friend.

Extract 4-39 INT11

185. pio11:   <u>so</u> ah (.) you went to <u>get</u> him and what did you tell
                (0.3) <u>Shane</u> ∧
186.   (2.3) <u>sorry</u> what did you tell <u>Bob</u> ∧

187.	SPT11:	(2.0) <u>nothin</u> just whether he wanted to come up for a <u>smoke</u> ∧
188.	pio11:	(4.6) is that all you <u>told</u> him ↑
189.	SPT11:	(1.0) yep⇒
190.	pio11:	and <u>what</u> did Bob <u>initially</u> say to you ↓
191.		did he <u>say</u> anything <u>initially</u> to you ↓
192.		did he say he <u>wanted</u> to come or he <u>didn't</u> want to come ↓
193.	SPT11:	(0.5) aw he wasn't <u>sure</u> ∧
194.		(1.2) then he went <u>inside</u> and he grabbed his <u>coat</u>
195.		and he <u>come</u> up ∧
196.	pio11:	(7.5) would this be <u>right</u> ⇒
197.		(0.5) or would this be <u>wrong</u> ↓
198.		you <u>kept</u> trying to <u>persuade</u> him to <u>go</u> ↓
199.	SPT11:	not <u>persuade</u> ⇒
200.		I asked him (0.6) <u>twice</u> ⇒

Perhaps it is pio11's on-record approach to the formulation as in lines 196–7: *would this be right or would this be wrong*, but SPT11 is careful to correct the police version from a potentially incriminating *persuade* to a more neutral *asked him twice*. It is rare in the data for a suspect to overtly attend to the language of a police formulation. Extract 4-40 from INT2 exhibits the more usual approach taken by participants to police formulations.

In the previous section, the segment presented below as Extract 4-40 was found to demonstrate a substantial alteration to the suspect's version where the reason given by SPT2 for the assault on his girlfriend was dismissed by pio2 and replaced with the police version that there was *absolutely no <u>reason</u>↓* for the assault.

Extract 4-40 INT2

276.	pio2:	(0.6) um↓ (.) was there any reason why you had to e::rm↓ (.) <u>treat</u> 'a this way at
277.	SPT2:	(1.2) it was a <u>combination</u> of things (.) y' know∧
278.		I↓ (0.4) didn't like the <u>fact</u> that↓ (0.4) y' know↑
279.		(0.6) here <u>I</u> am goin' out with a girl⇒
280.		and she⇒ (0.6) jumps into <u>bed</u> with (0.2) one of my⇒ so-called <u>mates</u>∧
281.	pio2:	(0.4) OK well regardless of that may have been the <u>case</u>∧
282.	SPT2:	auh-↓
283.	pio2:	um⇒ (0.6) not to say whether that the case or <u>not</u>∧
284.		but regardless of that <u>might've</u> been the case⇒

285.   (0.4) do you agree⇒ that that ah⇒ (.) <u>warranted</u> your
                   actions↑
286.   (0.4) by <u>draggin'</u> 'er out by the arm⇒
287.   (.) <u>pullin'</u> 'er by the hair⇒
288.   (0.8) // <u>forcibly</u>* removing 'er from the <u>house</u>∧
289.   SPT2:   nuo-* (1.0) nup∧

We have already seen that, in interactional terms, pio2 was able to achieve these changes through his access to topic management tools unavailable to SPT2, specifically, pio2's access to topic initiation devices which strongly obligate SPT2 to respond to the topic in favour of any topic SPT2 may raise himself. However, it is also pertinent that in order to dismiss SPT2's reason, pio2 employs a construction which juxtaposes SPT2's reason – *she⇒(0.6) jumps into <u>bed</u> with (0.2) one of my⇒ so-called <u>mates</u>∧* – with formulations of SPT2's actions and asks if the reason, already weakened through utterances such as *regardless of that <u>might've</u> been the case⇒* in line 284, warranted these actions.

As we saw in the previous analysis of extracts from INT1, it is clear that pio2 strengthens the supposition of unwarranted actions by introducing terms of violence as formulations of the suspect's prior turns. In lines 286–8, pio2 formulates SPT2's actions by using the verb phrases *<u>draggin'</u> 'er out by the hair, <u>pullin'</u> by the arm and <u>forcibly</u> removing 'er from the <u>house</u>*. In each case, the word that most emphasises the violence of the actions is stressed. This is particularly apparent in line 288 where the word *<u>forcibly</u>* is given greater stress than the main verb in the utterance, *removing*. By using these three utterances to formulate SPT2's actions, pio2 does, of course, edit out many other descriptions of the events offered by SPT2 during the interview. For instance, SPT2 describes 132/SPT2: *yellin and screamin at '<u>er</u>∧*, 161/SPT2: *<u>arguin</u> an' pushin' n' <u>pullin'</u>* and 219/SPT2: *<u>sitting</u> on the ground wif her after she (0.2) fell <u>o:ver</u>∧*, but none of these actions are included in pio2's formulation. It is noticeable that the first two examples from SPT2's version of events do contain terms of violence but they imply either non-physical violence – *yellin, screamin and arguin* – or interactional, two-sided actions – *<u>arguin</u>, <u>pushin</u> n' <u>pullin</u>*. These descriptions do not support the version pio2 is constructing of a level of violence perpetrated by SPT2 that is out of all proportion to the reason which SPT2 has supplied. The case pio2 builds is apparently very convincing and SPT2 takes up the TRP at the end of line 287, before pio2 has even finished his formulation, in order to indicate that his reason did not warrant these acts of violence. It is this acceptance of pio2's version by SPT2 that ultimately weakens

SPT2's reason for the assault to the extent that pio2 is able to formulate SPT2's reason as *absolutely no reason↓* despite the contradiction inherent in this claim.

Furthermore, in Extract 4-28 from INT3, examined in the previous section, pio3 uses the formulation 155/pio3: *but you ah can afford to (.) grow (1.0) the marijuana plants⇒* to associate SPT3's version of events with the criminal act of cultivating marijuana. The formulation also enables pio3 to imply that, financially, SPT3 prioritises the cultivation of marijuana over the legal pastime of cultivating ferns. By denying this SPT3 also places himself at risk of being accused of selling the marijuana to pay for its cultivation, which is one way of interpreting the comment that it 156/SPT3: *doesn't cost anything↓*. In this way, pio3 associates the suspect's version of events with criminality or anti-social behaviour through the use of formulations.

Finally, a segment from INT3 demonstrates that the question–answer pairs that dominate this interview do not appear to lend themselves as easily to the task of creating a police version of events.

Extract 4-41 INT3

221.	pio3	(0.8) all right (.) and <u>who</u> hung em up in the back shed↓
222.	SPT3:	<u>I</u> did↓
223.	pio3	(0.6) <u>how</u> did you do that⇒
224.	SPT3:	(0.6) tied em up with a <u>rope</u>∧
225.	pio3	(0.4) and <u>why</u> did you do that↓
226.	SPT3:	(0.9) so that wouldn't <u>go</u> everywhere↓
227.	pio3	(0.6) so they <u>wouldn't</u>∧
228.	SPT3:	<u>go</u> everywhere↑
229.	pio3	(0.4) oh <u>right</u>↓ (0.6) I'll <u>put</u> it to you that you <u>put</u> em there to <u>dry</u> out∧
230.		(0.8) for <u>later</u> use↓
231.	SPT3:	(1.1) no (0.2) just (0.2) to (0.4) get out of the <u>way</u>∧
232.	pio3	right⇒ (2.3) OK and then <u>explain</u> to me what <u>happened</u>

Pio3 is attempting to establish the reason why SPT3 tied the marijuana plants together and then hung them in a shed. Specifically, pio3 is proposing that SPT3 hung the plants in the shed with the intention of allowing them to cure, thus providing him with consumable material at some later stage. This interpretation of SPT3's actions would have the double implication of, firstly, casting SPT3's actions as suspicious and having criminal intent, and secondly, casting SPT3 himself as a heavy drug user, potentially in possession of a large quantity of cured marijuana.

However, SPT3's version has already minimised these interpretations as he has responded to pio3's questions about his actions by claiming that he only hung them up and tied them together to be a tidy shed user, as he explains in line 226/SPT3: *(0.9) so that wouldn't go everywhere↓*. By the time pio3 comes to formulate SPT3's version, SPT3 has already had the opportunity, by responding to the three prior content questions, to strengthen his version and to pre-emptively weaken pio3's formulation that SPT3 *put em there to dry out∧ (0.8) for later use↓*. Furthermore, pio3 prefaces this utterance with the phrase *I'll put it to you that* which does not have the effect of 'naturalising' the process of formulation in the way that pio1 and pio2 were able to do. We saw that in the extracts from INT1 and INT2, the police interviewers used utterances that implied that their construction of a police version was merely a restating of the suspect's version. This effect was achieved primarily through the use of formulation first pair parts to summarise the interviewee's prior talk. However, pio3 produces his utterance in lines 229–30 more transparently as a police version by using the police institutional construction *I'll put it to you that.* As in INT11 (see Extract 4-39), it appears to be less interactionally problematic for SPT3 to reject pio3's proposal and reiterate his own position (231/SPT3: *(1.1) no (0.2) just (0.2) to (0.4) get out of the way∧*) than it was for SPT1 or SPT2 to counter the claims made by pio1 and pio2 respectively.

It would appear that a more transparently institutional approach to the construction of the police version of events enables the suspect to have greater access to the interactional tools required to reject this version and maintain their own version of events. Nonetheless, the versions proposed by pio11 and pio3 have in common with the examples from INT1 and INT2 the purpose of presenting the suspect's actions as having criminal intent and of characterising the suspect himself as anti-social and violent.

4.5 Conclusion

The police discursive practices revealed through the analyses in this chapter represent an exploitation of an existing interactional structure – described by Frankel (1990) as a 'deference structure' – in order first to construct a police version of events and then to attempt to have the suspect align with this version in favour of a competing suspect version. Section 4.4.2 identified that both police and suspect participants engaged in the strategic use of evidence to support their version of events. Section 4.4.4 demonstrated that by utilising the topic management resources available to them, police interviewers are able to formulate a suspect's narrative as a police version which excludes contextual information provided by the suspect, introduces alternative versions which cast the suspect's actions as remiss or deficient and emphasises the violent or otherwise socially undesirable aspects of the narrative.

If we consider the institutional requirements which produce the interview turn structure, we see that it is the role of the police officer as 'elicitor' which is crucial in establishing a deference structure. Further, it is the use of a deference structure that provides the police interviewer with an interactionally unassailable position of authority in the interviews. That is, the preallocation of turn types ensures that the floor is returned to the primary interviewing officer at the close of any recognisable sequence of turns, generally a question–answer sequence. It is not possible, within this structure, for any other participant to 'hijack' the floor to undermine the intentions or authority of the primary interviewing officer. A successful attempt by the suspect, for instance, to take control of question initiations would constitute a breakdown of the interview procedure and would not be tolerated by the police institution – the resulting recording would not constitute a proper evidentiary interview.

An inherently authoritative position of the primary interviewing officer is made clear in the allocation of topic management tools. As discussed in the previous section, one of the results of the chain rule is that the role of interviewer affords the police officer a far greater range of topic initiation devices than the interviewee. Whereas the interviewee is only able to introduce new topics in ways which do not obligate the interviewer to take up a respondent role, the interviewer can introduce a new topic within any first pair part. The interviewee is therefore constrained to topic initiations that are minimally obligating and can be easily ignored, while the interviewer is able to introduce new topics within adjacency pair structures that maximise the obligation on the interviewee to respond 'on-topic'.

The recurrent application of a question–answer chain rule in interviews provides police officers with 'institutionally guaranteed' access to the floor to produce maximally obligating topic initiation devices. Given the relatively constrained contributions allowed by the suspect and, to a lesser degree, the secondary interviewing officer, the features of the primary interviewing officer's role which we have explored and described in this chapter provide him or her with an 'interactional authority' over the other participants.

Chapter 6 explores the relationship between the discursive practices identified in the analysis of the structural and interactional features of the interview, and instances of 'counterproductive' discursive behaviour constituting a police mythology about interviewing. The next chapter will consider the findings of a study involving a different type of interview data: police training interviews with children. The strategies employed by these police interviewers will provide a useful comparison to the strategies we have so far described in police-suspect interviews.

5
Interviewing Children: the VATE Approach

5.1   Introduction

This chapter presents a contrasting example of police discursive behaviour. This case study of police training interviews with children demonstrates that the police approach to interviewing adult suspects, as described in the previous chapter, is not the only questioning technique available to officers.

Thus far, we have seen that, as a form of institutional discourse, the language of police evidentiary interviews has generally been viewed in terms of its asymmetrical distribution of power and status between the dominant police participant and the subordinate witness participant (e.g. Auburn et al. 1995: 384; Thomas 1989: 137). In the previous chapter, this was supported by the analysis of topic management and turn-taking in police-suspect interviews which revealed that police authority is embedded in the institutional allocation of discursive resources. It might be expected therefore that when the witness is a young child, the difference in participant status would be clearly demonstrated through the prominence of features of asymmetrical institutional discourse. For instance, the use of discoursal indicators (Thomas 1989) and asymmetrical naming rituals (Lakoff 1990) by the dominant participants to maintain control over the discourse would be expected features of interviews between police officers and children.

Heydon (1997), however, finds that in certain discourse contexts it is not possible to make such predictions about the data based on our assumptions about the nature of police institutional discourse. In the interviews which are analysed here, features such as those described above are identified in the data; however, their role in enabling the asymmetry normally associated with police institutional discourse is challenged by the presence of features not normally associated with such asymmetry. These latter features are largely those which indicate the caring attitude of the police officer and a genuine concern for the comfort of the child, both by the interviewing officer and by the institution as a whole. Informal naming rituals and receipt markers (Atkinson 1992) are examples of such features. The complexity of the type of discourse found in these data reflects the unusual circumstances of the interviews and contrasts markedly with the approach of officers interviewing adult suspects.

As in the investigation of police-suspect interviews, adopting a theoretical framework which reveals the negotiation of meaning as achieved interactionally is an important consideration in this analysis. By focussing on the use of frames (Goffman 1974: 10–11) and participation frameworks (Goffman 1974: 517) to describe the data, as well as the use of discoursal indicators (Thomas 1989) and receipt markers (Atkinson 1992) this study furthers our understanding of how Interactional Sociolinguistics can be usefully employed to describe the way in which participants' goals are realised through their use of language. The analysis involving discoursal indicators and receipt markers demonstrates the problematisation of institutional discourse as necessarily asymmetrical. A more detailed discussion of these features and their relationship to institutional discourse can be found in Heydon (1997: 94–112).

5.2   The VATE project

The interviews transcribed for analysis in this study were conducted as a part of the Victorian Police Department's Video and Audio Taping of Evidence (VATE) project which has been in operation since 1993, and provides an alternative to the traumatic experience of testifying in court for vulnerable witnesses and victims of crimes, such as children. Instead of a court appearance, children under eighteen years and the mentally handicapped may give their evidence in the form of an interview with a police officer trained to elicit a narrative from the witness in a form acceptable to the court.

Part of the training for police officers involved in the VATE project involves conducting a videotaped interview with a child or mentally handicapped person. The object of the exercise is for the police officer to elicit as many details as possible about some, wholly innocuous, 'event' which the subject has recently witnessed. As these 'events' are set up in advance by the VATE project coordinators, the information elicited can be tested for accuracy against what was known to have happened.

Fourteen such training interviews were conducted at the Melbourne Police Centre in May 1997, and the videotaped recordings of seven of those interviews formed the basis for the data used in this study. The seven child participants were aged between eight and eleven years and were all students at a rural ballet school. The 'event' arranged by the researcher which they all witnessed (hereafter referred to as 'the Event') involved a man unknown to the children interrupting their ballet class and conducting a survey about after-school activities. (For a full description of the methodology employed in the study, see Heydon 1997: 20–8). The data were transcribed using a broader transcription methodology than the interview data already presented in this book and the reader should note that participant contributions are numbered according to turns rather than lines.

5.3   Summary of results of the analysis of the data

In analysing the data, this study identified several linguistic features which can be described as features of institutional discourse, such as the dominance of a question/answer structure, the fact that the goals of the interaction may not be apparent to the lay participants and the fact that there are constraints on displays of emotion (e.g. surprise, sympathy etc.) by the professional participants (Drew and Heritage 1992: 22–3). The tri-partite structural view of the three parts of the VATE interview (the Opening, the Information Gathering and the Closing) had linguistic implications and frame transitional utterances (Coupland et al. 1994: 93–4) were identified in each interview. These utterances marked the turn at which the interview moved from one part to the next (i.e. from the Opening to the Information Gathering, or from the Information Gathering to the Closing). As in the analysis of police-suspect interviews presented in Chapter 3, the frame and participation framework analysis (Goffman 1974) of the Opening and the Closing of the interviews found further evidence of police institutional discourse features, such as the roles of principal and author of the police officer's utterances in the Opening being assigned to the police institution rather than the speaker, the shifts in footing used in most of the interview Closings through which police officers were able to maintain a neutral stance during the review of the child's narrative, and the prevalence of discoursal indicators (Thomas 1989). These features and their implications for the power dynamics of the interviews will be discussed below. Two other features, discoursal indicators (Thomas 1989) and receipt markers (Atkinson 1992), which were identified in the data, will be discussed below in relation to issues of power, status and institutional discourse.

The interviews were further subjected to analysis in terms of the question forms being used by police officers to elicit information from the children. It was found that embedded requests for information of the form Can you ...? and Do you ...? (referred to as CY? and DY? respectively) had particularly high frequency in the Information Gathering part of the interview, although their presence in the Opening and Closing was also noted and analysed. Further analysis revealed that these embedded requests occurred with a narrow range of verb types and the various combinations of request form and verb type could also be analysed in terms of the types of response they elicited. It was found that the response types ranged across several categories, two of which, the substantive and the yes/no responses, indicated the two possible interpretations of the request: as a request for information in the case of the former, or as a question regarding ability in the case of the latter. The implications of this analysis for the functions of the requests and the issues of power and status mentioned above will be discussed further in this chapter and the implications for police institutional discourse more generally will be taken up in Chapters 6 and 7.

5.4   Features of police institutional discourse in VATE interviews

5.4.1   Participation frameworks of the tri-partite interview

In analysing the data it was found that the participation framework of the police on-record interview frame invoked at the commencement of the interview had a similar distribution of participant roles as were identified for the police-suspect interviews. In their opening statements, the police officers switch from speaking for themselves in the first utterance (e.g. V-INT3[13]: 1: VPO4 *You ready to go?...OK...this is a video taped statement at the Victoria Police Centre on Sunday the twenty-fifth of May 1997 and my name is Senior Constable (FN, SN)*) to speaking for another when they introduce the child (e.g. V-INT3: 1: VPO4 *and with me is (FN) who I'm gonna be speaking to*). As noted previously, in terms of Goffman's (1974: 517) participant roles, an *animator* is the person who physically produces talk. Thus in the opening statement, the police officer is the *animator* of the identification process. It was also noted in Goffman (1974: 517) that a *figure* is a person being spoken of, so we can see that by introducing the child at the end of the opening statement, the police officer assigns the role of *figure* to the child as the child is being spoken of.

As in the police-suspect interviews, however, the roles of *principal* (the person responsible for talk) and *author* (the person who creates talk) can be shown to belong to neither participant (Goffman 1974: 517). In the case of the opening statements, it is possible to argue that in making their statements to camera, the police officers themselves are only animators of a scripted statement which has been written by a third party representing the police force as an institution. If we consider Extract 5-1, we can see that in the first line of turn 1, VPO1 states that she is going to be reading from something.

Extract 5-1 V-INT6

1.   VPO1:   Here we go(..) ((sits)) OK (..) now I'm going to be reading
             from something. all right↑ so um. just bear with me. all
             right this is a video taped statement at the ah Melbourne
             Community Policing Squad today's um Sunday the
             twenty-fifth of May↑ (.) 1997↑ (.) can you tell the time
             Alison↑ (.) have you got a wa- oh very good can you tell
             me what the time is by your watch↑
2.   CH3:   Um. one past eleven↑
3.   VPO1:   So is mine (.) that's good (.) all right the time is one past
             eleven. my name is Senior Constable Alex Maxwell and
             I'm with Alison (..) Alison could you tell me what your
             full name is↑

This mention of reading from something clearly indicates that the statement made by VPO1 is not speech created by her, but rather a scripted statement created by someone representing the police force as an institution. Thus VPO1 is not the author of the statement and as the statements made by the other police officers in the VATE scheme at the commencement of their interviews are almost identical to this one, it would seem reasonable to postulate that none of the police officers occupies the role of author of this statement.

As to the role of principal of the statement, we must consider whether or not the police officer, as an individual, can be 'held responsible for having wilfully taken up the position to which the meaning of the utterance attests' (Goffman 1974: 517). As was the case for the police-suspect interviews, the police officer is not responsible for deciding whether or not to make the statement nor when it should be made and therefore cannot be considered responsible for any of the decisions which would place her/him in the role of principal of the statement.

We can summarise the analysis of the interview Openings by stating that the participation framework of the police on-record interview frame is one in which the speaker, the police officer, is assigned the role of animator of the utterances while the roles of principal and author seem to be assigned to an unknown third party which represents police protocol. In other words, the Openings in the VATE interviews are produced using the same distribution of participant roles as those of the police-suspect interview.

In discussing the Closing of the interviews, two different approaches to the participation framework were analysed and the first few turns of the Closings of two interviews – V-INT4 and V-INT7 – are reproduced in Extracts 5-2 and 5-3 below.

Extract 5-2 V-INT7

149.   VPO6:   Right (.) OK(.) certainly sounds very interesting(.)we'll
               stop the ah the tape there(.) but um just so I make sure
               I've got this right(.) so last Thursday you went to ballet↑
150.   CH7:   Yeah

Extract 5-3 V-INT4

67.   VPO7:   OK(.) I'm just going to go through what you've told me
              about this man OK and um I'd like you to just to make sure
              that I've got it right and if there's anything you want to
              add to what I've said you can just(.) interrupt me and add
68.   CH4:   Yep
69.   VPO7:   Or um if there's something that's wrong that I've said you
              can just tell me if I've got anything wrong(..)OK you said
              that at ballet school on Thursday at about six o'clock↑
70.   CH4:   Yeah

We see in the second of the above extracts that VPO7 made explicit to CH4 the purpose of the Closing and the roles to be taken up by the participants – that she would be reviewing the things said to her by CH4 and that CH4 was to feel that she could correct or affirm VPO7's assertions at any time. By comparison, VPO6 in the Closing of V-INT7 did not mention the roles to be played, only that he wanted to *make sure I've got this right*. If we compare this to the way in which a 'preferred version' is negotiated in police interviews with suspects (Auburn et al.

1995: 363–5) we may find some similarities, which might indicate that the approach of VPO6 is closer to the approach commonly identified as police institutional discourse.

The effect of this recognition of CH4's role in the Closing by VPO7 in V-INT4, seems to be that CH4 feels encouraged to make adjustments and additions to her narrative. Indeed, in turn 76 of V-INT4, VPO7's *circus* in the previous turn is adjusted to *[circus] dance* and in turn 86, CH4 adds to the description of the man as wearing an *old top* (turn 85) with *kind of like a T shirt or something*. However, in the Closing of V-INT7, CH7 does not add to or adjust any of the information presented by VPO6 (see V-INT7; 149–59 in Heydon 1997). This is in spite of the fact that VPO6 fails to mention many details which CH7 had supplied, such as the type and colour of the coat that the 'inspector' was wearing (see V-INT7; 118–24) and that he brought a video camera (see V-INT7; CH7: 140).

Clayman (1992) discusses shifts in footing used by media interviewers to maintain neutrality and shows how assertions are attributed to a source other than the interviewer as a means of distancing the speaker from such assertions. Thus we could argue that VPO7 in V-INT4 has maintained a neutral stance regarding the content of CH4's narrative by not taking personal responsibility for the utterances and referring to them only as things said by CH4. VPO6, on the other hand, appears to align himself more strongly with the content of CH7's narrative by not attributing his assertions about the Event to CH7.

This examination of the Closing of V-INT4 and V-INT7 indicates that when the police officer assumes the role of animator of the child's utterances, as in V-INT4, the child feels more able to adjust, if not actually challenge, the content of those utterances. By contrast, in not making the participation framework explicit, VPO6 in V-INT7 appears to have appropriated the child's narrative and reduced the possibility of CH7 offering any adjustment to his assertions.

In considering the participation frameworks of both the Opening and the Closing in terms of police institutional discourse we need to take into account the relationship between the police officer as an individual producing utterances which may be classed as police institutional discourse, and the institution represented by such discourse. It seems reasonable to assume that in their daily work, police officers are considered to be carrying out a duty and representing the police force as an institution, rather than representing themselves as individuals, and that this would be somehow incorporated as a feature of police institutional discourse.

We could therefore speculate that the distribution of roles in the participation framework of the Opening (i.e. the police officer as animator of utterances attributable to the police institution) and the stance taken up by VPO7 through the shift of footing which places her in the role of animator of CH4's utterances, both conform to a notion of the police officer as a functionary of the police institution. Before discussing this issue further, we shall consider what influence discoursal indicators have on the nature of the institutional discourse being discussed here.

5.4.2 Discoursal indicators

If we analyse the use of discoursal indicators (Thomas 1989) by police officers we find that this feature is employed to delineate the parameters of the discourse and restrict the allowable contributions of the child to within those boundaries. For instance, by stating at the commencement of the Information Gathering that *I want to talk to you about ballet class, um, on Thursday* (V-INT4, VPO7; 15), the police officer has restricted the topic of the subsequent conversation to one particular ballet class on one particular day.

Furthermore, when the police officers use the discoursal indicators to describe the boundaries of the discourse to follow, they often place themselves in the position of speaker: V-INT3, VPO4; 19: ... *I'm going to be speaking to you* ...; V-INT1, VPO2; 41: ... *I'd like to talk to you* ...; V-INT4, VPO7; 15: ... *I want to talk to you* ...; V-INT2, VPO3; 7: ... *I'll be speaking to you* ... In V-INT5–7 the police officers do not overtly place themselves in the position of speaker in this way but rather indicate that they will be asking the child questions, which is another form of discoursal indicator (see V-INT5, VPO5; 17; V-INT6, VPO1; 11; and V-INT7, VPO6; 27 & 31).

Given that these discoursal indicators are used by dominant participants, their use by the police officers at the transitional points of the interview would seem to indicate that the police officers are reiterating their dominance in the interview at these crucial moments presumably as a way of guiding the structure of the interview. This would seem to be a feature of police interview discourse, and perhaps police institutional discourse as a whole,[14] where it is the responsibility of the interviewing officer to maintain the relevance of the interviewee's contributions. As such, the police officer would have need of discoursal indicators to guide the interviewee so that each contribution by the interviewee adds to the narrative in a meaningful way.

Thus we have established that discoursal indicators may be considered another feature of police institutional discourse and that their function in these interviews is to maintain the police officer's dominance such that contributions made by the interview subject will be kept within the boundaries of what is deemed relevant by the police officer. This issue will be discussed further in Chapter 6 where the police assertion of 'discursive authority' in the interview will be considered in relation to other institutional requirements, such as the need to obtain a voluntary statement from the interviewee.

In the following section, we shall explore the methods used by the police officers to balance their dominant role in the discourse with the need for the child to express herself freely and not feel restricted in her narrative.

5.5   Features of informal institutional discourse in VATE interviews

5.5.1   Naming rituals

One feature of the interviews which has been mentioned but not yet analysed is the use of naming rituals, particularly in the Opening. It can be seen from the data that it is a necessary part of the opening statement to camera that the police officer states her/his name and rank (see Extract 5-4 below).

Extract 5-4 V-INT2

1.   VPO3:   OK this is a video taped statement at the ah (.) Victoria Police Centre↑ on Sunday the twenty-fifth of May 1997 and the time now is eleven thirty one in the morning (.) my name's **Senior Constable John Robertson**↑ and with me today is Sarah↑(.) Sarah can you tell me your full name please(.)
2.   CH2:   Um (.) Sarah (.) Jane(.) Miller

We can see from this extract that as a part of the opening statement, the police officer is required to name her/himself and introduce the child. If we examine turn 1 of Extract 4, we notice an inequality in the status assigned to the participants through the naming ritual. While PO3 is identified by a title which denotes a position within the police institution as well as by his first name and surname *Senior Constable John Robertson*, CH2 is referred to only by her first name *Sarah*. Inequality in naming rituals is identified by Lakoff (1990)as a part of the doctor–patient relationship and can be seen as representative of the 'necessary asymmetry' of institutional discourse. Furthermore, CH2 is given a subordinate position relative to PO3 through the use of the utterance *and with me today is* preceding her first name, which implies not only that PO3 is the dominant participant accompanied by the child, but that CH2 is one of many children that PO3 has spoken to and just happens to be his interview subject today. This latter issue is indicative of institutional discourse where the lay person's experiences, which are unusual and unique to them, are treated as one case of many that the professional participant has cause to deal with (see Drew and Heritage 1992: 50–1). Thus it seems that the naming ritual taking place in the police officer's opening statement is part of the set of features that comprise several other forms of institutional discourse.

However, this picture of the VATE interview as a form of institutional discourse containing the same features as other forms of institutional discourse is incomplete. It does not take into account several features which can be shown to distinguish the VATE interview at least from other types of police interview. For instance, we have just considered the naming ritual found in the police officer's opening statement as representative of asymmetry in institutional discourse. But can the same be said about the remainder of the Opening, or indeed the remainder of the interview as a whole? To start with, the use of the police officer's full name and rank is dropped by the police officer almost immediately following the opening statement. Consider PO3's statement highlighted in turn 11 shown in Extract 5-5 below.

Extract 5-5 V-INT2

11.   VPO3:   we'll be asking questions(.) now also(.) if when I'm asking questions(.) if I ask a question and you don't understand it↑ **just say hey I don't understand John** can you ask me that question again or can you ask it in another way↑ also if you don't know the answer just say I don't know(.)

12.   CH2:   Mm

Here PO3 is instructing CH2 to indicate if she does not understand a question. In order to make himself clear, PO3 animates the sort of statement he expects CH2 to make in case of such a misunderstanding: *hey I don't understand* and then adds his own first name to the end of the animated statement *John*. Here then PO3 has clearly demonstrated to CH2 that she is to address him using his first name. Similarly in V-INT3, V-INT6 and V-INT7, the police officers use the same device, explicitly demonstrating to the child that she is to address the interviewing officer by her/his first name (see V-INT3, PO4; 13; V-INT6, PO1; 19; and V-INT7, PO6; 23).

This alternative naming ritual is supported as the dominant paradigm for naming in the interview procedure as a whole by the fact that all of the interviewing officers and children wore large name tags on which was written only the first name of the wearer.

Thus in the interviews we have evidence of two different naming rituals which seem to correspond to two separate 'orders' of discourse (Fairclough 1989).[15] One of these is represented as the normal police institutional discourse style and contains features such as asymmetry in the naming ritual. The other seems to be connected to a more empathetic discourse style and has at least one feature of equality which is the use of first names by both participants.

The use of receipt markers by the police officers as a way of acknowledging the child's contributions was also found to be a feature of the interview data. In light of the above discussion about the formality of discourse being employed by the VATE police officers, this feature and its implications for the way we define the discourse of the interviews will be discussed in the following section.

5.5.2   Receipt markers

The use of an utterance such as *OK, certainly* or *right* was found to be very common in the interviews as a way of acknowledging receipt of the child's response to a question. It was noted that this feature is identified by Atkinson (1992) as a receipt marker used by arbitrators in informal court proceedings. Atkinson (1992) compares this strategy to those employed in other types of court proceedings such as cross-examination, where a response to one question is frequently given no acknowledgment and is immediately followed by another question. This technique is found to disorient and distress witnesses being so examined because there is no indication of how their response has been received. Atkinson notes that:

> By contrast, the arbitrator's practice of acknowledging receipt before going on to the next question may be one way of helping to reduce or mitigate the kind of uncertainty that is involved in situations where the only acknowledgment an answer receives is an unprefaced next question. (1992: 202)

That such a device is so prominent in the data for the VATE study indicates that while these police officers may occupy a dominant participant role in the discourse, they are aware of the need to reduce the uncertainty that the children may feel in the interview. Furthermore, this device, as Atkinson notes, does not signify the user's opinion of the response being acknowledged, only that the response has been heard and understood. This is an important aspect of the VATE interviews where police officers are required to maintain a neutral position in regard to the child's narrative and not make judgmental remarks about the quality or content of the information elicited (see Powell and Thomson 1994: 207).

Although the police-suspect interviews discussed in this book were not specifically analysed for the use of receipt markers, upon listening to the interviews it is clear that receipt markers are much less common in these 'standard' police interviews with adults. Certainly Atkinson (1992) notes that it is not a feature of usual court proceedings (see above), but rather indicates a less formal style of discourse.

So far we have seen that the VATE interviews contain features of both formal and informal institutional discourse. The participation framework of the police on-record interview frame was shown to be a feature of formal police institutional discourse, where the police officer takes up the position of a functionary representing the police force and assumes only the role of animator of utterances scripted by the police institution. Further, the use of discoursal indicators to restrict contributions made by the subordinate participant was also shown to be a feature of police institutional discourse, as was the asymmetrical naming ritual contained in the opening statement of the interview.

On the other hand, the widespread use of first names by both participants and the use of receipt markers by the police officers were both found to be features of a less formal discourse.

This study included a detailed analysis of embedded requests for information used in the Information Gathering part of the interviews. In a later section below, we will consider the findings of this analysis in relation to the issues of asymmetry and status in the discourse described above.

5.6   Embedded requests in the VATE interviews

5.6.1   Functions of embedded requests

In the analysis of the data, the two main forms of embedded requests found in the interviews. *Can you____?* (CY?) and *Do you____?* (DY?) requests were considered according to their distribution, the verbs which occurred with them and the types of responses they elicited. Extract 5-6 below contains some examples of these request forms being used in the Opening. Regarding the types of responses elicited by the different request forms, it was noted that police officers would be most likely to expect substantive responses as these types of request are primarily requests for information. Departures from substantive responses, in particular yes/no responses, indicated that the child may have interpreted the request as a question regarding ability and thus the request had not fulfilled its function of eliciting information.

Of the CY? requests, it was found that those used with the verb *remember* were most likely to elicit a yes/no response, while those with *tell me* or *describe to/for me* were the least likely to elicit a yes/no response. Further, it was suggested that the use of a verb which implied talk of some kind with the personal pronoun me, such as in *can you tell me … ?* acted to encourage the child, reassuring her that the information she gave was of personal importance to the police officer. This may have partially explained the effectiveness of these types of response in eliciting substantive responses.

The DY? requests were found to occur with two verbs, *know* and *remember* in 97 per cent of cases (see Heydon 1997: Table 4.9, p. 85). Of the occurrences with these two verbs it was found that DY? requests with *know* were more likely to elicit yes/no responses than DY? requests with *remember*, and furthermore, there was no evidence to suggest that the DY? *remember* requests were being interpreted by the children as questions regarding ability as they were never given an affirmative yes/no response. The DY? *know* requests, however, elicited several affirmative yes/no responses indicating that the children felt the request could be regarded as a question about knowledge/ability and could be responded to with an agreement token.

One aspect of the interviews which demonstrates quite clearly the difference between the various request forms and their possible interpretations is their function in the Opening of the interviews. As mentioned above, the Opening consists of a statement by the police officer followed by requests for the child's full name and date of birth. To obtain the child's date of birth, many of the police officers asked the child to give their age first and then their birthday (see Extract 5-6 below).

Extract 5-6 V-INT2

1. VPO3:   OK this is a video taped statement at the ah(.) Victoria Police Centre↑ on Sunday the twenty-fifth of May 1997 and the time now is eleven thirty one in the morning(.) my name's Senior Constable John Robertson↑ and with me today is Sarah ↑ (.) Sarah **can you tell me your full name** please(.)

2. CH2:   Um(.) Sarah(.) Jane (.) Miller

3   VPO3:   OK↑ now(.) **can you tell me how old you are** please Sarah

4.   CH2:   I'm nine(.)
5.   VPO3:   And **do you know when your birthday is**↑
6.   CH2:   Yeah(.) the fourteenth of March

What is noticeable about each of these Opening requests, is that while a CY? *tell me* request can be used to obtain any of the pieces of information mentioned above, the DY? *know* request can only be used to elicit the child's birthday, and is never used to elicit the child's age or full name. Often a direct request is used to elicit the child's age (eg. V-INT7, PO6; 7: *And how old are you Jacqui*) but never to elicit the child's birthday; here an embedded request is always used and it is most commonly a DY? *know* request. (See V-INT1, PO2; 9; V-INT2, PO3; 5; V-INT4, PO7; 5; V-INT7, PO6; 9 in Heydon 1997.) DY? *remember* and CY? *remember* requests are never used in this part of the Opening.

This indicates that *Do you know your full name?* or *Do you know how old you are?* are not appropriate requests for children of this age because such questions imply that they may not know their full name or their age and this is very unlikely. *Can you tell me your full name?* has none of these implications in the interviews and receives a substantive response every time it is uttered with no agreement token which might indicate that it has been interpreted as a question regarding ability.

It seems then, that the CY? *tell me* requests can be used in situations where the child's ability to answer the question is not at stake because they are more likely to be interpreted as requests for information. Conversely, the DY? *know* requests are more likely to be used in situations where the child's ability to answer the question may not be taken for granted, such as in requests for the child's date of birth or birthday. (The data show that many of the child participants did not know the year of their birth, though they were all able to give their birthday.) Furthermore, the DY? *know* requests cannot be used in situations where the child is reasonably certain to be able to answer the question because they are more likely to be interpreted as questions regarding ability/knowledge which would be inappropriate when requesting a ten-year-old's full name, for instance.

Thus the first few turns in the Opening of the interviews reveal some definite differences in the functions of CY? *tell me* and DY? *know* requests. While the former functions most strongly as a request for information, the latter can easily function as both a question regarding ability and a request for information. This difference is recognised by the police officers who avoid the use of DY? *know* requests when↑ no question regarding ability is to be implied. This finding strongly suggests that the more yes/no responses an embedded response elicits, the more likely it is to be functioning both as a request for information and as a question regarding ability, such as was found to be the case with the DY? *know* requests. The CY? *tell me* requests, which were more successful in eliciting substantive responses, do so because they function more strongly as requests for information.

While Ledbetter and Dent (1988: 232) classified both CY? *tell me* and DY? *know* requests as embedded requests for information and noted that they may be interpreted as questions regarding ability by young children, they did not differentiate between the forms of request within this classification in terms of the responses they may elicit. This study finds that at least these two different types of embedded request can be ordered according to the likelihood of their being interpreted as questions regarding ability.

If we now consider the other types of embedded request found in the data, we may be able to find where they fit in terms of a hierarchy such as that mentioned above. It was found in the analysis of the data that CY? *remember* requests elicited three yes/no responses out of a total number of six occurrences of the request, and that one of these was an affirmative response, whereas of the two instances of CY? *describe to/for me* request both were found to elicit substantive responses. We can therefore place the CY? *remember* requests closer to the DY? *know* requests in the hierarchy and CY? *describe to/for me* requests closer to the CY? *tell me* requests. DY? *remember* requests were found to be much less likely to elicit a yes/no response than DY? *know* requests, and never elicited an affirmative response. Therefore DY? *remember* requests could be placed nearer to the CY? *tell me* requests. Taking all this into account, our hierarchy would then look something like the following:

Least likely to be interpreted as a question regarding ability	CY? *describe to/for me*
	CY? *tell me*
	DY? *remember*
	CY? *remember*
Most likely to be interpreted as a question regarding ability	DY? *know*

The CY? *describe* requests can be considered least likely to be interpreted as questions regarding ability as they only elicited substantive responses. CY? *tell me* requests have been placed above DY? *remember* requests because of the use of the former in the Opening, as described above, which strongly suggests that they are seen to function primarily as requests for information by the speaker. Additionally, CY? *tell me* requests elicited fewer yes/no responses than DY? *remember* requests. DY? *know* requests are most likely to be interpreted as questions regarding ability because of the high number of yes/no responses which they elicited in the interviews. Their use in the Opening as questions regarding ability (see above) also contributes to their position in the hierarchy.

5.6.2   Embedded requests as indicators of obligation

Having established the relevance of such a hierarchy, we might now consider another type of hierarchy which describes the way in which responses are elicited by different types of illocutions. Thomas (1989: 152) asserts that some illocutions are more obligating than others and proposes a hierarchy of obligatingness. At the top of the hierarchy, Thomas places illocutions such as greetings, summonses, naming addressee, direct questions and direct requests. These are considered to be more obligating because they are more likely to require a response from the addressee. Those illocutions which are considered minimally obligating and therefore less likely to require a response from the addressee are assertions about events and phatic communication. Thomas considers the type of response as a gauge of the obligatingness of an illocution. If we consider the responses to the question types mentioned above in terms of the obligatingness of the illocution, we could perhaps establish a hierarchy of obligatingness between these five types of embedded request. Given that all the requests in the data were of a type which elicited some kind of response, to establish a hierarchy of obligatingness it is necessary to consider the type of response elicited by each CY? or DY? request and whether it was a substantive response or an agreement token. As the previous hierarchy, that of the likelihood of the request being interpreted as a question regarding ability, was based in part on the number of substantive responses elicited by the request, a hierarchy of obligatingness places the requests in the same order.

Highly obligating	CY? *describe to/for me*
	CY? *tell me*
	DY? *remember*
	CY? *remember*
Minimally obligating	DY? *know*

While it is perhaps not surprising that some types of embedded request are more obligating and more likely to elicit a substantive response than others, it is the nature of the requests themselves that is consequential in this study. It is apparent that those types of embedded request which occupy the highest positions in both the hierarchies discussed above, CY? *describe to/for me* and CY? *tell me*, have two features in common: they both mention talk (*tell/describe*) and they both include some mention of who the talk is for (*me*). Furthermore, the latter of these features functions to reassure the child that the police officer is personally interested in the child's responses. Both these requests can therefore be seen to explicitly direct the child to talk and to confirm that the interviewer is receptive to this talk. If we consider this in the light of the hierarchies constructed above, we can postulate that those requests which contain these two features will be more successful in eliciting substantive responses than those which do not.

5.7   Summary

This chapter has presented the findings of an earlier study which investigated the role of various discursive features in police child training interviews. We have seen that these interviews have in common with the police-suspect interviews certain institutional features, such as formal and asymmterical naming rituals. In particular, we have seen that all the interviews share the participation framework labelled PI2R (see section 3.3.4) in the Opening and Closing.

In contrast to the police-suspect interviews, however, the police child interviews were found to contain features typical of a less formal order of discourse, such as informal naming rituals and receipt markers. Supporting this less formal approach was the frequent use by the VATE officers of indirect, embedded requests such as *can you tell me ... ?* and *do you know ... ?* The various forms of embedded request found in the data were arranged in a hierarchy indicating both the likelihood of obtaining a yes/no response and the degree to which the interviewee would feel obliged to respond. Forms of request that were most 'obligating' – the *can you tell me* type – were found to contain an explicit direction to the child to talk and a casting of the police officer in the role of listener. The relevance of this finding to the critical analysis of police-suspect interviews with adults will be the focus of section 6.3 in the following chapter, which explores three 'myths' relating to police interviewing.

6
Myths about Police Interviewing

6.1 Introduction

The discussion of prior research into police behaviour and interviewing in Chapter 2 identified a number of studies that directly or indirectly highlighted the potential for an institutional 'mythology' about police interviewing. For instance, Baldwin (1993) specifies a number of police beliefs that he finds to be erroneous or based on false assumptions and therefore directly contributes to our understanding of a police interviewing mythology. On the other hand, a number of forensic linguistic studies of police interviews with non-native English speakers were found to be based on expectations about interviews with native English speakers that have not yet been investigated. These studies suggest indirectly that there may be institutionally held beliefs about the process of police interviewing which require further study. The findings of these prior studies will be drawn upon in different ways to provide a starting point for the exploration of a number of specific 'myths' underlying the discourse of the interviews. Once the nature of a myth has been described, a salient discourse feature, or set of features, identified in the previous three chapters will provide a framework through which the effect of this myth on the discourse can be analysed. The implications of a mythology for the role of police institutional discourse in the interview will be discussed in the next chapter in relation to power relations and institutional requirements.

6.2 The myth of comprehension

In Chapter 2, a number of Australian studies were mentioned whose common focus was the problems that can occur in interviews between native English-speaking police officers and non-native English-speaking, or non-English-speaking, suspects (e.g. Cooke 1996; Eades 1982, 1994; Gibbons 1996; Jensen 1995). It was suggested that these studies rely to some extent on assumptions about the adequacy of police interview procedures when dealing with native English-speaking suspects. For instance, where changes are recommended to the interview procedure, such as developing the evidence through narrative forms rather than question–answer sequences in interviews with Aboriginal suspects (Cooke 1996), these changes are assumed to promote equality before the law for Aboriginal suspects. Cooke finds that Anglo-Australian suspects are likely to have been exposed to the question–answer form of interviews through education and the media and are therefore unlikely to experience the same problems with this form of talk as Aboriginal people who may be less familiar with its rules and requirements. This seems to be a reasonable assumption to make about Anglo-Australian culture and its linguistic norms; however, Cooke's finding that 'narrative testimony . . . appears conducive to a more thorough elicitation of evidence' (1996: 279) is equally true of police interviews with native English speakers according to Braithwaite, Brewer and Strelan (1998) and Shuy (1998) (see section 6.4).

Gibbons (1996) makes several important observations about the vulnerability of non-native speaking suspects to police practices that are found to distort the evidence in videotaped interviews. One example of a Tongan man being interviewed in relation to a murder case demonstrates that the suspect's lack of understanding of police procedures and the complex language being used in the interview both contribute to a distortion of the evidence by the interviewing officers.

A rigorous corpus-based analysis of the language use of police interviewers compared with general language use in an English-speaking context (Fox 1993) has found that certain discourse structures common to the speech of police interviewers are extremely infrequent in general speech. For example, the use of *then* following a subject noun phrase, as in *I then walked into the shop*, is common in police statements and yet was found to be very rare in the corpus database. This demonstrates not only the influence that police officers have over the language used in statements of evidence (supposed to be transcriptions of the suspect's utterances) but also the wide gap that exists between 'policespeak' and everyday language use for native and non-native English speakers alike.

These findings suggest that difficulties in comprehension experienced by non-native speakers of English in police interviews reflect an inherent communication problem arising from the use of 'legal jargon'. Although prior studies acknowledge to some extent the generalisability of their findings to the broader population, the fact remains that discussion of the issue of comprehensibility in police interviews has been dominated by research into the experiences of non-native speakers and other vulnerable suspects such as children. While there can be no doubt that this is an important priority, assessing the extent of the problem for adult native speakers may contribute to a better understanding of the issues involved. This is especially relevant if the adult native speaker experience is being drawn upon as a baseline for determining equality before the law for disadvantaged groups.

Through an analysis of clarification sequences in the police-suspect interviews, I will demonstrate that these Anglo-Australian suspects face issues concerning the interview process and specialised language use which are not dissimilar to the issues faced by non-native English speakers in the studies mentioned above.

6.2.1   Comprehending 'policespeak'

In section 3.3.1, an analysis of the institutional language used to construct the Opening and Closing of the interviews found that police officers displayed a reluctance to vary the wording of the Formal Statements, which are based on police Standing Orders and memorised or read out from forms. Clearly there is an organisational advantage to this approach as it is intended to minimise the risk that the interview will be disallowed as evidence due to a failure to meet the legislative requirements. However, an example from the Closing sequence of INT2 demonstrated that this inflexibility contributed to a failure on the part of the interviewing officer to adequately explain the fingerprinting procedure despite evidence that the suspect did not understand certain aspects of the caution.

This phenomenon can be seen even more clearly in INT8, where a lengthy clarification sequence is undertaken by the participants following the articulation of the formal request for consent to obtain the suspect's fingerprints. The sequence has been reproduced in full as Extract 6-1 which, although rather lengthy, provides a valuable insight into the problems associated with institutional discourse in clarification sequences.

Extract 6-1 INT8

468.	pio8:	or you are found not <u>guilty</u> of the <u>offense</u>
469.		or any other relevant offense before the end of that <u>period</u> ⇒
470.		then the <u>fingerprints</u> will be destroyed ↓
471.		do <u>you</u> understand this <u>information</u> ↑
472.	SPT8:	so have I got a <u>choice</u> whether I get fingerprinted or <u>not</u> ↑
473.	pio8:	<u>do</u> you do you wish to <u>comment</u> o- on this information ↓

474.		do you understand what I've <u>said</u> to you ∧
475.	SPT8:	not really <u>no</u> ↓
476.	pio8:	would you like me to <u>read</u> it to you <u>again</u> ↓
477.	SPT8:	no I just <u>I'm</u> asking <u>you</u> ⇒
478.		do d- have I got a <u>choice</u>
479.		do I <u>have</u> to be fingerprinted or <u>don't</u> I ∧
480.	pio8:	you <u>do</u> you do have a <u>choice</u> ∧
481.		you can say you can <u>agree</u>-ee to have your <u>fingerprints</u> taken ⇒
482.		or you can <u>disagree</u> to have your fingerprints taken↓
483.		(1.7) if you (2.1) <u>disagree</u> to have your <u>fingerprints</u> taken ∧
484.		then the poli- then the <u>police</u> can enter into a <u>certain</u> course of <u>action</u> ↓
485.		and that's a course of <u>action</u> I've <u>detailed</u> in this ah
486.		(0.9) in this ah (0.3) <u>paragraph</u>
487.		would you like me to <u>read</u> it to you <u>again</u> ↓
488.	SPT8:	no it's o<u>kay</u> ∧
489.	pio8:	(3.2) do you under<u>stand</u> the <u>information</u> which I've <u>read</u> out to you ↓
490.	SPT8:	yes ⇒
491.	pio8:	do you wish to <u>comment</u> on this information ↓
492.	SPT8:	(3.2) um (2.1) nah I don't want to be <u>fingerprinted</u> ∧
493.	pio8:	you <u>don't</u> want to be fingerprinted ↓
494.		oh well that's me next <u>question</u> ↓
495.		do you <u>consent</u> to giving your fingerprints ↓
496.	SPT8:	no ↓
497.	pio8:	you <u>don't</u> ↓
498.		all right↓
499.	(sio8):	(do you wa-)
500.	pio8:	do you have any <u>reason</u> for not consenting to giving your fingerprints ↓
501.	SPT8:	I just don't <u>want</u> to ↓
502.	pio8:	okay↓
503.		(2.3) are you <u>aware</u> (1.0) and do you <u>recall</u> me <u>saying</u> during that paragraph ⇒
504.		that if you <u>refuse</u> to give your fingerprints <u>voluntarily</u>
505.		(.) a member of the <u>police</u> force <u>may</u> use <u>reasonable</u> force to <u>obtain</u> them ↓
506.		did you <u>hear</u> me say //that* ↑
507.	SPT8:	yeah* ⇒
508.	pio8:	and are you <u>aware</u> of what <u>reasonable</u> force is ∧
509.	SPT8:	no ∧

The extract begins with the last part of the statement of the suspect's rights and obligations regarding fingerprinting. As we saw in section 3.3.1, the fingerprinting statement is very long and complex even by police standards and it would be reasonable to expect that suspects might not understand every aspect of this caution. This is recognised by the police institution and the police interviewer is required to ask the suspect if they understood the preceding statement (as in line 471 above). The problem in this sequence arises when pio8 seems to do anything to avoid answering the very direct question asked by SPT8 in line 472: *so have I got a choice whether I get fingerprinted or not.* In fact, pio8's 'explanation' of the suspect's rights is so indirect that SPT8 believes she has a choice not to be fingerprinted when no such choice exists. It appears that pio8 is aware that a misunderstanding has occurred, but he is unable to address the problem within the scope of the institutional discourse of the Closing. In fact, it takes another 51 lines of transcribed talk to sort the problem out, at which point the suspect, in agreeing to the fingerprinting, states quite succinctly SPT8/560: *yeah I'm not going to be held down* – a clarification which might have occurred some five minutes earlier if the police interviewer had been more flexible in the construction of his explanatory utterances. The constraints of police institutional discourse on effective interviewing will be investigated in the next chapter, but a further example from INT1 will demonstrate the complexity of comprehension problems in the Closing.

Extract 6-2 NT1

527.	pio1:	(0.4) then the <u>fingerprints</u> will be des<u>troye</u>d↓
528.		(0.5) do you under<u>stand</u> that infor<u>mation</u>∧
529.	SPT1:	°yes I <u>do</u>° ((barely audible))
530.	pio1:	do you wish to <u>comm</u>ent on any of this information∧
531.	SPT1:	no↓
532.	pio1:	do you cons<u>ent</u> to giving your fingerprints↓
533.	SPT1:	no∧
534.	pio1:	(1.5) did you under<u>stand</u> this (.) infor<u>mation</u>↑
535.	SPT1:	yep↓
536.	pio1:	(0.6) right↓ I'll just (0.4) <u>read</u> it to you (0.2) again slowly⇒
537.	SPT1:	°all righ°
538.	pio1	your <u>fingerprints</u> are required for the <u>pur</u>pose of en- identi<u>fication</u>↓
539.		(0.4) your fingerprints <u>may</u> be <u>used</u> in evidence at court↓
540.		(0.5) if you re<u>fuse</u> (.) to give your fingerprints volun<u>tar</u>ily ⇒

541.   (0.2) a member of the poli<u>ce</u> <u>force</u> <u>may</u> use <u>reasonable</u>
                 force to ob<u>tain</u> them↓
542.   SPT1:   (0.7) oh right <u>yeah</u> //(that's ri-)*
543.   pio1:   you* understand that∧=
544.   SPT1:   =I under<u>stand</u> yeah⇒
545.   pio1:   right↓ (0.4) <u>do</u> you consent to giving your fingerprints∧
546.   SPT1:   °<u>no</u> I don't°
547.   pio1:   (0.7) you under<u>stand</u> about <u>reasonable</u> force to obtain
                 them ⇒
548.   SPT1:   °yeah°
549.   pio1:   (0.6) and if you're <u>not</u> charged within six months they
                 get destroyed <u>anyway</u>∧
550.   SPT1:   right↓ (0.9) yep∧
551.   pio1:   (0.3) you understand all <u>that</u>↑
552.   SPT1:   yep⇒
553.   pio1:   and you still don't consent↓
554.   SPT1:   (1.0) nah⇒ I'll <u>give</u> 'em∧
555.   pio1:   (0.3) oh you <u>do</u> consent
556.   SPT1:   <u>ye::ah</u>∧ (.) oh∧ right↓ yeah↓ (.) no↓ look⇒ (0.2)
                 yeah⇒ I do⇒
557.   I'll <u>give</u> 'em⇒ no <u>worries</u>⇒

While the example of misunderstandings in the Closing of INT8
related to the confusing language of the caution, Extract 6-2 from INT1
demonstrates that issues of comprehensibility are not always so predictable. While SPT1 indicates that he has understood the caution, pio1's
request for SPT1's consent to undertake the fingerprinting procedure is
met with a refusal 533/SPT1: *no*∧. Perhaps because this is not the preferred
response (Sacks 1987), pio1 does not immediately accept this refusal
and instead she initiates a clarification sequence in which she attempts
to ascertain SPT1's level of understanding of the caution.

In lines 538–41 we can see that pio1, like pio2 and pio8, does not
define any of the terms she is using, but rather checks with SPT1 that he
understands them. She continues to try to resolve the problem in this
way, despite the repeated assurance from SPT1 that he understands the
caution. As we saw in INT2, the interviewing officer relies heavily on
the words and phrases used in the Police Manual when attempting to
clarify a misunderstanding. In INT1, this is ineffective in itself and only
a chance expansion of SPT1's negative response (551/SPT1: *nah*⇒ *I'll*
give 'em∧) sheds light on the cause of the misunderstanding: SPT1 has
apparently interpreted *consent* as something like *object*, and produced
responses appropriately.

The clarification produced by pio1 could not have ensured the resolution of the problem because it was based on a faulty, though understandable, assumption about the relative comprehensibility of police institutional discourse. That is, the institutional design of the police interview assumes that something like the fingerprinting caution will be difficult to understand whereas something like the question *do you con<u>sent</u> to giving your fingerprints*↓ will not cause any misunderstandings. This is, as mentioned, a legitimate assumption to make; however, if it is applied too rigidly then it becomes much more difficult for police officers to resolve a problem such as experienced by the participants in INT1. Instead of considering a range of possible causes of the misunderstanding, pio1 seems only able to focus on the institutionally recognised cause – that the suspect has not properly understood the caution. Even when faced with the prospect of having to *use reasonable force to obtain* the suspect's fingerprints, pio1 does not attempt to replace the words and phrases of the Formal Statements with a significantly less institutional set of terminology, despite being able to recognise that some kind of problem has occurred. In the case described here, the problem is eventually resolved. However, one can well imagine the confusion and aggravation that may have resulted had the misunderstanding not been clarified by the suspect and had the police officers proceeded to use force to obtain SPT1's fingerprints.

These examples from INT1 and INT8, and SPT2's request for clarification discussed in section 3.3.1, are not the only cases of suspects failing to understand police institutionl talk. In INT3, a number of routine or institutional questions are asked in accordance with legislative requirements but their purpose remains obscure to SPT3, as the following extract demonstrates.

Extract 6-3 INT3

400.	pio3:	what's your <u>reason</u> for <u>having</u> those items↓
401.	SPT3:	a:h antiques⇒ (.) you know⇒ (.) <u>family</u> stuff∧
402.	pio3:	(1.4) ar- are they <u>registered</u>↑
403.	SPT3:	(0.3) no↓
404.	pio3:	(0.5) OK what's your reason for ah possessing a
405.		(0.5) um (0.3) unregistered <u>firearm</u>↑
406.	SPT3:	(2.8) didn't I just <u>answer</u> that↑
407.	pio3:	(1.0) °I'm asking you your <u>reason</u> for possessing a°
408.		(1.0) ah unregistered <u>firearms</u> ↓
409.		two <u>unregistered</u> firearms↓
410.	SPT3:	(0.2) I just <u>forgot</u> about them↓ I

411.   (.) you know just↓
412.   pio3:   (3.6) did you have any <u>intentions</u> to register them↑
413.   SPT3:   (1.6) <u>yes</u> if I had have <u>remembered</u>↓

Those items referred to by pio3 in line 400 are the firearms found in SPT3's attic. After confirming that they are unregistered in line 402, pio3 then asks SPT3 to provide a reason for possessing *unregistered firearm*[s] in line 405. This is an unnecessarily repetitive question as far as SPT3 is concerned and he expresses this with a straightforward query 406/SPT3: *(2.8) didn't I just <u>answer</u> that*↑ after a long pause for consideration. However, pio3, like pio1 and pio2 in the previous examples, does not clearly explain why he is asking the question and instead simply repeats the phrase he has used, with an added emphasis on *unregistered* in the hope that this will adequately convey that what he is really seeking is an explanation of why SPT3 has not registered the guns. This approach appears to work, and yet it seems to be an unusually clumsy approach to clarifying the nature of the question. An obvious alternative would have been to say *yes, but why didn't you register them* or indeed to have simply asked that question in the first place (in line 404) instead of relying on an inefficient and confusing institutional format.

Another example from INT1 concerns the important process in the Closing where the criminal charges are laid. This sequence and the misunderstanding it displays were discussed in section 4.2.1 where it was noted that SPT1 responds only minimally when he signals his understanding of the charging process. Given SPT1's minimal reponse, it is unclear whether he believes himself charged with criminal damage (for breaking the shop door), or he believes that he will be charged for the damage in a monetary sense. Pio1 seems prepared to proceed to the next stage of the Closing without obtaining a clear confirmation from SPT1 that he understood the nature of the charges made against him. This is a serious failing in the interview process and one which was caused by police assumptions about the interview process which were not shared by the suspect. For instance, we saw in section 4.2.1 that pio1's attempt to clarify the charge issue (504/pio1: *(0.5) but you //<u>understand</u> * that there's <u>charges</u> pending as well*⇒) does not even use the construction *charged with* that would highlight the criminal meaning of *charge*. Therefore, line 504 can only work as a clarification of her original statement by reference to a structural rule of the interview – that information relating to events is not discussed in the Closing. This rule can be described as a type of contextualisation cue (Gumperz 1982) through which the meaning of the utterance can be understood. By reference to a contextualisation cue such as this rule it becomes evident that the phrase *charges pending* must relate to criminal charges, and not to the financial arrangements between SPT1 and the shop owners as this latter interpretation would be introducing event information into the Closing. However, contextualisation cues are not always accessible to both participants and, in this case, pio1 is relying on a contextualisation cue for the valid interpretation of her utterance that is not available to SPT1. Without access to the appropriate cues, SPT1 is unable to correctly interpret pio1's clarification.

It is not suggested here that pio1 makes a deliberate decision to draw on a rule of the interview structure to clarify the charge issue, only that her discursive practices reveal an assumption underlying the utterance that the suspect will have access to this institutional knowledge. SPT1, however, appears to be unaware that event information is not being discussed at this point and continues to refer only to the financial meaning of *charges*.

6.2.2   The case for a myth of comprehension

The discussion above has clearly demonstrated that misunderstandings and other communicative difficulties can easily occur in police interviews between native Australian English speakers. It is likely that such misunderstandings would vary between speakers of different sociocultural backgrounds and education levels; however, it is beyond the scope of this study to attempt any differentiation of the findings on the basis of social class. Importantly, it was found that police jargon and complex legal language are not solely responsible for communicative difficulties. Nonetheless, this appeared to be commonly assumed and, in at least one case in INT1, caused the police interviewer to overlook other sources of the misunderstanding.

However, this assumption seems inconsistent with the interviewer's rigid adherence to police institutional discourse during clarification sequences. That is, on the one hand, the police themselves acknowledge that legal language is likely to be problematic or incomprehensible to suspects, but on the other hand they consistently rely on institutional words and phrases when they are attempting to explain some prior legal jargon. It seems, therefore, that police officers have only a limited understanding of how to clarify institutional talk whilst still maintaining the legislative requirements of the interview. In some interviews, such as INT1 and INT8, these assumptions and misconceptions about legal language are combined with a failure to correctly identify non-institutional talk as a possible source of difficulty. The effect is a serious breach of the legislative requirements during the charging process and a narrowly avoided physical encounter with the suspect over the finger-printing procedure.

The beliefs about language use and comprehensibility displayed by the police officers in these interviews can be described as a myth about comprehension insofar as these beliefs and assumptions are contradicted by the actual behaviour of suspects. Analysis of the data demonstrates that suspects can misunderstand ordinary words as well as institutional jargon. We have also found that the approach taken to clarification by police officers is inadequate and their failure to provide plain language explanations contradicts an institutional assumption that legal jargon is difficult to understand.

6.3   The myth of threatened authority

In section 2.2.2, it was noted that according to prior studies, more effective police–citizen communications can be achieved both in everyday interactions (Braithwaite et al. 1998) and in evidentiary interviews (Shuy 1998) if police officers are prepared to engage in a more 'conversational style' of speech. In the case of interviews in particular, Shuy (1998) notes that a conversational style encourages suspects to produce confessions spontaneously. Both studies found that an inherent asymmetry in power between the police officers and the suspects can be addressed by police officers through the use of discourse features such as receipt markers, which indicate that the police officer is receptive to the citizen's contributions. Finally, it was noted that these prior studies both suggested a conflict for police officers between maintaining an authoritative role in the interaction and providing an appropriate environment for the achievement of institutional goals, i.e. obtaining a voluntary confession from the suspect.

As discussed in section 2.1.1, the theoretical framework of the present study is one in which the distribution of power among participants in an interaction is not viewed as a fixed arrangement. Rather, power is something that is considered to be negotiated by the participants and patterns of power distribution will be continually reproduced through the interaction. Authority, on the other hand, is understood to be the power that is granted to the police officer through legislation via the police regulations. Thus an 'authoritative voice' is a term denoting the discursive role assumed by the police interviewer as a necessary tool for the job of interviewing a citizen. A CA approach to the data in Chapter 4 revealed that there is a clear asymmetry in the distribution of interactional resources available to the different participants according to their role in the interview. In this sense, the police interviewers were found to have access to resources that facilitated an 'authoritative voice'. By drawing on these resources, police interviewers are able to display this authority to suspects and in doing so, control the contributions they make. The continual production of an authoritative voice through the turn-by-turn construction of the interview allows police officers the opportunity to continually exert power over the interaction, but it also gives them the choice not to use all the available resources and instead, as Braithwaite et al. (1998) and Shuy (1998) have suggested, forgo some of their power to promote a less formal environment.

The findings of prior research mentioned above suggest a complex relationship between police beliefs, the inherent features of interviews and achieving the ideal communicative environment. The issues raised by Shuy (1998) and Braithwaite et al. (1998) will be addressed in an analysis of the relationship between oriented-to behaviour patterns and institutional requirements. More specifically, the findings presented in section 3.6, which described the approach taken by each of the police interviewers to the shift from Opening to Information Gathering, will be re-examined to reveal the discursive practices of each police officer in the management of their authority at this critical stage of the interview. Through this investigation we will ascertain the validity of police concerns that their authority in interviews is threatened by the behaviour of suspects.

6.3.1   The management of police authority

The identification of the target Participation Frameworks in the tri-partite interview structure in Chapter 4 provided the basis for an analysis of the shift from Opening to Information Gathering in section 3.6. In that analysis we saw that despite some consistencies in the move towards the target participation framework (S3R), each of the suspects responded differently to the process of frame shift. The analysis of these differences resulted in two major findings. Firstly, a clear statement of intention by the interviewing officer in the initiation of the Information Gathering was found to predict accurately the nature of the subsequent discourse. Whereas pio2 indicated that his role was that of a recipient of information given by the suspect in his own words, pio3's statement identified his role as that of an 'asker of questions'. In each of these two interviews, the suspects oriented to the participation frameworks (S3R and P2RA respectively) which most closely related to these police officer roles. In INT1 where no clear statement of intention was made, the

Information Gathering began with different frameworks being invoked by the two main participants before they found some alignment after several turns.

The second major finding followed a close analysis of the first forty lines of the Information Gathering in INT1. The shifts made by the participants through different participation frameworks were examined and then compared to the frameworks invoked in INT2 and INT3. It was found that the failure of the interviewing officer to invoke the S3R framework immediately upon initiating the shift into the Information Gathering appeared to result in a lack of commitment to that framework thereafter. In INT1 this was particularly interesting as the suspect displayed a strong, spontaneous commitment to S3R at first, but shifted to P2RA following the police officer's continued invocation of that framework. Finally, when the police officer did attempt to invoke S3R, SPT1 showed only a minimal orientation towards it.

Thus the investigation of uptake of the S3R framework by suspects as the interview shifts from the Opening into the Information Gathering found that the success of this shift in footing appears to be related to the discursive activity of the police interviewer. For instance, pio2, who emphasises his role as a recipient of suspect-produced information and not as an asker of questions, shifts most successfully into the target participation framework.

These findings would suggest that aspects of the police officers' institutionally endowed interactional role are not necessarily conducive to a successful uptake of the S3R framework by suspects in the Information Gathering. Because they are undertaking an interview, the police officers have as one aspect of their interactional role the purpose of 'asking questions' (i.e. binary and content questions, as opposed to non-specific requests for information). However, they are also engaged in facilitating a confession by the suspect, and as such another aspect of their role is that of 'receiving information'. These two aspects of the police officers' role involve different levels of access to interactional resources.

An 'asker of questions' has at his or her disposal a number of tools that provide power over the discourse, especially in the area of topic management. As we saw in section 4.3, police interviewers, particularly primary interviewing officers, frequently draw upon the resources available to an asker of questions to decide the topic of the suspect's turns at talk. Section 4.4.2 demonstrated that interviewing officers make use of a wide range of topic initiation devices, predominantly forms of request, to dismiss a topic that the suspect had initiated through stepwise transitions and assert a police-preferred topic. In such situations, police officers use forms of request that strongly constrain the content of the response, such as binary or yes/no questions and WH-questions, thus greatly increasing their influence over the topics available to the respondent. The aspect of the police interviewer's role that involves asking questions is therefore one that maximises police interactional power.

By comparison, the aspect of the police role that emphasises police reception to a suspect confession involves a very different set of interactional tools. This difference is primarily a result of the need for a suspect to be able to initiate talk on topics which they feel are most relevant to the criminal activity. As an interviewee, a suspect is already constrained to produce talk that is topically consistent with the interviewer's turns. In order to introduce new topics, suspects may produce 'stepwise topic transitions' (Jefferson 1984a) within one turn at talk. This resource, which is accessed by the suspects in almost all of the interviews, was exemplified in a number of extracts presented in sections 4.3.1 and 4.4.2. For the police participant engaged in displaying receptivity to suspect initiations, it is important that she or he withholds turns which are topically disjunctive and produces turns which encourage the suspect to continue talking, such as receipt markers or continuers (e.g. *mm hm, go on, right*). Given that this behaviour may lead to the suspect having greater control over the topic of talk, it can be seen that this aspect of the police interviewer's role is one that minimises police interactional power. These findings appear to be consistent with those of the prior research mentioned in the section above. That is, in order to encourage the suspect to produce a confession voluntarily, police officers need to emphasise an aspect of their role that minimises their authoritative voice and interactional power.

If we return now to the findings of the data analysis concerning the shift from Opening to Information Gathering, it is possible to see that issues of police authority are highly relevant to the success of this transition. The environment conducive to voluntary confession by the suspect has already been identified as the S3R participation framework and an equivalence has been established between the availability of this framework to suspects and their access to topic initiation devices. As discussed in section 3.6 and reiterated above, the success of the transition into the Information Gathering can be measured by the extent to which the suspect displays an orientation towards the three roles of *author, animator* and *principal* in relation to utterances concerning the alleged criminal activity. However, it is now apparent that this measure of success also indicates the extent to which the police officer is able to orient to a position that minimises her or his authoritative voice in the interaction. Furthermore, if we consider that the construction of the 'frame transitional utterance' (Coupland et al. 1994) was found to be critical to the success of the transition as a whole, then an examination of the management of authority displayed through those transitional utterances might reveal something about police beliefs about their authoritative voice in the Information Gathering.

The transitional utterance produced by pio1 does not display any particular orientation to either a 'questioner' role or a 'recipient' role; but in the subsequent turn, SPT1 spontaneously initiates a new topic and in doing so invokes the S3R framework. However, this arrangement does not last because pio1 interrupts SPT1 to commence a series of direct questions that forestall the invocation of the S3R framework. Several turns later, pio1's attempts to reinvoke S3R are met with limited success.

In relation to issues of police power in the discourse, two things are immediately apparent from these findings. Firstly, in the absence of any display by pio1 of her orientation to either a questioner or recipient role in her transitional utterance, the suspect effectively assigns pio1 the role of recipient by initiating a new topic and providing information not requested. In other words, SPT1 freely chooses the framework most conducive to a voluntary confession and in doing so assigns pio1 a role that minimises her power over the interaction. Secondly, pio1 rejects this assignation of the recipient role by immediately accessing the interactional resources available to her (i.e. the capacity to interrupt the suspect with a topically disjunctive turn) and in doing so she displays her orientation to the questioner role which in turn maximises her interactional power. Throughout the subsequent negotiations of the participation framework, pio1 maintains her orientation to the role of questioner and her eventual assumption of the role of recipient is initiated through her own attempts to invoke the S3R framework, and not in response to any such initiations by SPT1. Pio1's behaviour is specifically designed to obstruct SPT1's attempt to invoke the S3R framework and to assert her police authoritative voice until she has regained the power over the interaction that was minimised through SPT1's actions. This interpretation is supported by reference to the content of the contributions by each participant throughout the sequence. As discussed in section 3.6, pio1 interrupts SPT1's initiation in the S3R framework in order to ask questions in the P2RA framework, questions to which she already knows the answer. Pio1's behaviour clearly prioritises the assertion of her authoritative voice over the eliciting of voluntary contributions from SPT1.

Similarly, pio3 displays his preference for a framework that maximises his power over the discourse by using a transitional utterance that aligns him with the role of questioner. He follows this with a series of binary and content questions to which SPT3 responds with the minimal required information. As noted above, pio3 is not successful in engaging SPT3 in an S3R framework beyond two lines comprising an extremely general comment about the events of the day. Pio3's strong commitment to a P2RA framework in the early stages of the Information Gathering ensures that SPT3 is unable to initiate turns that might diminish the power of his authoritative voice, such as the initiation produced by SPT1. However, in doing so, pio3 sacrifices the opportunity of obtaining a voluntary confession produced by SPT3 in an S3R framework.

INT2 was found to contain the most successful transition into an Information Gathering featuring suspect utterances produced within an S3R framework. This was linked to pio2's frame transitional utterance, which displayed his close alignment with a role of information recipient. Furthermore, pio2's later turns in a P2RA framework were produced at a TRP in SPT2's turn and not interruptively, as in INT1. Through his actions, pio2 first indicated that he was prepared to minimise his authoritative voice to listen to SPT2's version of events and then demonstrated that he was respectful of SPT2's turn space, even when he was assuming the role of questioner. In contrast to pio1 and pio3, pio2 prioritises the invocation of the S3R framework at the commencement of the Information Gathering and avoids utterances that maximise the power provided by his authoritative voice.

The analysis of data gathered from the VATE training interviews with children revealed another way that police officers can approach the issue of embedded authority in the interview structure. In the following section we return to the findings of the previous chapter concerning the use of embedded requests in VATE interviews and further explore the functions performed by these requests in relation to varying levels of formality in the interview discourse.

6.3.2   Duality in the functions of embedded requests in VATE interviews

In Chapter 5, the analysis of police child VATE interview data established that the embedded requests which enjoyed the most success in eliciting information were those which were considered highly obligating and which combined two functions: explicitly directing the child to talk and confirming that the interviewer is receptive to this talk. What we notice about these two functions of the most obligating requests is that they correspond almost exactly to two of the features described in Chapter 5 as indicating different orders of discourse. In the first instance, the direction to the child to talk can be seen as a form of discoursal indicator, an utterance which overtly guides the response of the interviewee, and as such could be considered a part of police institutional discourse. There is a clear parallel between this function of the embedded requests and the transitional utterances used as discoursal indicators by the police officers in the interviews with adult suspects. But the other aspect of the request form, that which functions to confirm that the speaker is receptive to the respondent, has similarities with another feature discussed above – the receipt marker – which also functions to reassure the respondent that her/his response has been heard and understood. Thus the *can you tell me* request form belongs to a less formal institutional discourse which is more concerned with the reassurance of the lay participant than is usual in police institutional discourse. The implication of this finding is that the request form which is most effective in eliciting information happens to be one which combines aspects of both a formal and an informal style of institutional discourse.

Considered in light of the fact that we previously identified several features common to the VATE interviews belonging to different orders of discourse, this last finding is a most interesting development. Given that the interviews are, above all, information seeking, a request form which functions efficiently to elicit information might be considered a fundamental element. The fact that the features which make this request form so effective display a combination of discourse types being used would tend to indicate that the duality of discourse is itself fundamental to the VATE interviews.

This last assertion is supported by the context in which the VATE interviews take place. While the transcripts used as data in this study were made from interviews conducted as a part of a training course, in terms of the skills displayed and the approach used by the police officers these training exercises are assessed by the VATE course supervisors as though the interview were a genuine evidentiary interview. Thus, if the training scheme is successful, it is reasonable to assume that the same features which are identified by this study would appear in a genuine evidentiary interview with a child witness. In such a context, the regular police interview discourse features, such as those displayed in the opening statements, would be a necessary requirement if the interview is to be used in court where accurate and reliable identification of participants is vital to the evidence being considered admissible.

On the other hand, the ultimate purpose of the VATE interview is to reduce the stress on the child normally associated with a court appearance. Thus it would be redundant in the extreme if the interview were to conform exactly with normal police procedure, which would no doubt be just as confrontational and confusing to the child witness as the proceedings of the court are considered to be. Instead the VATE interview is designed to put the child at ease and encourage their trust in the police officer, so the importance of the police officer demonstrating their personal interest in the child's story is a very real consideration as well as being one not normally associated with police institutional behaviour. As we have seen in the analysis of police-suspect interviews, it is more usual for police officers as individuals to display a minimal amount of personal interest in an interview subject as their personal interests are considered secondary to the interests of the institution they represent.

We can conclude that in the case of the VATE interviews the apparent duality of discourses represents the intersection of the requirements of the court, as expressed by the police force as an institution, and the needs of the child witness being interviewed under the VATE system. This stands in marked contrast to the approach taken by interviewing officers in regular interviews with suspects. It is not merely that *can you tell me?* questions are rare in police suspect interviews, but the concerns that they represent are similarly absent from the agenda of most of the police officers. The overwhelming prevalence of disjunctive topic shifts, for instance, is indicative of a failure by police interviewers to consider the benefits of a more conversational and less asymmetrical approach to questioning – benefits obviously appreciated by the VATE interviewing officers. This section has demonstrated that casting oneself as a recipient of talk is of central importance in an information-seeking interview, and yet the behaviour of pio1 and pio3 in the police-suspect interviews indicates that this priority may be overridden by a perceived need to emphasise police authority. We will now return to the police-suspect interview analysis to draw conclusions about a myth of threatened authority.

6.3.3   The effects of displaying power

By relinquishing a more powerful role in the interaction at the point of transition into the Information Gathering, pio2 does not permanently deny himself access to the tools provided by his authoritative voice. On the other hand, after asserting a maximally powerful role in the frame transitional utterance and subsequent turns, pio3 is unable to obtain the necessary co-operation from SPT3 that would allow him to forgo his position of questioner and assume the role of recipient.

Pio1 enjoys a partially successful invocation of S3R following her initial assertion of a powerful role, but the most pertinent aspect of that interview is that it reveals so clearly pio1's fear of losing any amount of control over the interaction. Despite being offered an ideal environment for voluntary confession by SPT1's topic initiation at the very beginning of the Information Gathering, pio1 curtails this invocation of the S3R framework and focuses on reversing any resulting decrease of her power.

It is also worth noting that the success of pio2's transitional turn is not simply due to his personality. If we compare this police officer's behaviour in INT2 with his behaviour in INT3 as the secondary interviewing officer (sio3), we can see that he strongly aligns himself with the role of questioner as sio3 (see section 4.3.3). When engaged in behaviour that maximises his power, he is no more successful than pio3 in moving the suspect, SPT3, into an S3R framework.

It appears that the frame transitional utterance provides an optimal moment for police interviewers to minimise the effects of their authoritative voice and encourage the suspect to take up the S3R framework. Furthermore, the findings of text analyses from later stages of INT2 demonstrate that the underlying authority of pio2's police voice is not diminished by his alignment with the role of recipient early in the interview. In 4.3.1, for example, it was found that SPT2 maintains an alignment to the distribution of topic management tools in favour of pio2 by displaying reluctance to initiate topics other than by stepwise transition.

By using this 'optimal moment' to prioritise the display of their authoritative voice and maintain maximum power over the interaction, pio1 and pio3 deny themselves the opportunity of moving easily into the S3R framework at the outset of the Information Gathering. In the case of pio1, it is clearer that this choice is made in response to SPT1's initiation. By initiating a new topic at the start of the Information Gathering, SPT1 'casts' pio1 in the role of listener, thereby minimising her power in the interaction. For both pio1 and pio3, a belief that it is necessary to strengthen their authoritative voices at the outset of the Information Gathering serves to undermine the success of the transition into an ideal speech environment that might promote voluntary confessions from the suspects. Pio2, whose conduct in the transitional stage displays a disregard for concerns about his authoritative voice, successfully establishes a conversational style in the Information Gathering and does not appear to suffer any reduction in the authority of his police voice at a later stage in the interview. This is consistent with the findings of Braithwaite et al. (1998) and Shuy (1998), noted earlier, that a conflict may arise between police beliefs in maintaining a powerful image and ideal police conduct that encourages a more 'conversational style'. However, the case study of police VATE interviews with children offers an alternative to the authoritative approach, while at the same time highlighting that it is unnecessary to emphasise a powerful police role in the interview.

In conclusion, we have found through the detailed analysis of the text, evidence for the existence of a police myth that turn initiations by suspects pose a threat to the police authoritative voice.

6.4   The myth of persuasion

One aspect of the 'mythology' of police interviewing presented by Baldwin (1993) is the police officers' belief that suspects can be persuaded to change their story or confess to crimes in which they had previously denied involvement. Baldwin's analysis demonstrated that these beliefs were ill-founded, since less than 4 per cent of the suspects in a study of 600 interviews were persuaded to change their story (pp. 332–3). His findings are supported by the social cognitive approach to racist discourses developed by van Dijk (1987), who finds that '[b]ecause attitudes are usually rather complex cognitive structures, they simply don't change that easily, and rarely after one persuasive communication' (p. 265). Van Dijk finds that a failure to recognise this relationship between persuasive behaviour and attitude change is one reason that 'classical persuasion research' has been largely inconclusive as to the effects of persuasion (van Dijk 1987: 250–68). However, Baldwin's study, though based on a large corpus of data, does not report any findings relating to the actual discursive practices of interviewing officers undertaking an attempt at persuasion, nor is there any specifically linguistic analysis of precisely what constitutes a change in the suspect's story. By contrast, van Dijk proposes that we analyse the 'discourse dimension' of persuasion, and consider 'social acts performed by participants in communicative contexts' (p. 251).

In order to investigate this myth more thoroughly, we will therefore draw on the findings of the analysis presented in section 4.4. This will permit us to discuss the issue of police tactics of persuasion in terms of the negotiation of police and suspect versions of events and avoid the rather vague notion of 'suspects changing their story'. Most importantly, a description of participant role distribution provides us with an analytic framework through which we can demonstrate the effectiveness of the police tactics. As we have already seen in the previous chapter, a negotiation of competing versions can be viewed as an attempt to persuade the suspect to produce utterances within an S3R framework that agree with the police version.

The analysis in 4.4.2, found that the discursive practices of police officers when negotiating competing versions were characterised by the presentation of previously concealed evidence as a 'my side' telling (Pomerantz 1980) and requests for the suspect to account for the evidence. In 4.4.4, it was found that police interviewers routinely produced formulations of the suspects' prior turns in which violence or criminality were emphasised. The formulations were used to support a police version of events at the expense of the suspect version. Both of these practices will now be considered in terms of their effectiveness in persuading the suspect to produce the police-preferred version of events within an S3R framework. Since we are specifically interested in whether or not the police discursive practices effect a change to the suspect's story, the police-preferred version must be seen as an alternative to a stated suspect version of events. A successful act of persuasion will not be deemed to have taken place where the suspect had not yet made any comment on the issues being discussed.

6.4.1   The effectiveness of persuasion

In section 3.4, it was found that the presentation of previously concealed evidence to counter a suspect claim exposes the police officer to an invocation of the P3R framework. In fact the presentation of police evidence in competition with the suspect's version of events is by definition a shift away from the S3R framework – the police officer is producing an utterance that the suspect has specifically not written or taken responsibility for.

However, it is useful to consider whether the police officer, by invoking the P3R framework, is able to move from this undesirable framework into one more conducive to voluntary confession. After all, the aim of the discursive practices we have identified is to negotiate the competing versions in favour of the police version and this means that both participants have to display an orientation towards this version as the accepted version of events. Thus, an assertion made within the P3R framework will need to be ratified by being produced in the P2RA framework where the suspect takes up the role of *principal* in relation to the information contained therein. The suspect, in other words, has to agree that the evidence presented by the police officer represents a version of events which he (the suspect) accepts as his own version of events.

The analysis of data in section 4.4.2 indicated that police interviewers present evidence as an indirect elicitation device (a 'fishing' device), but that they subsequently produce more direct requests if the suspect fails to account for the evidence presented. Therefore, in order to demonstrate whether or not the participants move into a P2RA framework following the presentation of previously withheld information, it is necessary to examine the interactional moves that make up this type of sequence. For this purpose, a segment has been chosen from INT1 that contains a particularly complex example of the practice.

Extract 6-4 INT1

209. pio1:   can you just* <u>explain</u> to us who <u>Ian</u> is∧ (.) like⇒
210. SPT1:   (0.4) I don't <u>know</u> him↓
211. pio1:   °I don't know↓°
212.   he's um Betty's new <u>de facto</u> is he or something↓
213. SPT1:   //just a <u>friend</u> ⇒*
214. pio1:   a <u>boy</u>friend∧* or⇒
215. SPT1:   //<u>she</u> says anyway↓*
216. pio1:   just a friend↓* and he just <u>works</u> there↓ every now and <u>then</u> ⇒
217.   to help her out when she's <u>busy</u>↓
218. SPT1:   no he just <u>goes</u> there⇒
219.   just to stay <u>around</u> er (0.2) //(I)*
220. pio1:   but he serves* at the <u>counter</u> and stuff <u>doesn't</u> he↓
221. SPT1:   <u>yeah</u> just helps //<u>out</u> a *bit there
222. pio1:   he <u>assists</u>:* the sales↓
223.   all <u>right</u> so it's <u>Ian</u> <u>Flemmings</u>↑
224. SPT1:   (0.6) I- I don't <u>know</u> him∧
225.   I <u>honestly</u> don't know him∧
226. pio1:   right↓
227. SPT1:   I //don't know (where he comes from or)*
228. pio1:   his <u>name's</u> Ian Flemmings* ⇒
229.   <u>you</u> only know him as <u>Ian</u>↓
230. SPT1:   that's <u>it</u>⇒

Like the examples discussed in 4.4.2, the sequence in the extract above begins with an adjacency pair through which the participants display a conflict between the suspect and police versions. In this case, pio1 makes a request for information about Ian's identity (in line 209) but SPT1 claims not to 'know' this man (line 210). Faced with SPT1's unwillingness to supply the requested information, pio1 produces a series of 'my side' tellings concerning Ian's identity. Pio1 suggests that Ian may be Betty's new partner and that he appears to work at the shop. Pio1 is able to elicit accounts from SPT1, which are produced in the S3R framework in lines 213, 215, 218 and 219. SPT1's version accounts for parts of pio1's evidence by confirming that there is a man who helps Betty at the shop and generally keeps her company as a friend. These utterances do not exactly agree with the version of events that pio1 has suggested in the turns which precede them (lines 212 and 216), but they do support a version of events where SPT1 'knows' Ian. Pio1 then revises her approach and instead of the indirect 'fishing devices', she directly requests from SPT1 confirmation that this man's name is Ian Flemmings. SPT1 responds by immediately returning to his own version that he does not 'know' Ian and strengthens his commitment to this version: 225/SPT1: *I honestly don't know him*∧.

SPT1 reacts to pio1's direct elicitation by rejecting the role of *principal* in relation to the information pio1 has revealed. That is, the move towards a police version encounters resistance from the suspect when pio1 engages in more direct elicitation devices with less regard to 'propriety' than the original 'fishing devices' (Pomerantz 1980). There is no sense in which the suspect could be said to accept the police version in the P2RA framework once the interviewer has moved to a direct elicitation device.

Furthermore, a brief examination of the data finds that this response is indicative of the suspects' behaviour whenever the device is employed. For example, we have already seen in the previous section that in INT2, when SPT2 is told by pio2 about the bruising to both Leila's arms, SPT2 does not take up a *principal* role in relation to this information and instead maintains his own version of events. The point at which SPT2 can be observed to reject the police version is following the move from a less direct 'fishing device' (239/pio2: *a::hm*⟹ *(2.0) it's a::h*⟹ *(.) she's had (.) some injuries on 'er arm*⟹) to a direct question (242/pio2: *at some stage*↓ *(0.2) didju have hold of 'er other bicep*↑). In response to the 'fishing device', SPT2 offered a minimal response (241/SPT2: *mm hm*∧), but his response to the direct question was a clear rejection of the suggestion (245/SPT2: *not that I can remember*⟹).

It is interesting to compare these findings with those of Bergmann (1992), who claims that these 'information-eliciting tellings can successfully be used as a lie-detection device and are therefore highly suitable for exploratory interviews, examinations and interrogations (e.g. police interviews)' (p. 146). It is true that these devices can be used to ascertain whether or not a suspect might produce a lie, but it remains impossible to judge the veracity of the suspect's response to a question if the requested information is not already known to the interviewer. If we now consider the effect of this discursive practice on the negotiation of versions, it is noticeable that the initial reliance on 'fishing' devices demonstrates an orientation by the police officers to an indirect approach to the negotiation of competing versions. Presenting evidence that supports a police version and requiring the suspect to account for this evidence in some way is intended to weaken the credibility of the suspect's version. However, to achieve this, the discursive practice relies upon an assumption that the suspect will feel sufficiently obligated to provide an account. The findings presented thus far, however, suggest that such an assumption is ill-founded. For instance, SPT2 does not appear to feel obliged to explain the bruises to Leila's left arm in line 241 and SPT1 does not attempt to offer an account explaining why witnesses claimed that he had slammed the door the second time he closed it (line 489). Whether or not the indirect elicitation device has provided a means of 'lie-detection' Bergmann (1992), the police officer is ultimately unsuccessful in persuading the suspect to orient to the police version. As such, the knowledge that the suspect may be lying is not particularly useful.

The analysis in 4.4.2 also found that in the two cases mentioned above, the failure of the 'fishing' devices to elicit an account from suspects was oriented to by the police officers. Pio1 and pio2 both produce formulations in which they request confirmation that the suspects are failing to provide an account (246/pio2: *so you can't explain⇒ how those⇒ (.) marks would 'ave got there↑* and 490/pio1: *(0.6) you've got nothing * to say to that∧*). In both cases, the suspects provide confirmation and continue to withhold an account.

It should be noted that it is not the case that suspects routinely dismiss or challenge the police version of events. For instance, in relation to Extract 6-5 below, SPT2 has not volunteered any information about Leila's state of mind within an S3R framework to this point in the interview, so pio2's assertion in line 271 cannot be said to form part of SPT1's version of events. Yet SPT1 accepts the statement within a P2RA framework in line 272 despite the ease with which he could have simply denied any knowledge of Leila's feelings at the time.

Extract 6-5 INT2

271. pio2: (1.0) do you agree that she would've been <u>frightened</u>↑
272. SPT2: (1.4) ye:p∧

As a way of assigning the *principal* role to the suspect in relation to a piece of information, indirect elicitations such as fishing devices are largely unsuccessful. However, moving to a more direct approach appears only to provoke a stronger rejection of the police version by suspects. In a final attempt to weaken the suspect's version of events, the police officer may formulate the suspect's responses as lacking an account for the evidence, but as this does not alter the suspect's overt alignment to the police version, it is ultimately an approach which does not serve to invoke or maintain the S3R framework, or even a P2RA framework.

Nonetheless, it is worth considering what this 'last resort' police move may be seeking to achieve. Formulations display a preference for confirmation of the proposed state of affairs (Bilmes 1988). Therefore, the formulations produced by pio2 and pio1 cannot be seen as continued attempts to obtain an S3R statement from the suspect that will account for the evidence and support the police version, since they are designed to confirm that no such account can be offered. Instead, the production of these formulations presents the suspect as uncooperative for failing to provide the requested account and the suspect's version of events is made to appear inadequate. This is illustrated quite clearly in INT12, from which the following extract is taken.

Extract 6-6 INT12

759. pio12: do you remember throwing a <u>lolly</u> machine ↑
760. SPT12: <u>no</u> ↑
761.   (2.2) cause I know I <u>wouldn't</u> have done that ↓
762.   and I know I <u>didn't</u> ∧
763. pio12: (3.5) you know you <u>definitely</u> didn't ↓
764. SPT12: ye ep ∧
765. pio12: and yet so much <u>else</u> is (0.5) <u>vague</u> to you ↓
766.   can't <u>remember</u> ↓

After obtaining confirmation that SPT12 cannot account for the evidence (in this case an allegation made in a witness statement) in line 763, *you know you definitely didn't*, pio12 goes on to comment that the suspect's certainty stands in contrast with his prior vagueness. That is, by asserting that the suspect has previously been unable to remember details of the events, the police interviewer implies that it is unlikely that he will be able to remember this event with any more clarity and he must therefore be lying when he says that he *know[s] he wouldn't have done that*. In fact, the suspect has not been particularly vague in his earlier descriptions, but his version of events has diverged significantly from the police version and he has been unwilling to agree to details in their version. Shortly after this sequence, pio12 again formulates the suspect's version and confirms his refusal to agree with the police version:

Extract 6-7 INT12

779.	pio12:	so you're saying you were <u>nowhere</u> <u>near</u> the kiosk area ↓
780.	SPT12:	no ∧
781.	pio12:	at <u>any</u> stage ↑
782.	SPT12:	the <u>closest</u> I would have <u>been</u> was that <u>centre</u> pole
783.		(0.3) thing

The detailed text analysis in section 4.4.4 found that formulations were frequently used by police officers in the negotiation of competing version of events in order to associate the suspect's version with violent or anti-social behaviour. This discursive practice contributed to a recognisable pattern in the differences between police and suspect versions of events such that police versions were consistently more violent or incriminating than suspect versions. There appears to be a relationship between this discursive practice and that described above, in the sense that they both attempt to malign the suspect's version of events through negative connotation, presumably with the expectation that this will facilitate their alignment to the police version.

The analysis in section 4.4.4 found examples of 'negative association' being used in all the interviews, yet it appears to have no effect on the participation frameworks invoked. It does not result in the suspect relinquishing his S3R alignment to his own version of events and taking even a P2RA alignment in relation to the police version. One instance of this practice being employed by pio3 in line 155 of INT3 (see Extract 6–8 below) appears to strengthen, rather than weaken the suspect's adherence to his version.

Extract 6-8 INT3

152.   SPT3:   no↓ (0.4) there was going to be <u>ferns</u> and that in there↓
153.   (1.4) and I put <u>those</u> in there because we couldn't afford (0.3) <u>ferns</u>
154.   and (.) stuff like that (0.5) so↓
155.   pio3:   (1.0) but you ah can <u>afford</u> to (.) grow (1.0) the marijuana plants⇒
156.   SPT3:   doesn't <u>cost</u> anything↓

SPT3's response in line 156 is one of the rare occasions when he invokes the S3R framework – another being the account he gives of the watering system placement in lines 152–4. This is in response to pio3's indirect request for an account, as discussed in the previous section. That he chooses to do so at this point seems to indicate that pio3's attempt to engage this strategy has only succeeded in causing SPT3 to display an even stronger alignment to his version of events.

In one case examined, the findings appeared to suggest that pio2 successfully persuades SPT2 to accept the police version that there was *no reason* for the assault on Leila and abandon his (SPT2's) original version that the reason was Leila's infidelity. It is pertinent to note, however, that this agreement is only temporary. When the question is asked a second time during the Closing of INT2, the suspect returns to his original version that his reason was SPT1/326–8: *just the <u>fact</u> that↓ (1.2) h y' <u>know</u>∧ that (1.6) she got into <u>bed</u>⇒ with me⇒ (0.4) so called <u>mate</u>∧*. The attempt to have SPT2 align with the police version of *no reason* in the S3R framework must therefore be considered a failure.

6.4.2   The case for a myth of police persuasion

In summary, the analysis of the data and the consideration of the activities undertaken by participants as they negotiate competing versions of events demonstrate that once a suspect has displayed his alignment to a particular version, no discursive practice identified in the analysis was successful in altering that alignment or shifting it to a different, police version of events.

It is interesting to note that the belief in persuasion as a legitimate tactic in interviews is not confined to police institutional interviews. For example, Fisher and Todd (1986a) find a similar phenomenon existing in medical interviews with women, such that '[f]or doctors, persuasion is often seen as part of the job they have to do' (p. 3). Furthermore, Fisher and Todd (1986a) note that 'those in the women's health movement have argued that doctors' use of persuasion, while friendly, may not be in women's best interests' (p. 4).

The findings of the analysis in this study can be summarised in lay terms as 'the suspect will never change their story'. Once a police version is presented in competition with a suspect version, the suspect will never align with the S3R framework, or even the role of *principal*, relative to the version in subsequent role negotiations. In relation to the presentation of previously concealed evidence, it seems pertinent to recall the advice of Grice (1975) that 'the best way of negotiating one's position is to be sincere and clear, to tell only the relevant things, not conceal or with-hold truth' (p. 66). The preceding analysis supports this view, which is generally expressed as the Gricean maxim of Quality, and exposes as a myth the belief that it is possible to 'trick' the suspect into making a voluntary confession once some aspect of that would-be confession has already been denied by the suspect. Moreover, we might also recall that Fairclough (1989), when describing the function of formulations from a CDA, rather than a CA, perspective finds that their use limits the recipient's 'options for future contributions'. It is not difficult to see how this might be counterproductive in the Information Gathering phase of a police interview.

6.5 Conclusion

This chapter has identified three different aspects of a mythology about police interviews and to some extent the discussion has already addressed the impact of the mythology on the interview, and in particular, on the achievement of institutional goals. However, it is worth synthesising those findings before we move on to a discussion of the mythology as a social activity in the following chapter.

In relation to the first myth identified, the myth of comprehension, it was found that assumptions about the complexity of legal jargon in the interviews could cause police officers to ignore the potential for confusion arising from more mundane language use. These assumptions were supported by the institutional requirements to check the suspect's comprehension of legal jargon, but not other aspects of the interview. Furthermore, assumptions about how best to fulfil legislative requirements resulted in police officers continually producing specialist language rather than substituting lay terms, at the expense of a successful clarification sequence. Both of these assumptions resulted in police behaviour that had the potential to seriously undermine the success of the interview through a failure of the police to uphold the very legislative requirements that they were attempting to fulfil. Regarding the second aspect of the myth in particular, the reluctance of police officers to substitute lay terms for the legal jargon of 'cautions' (because lay terms may be insufficiently precise to convey the legislative requirements) is self-defeating since their failure to use lay terms can result in a failure to meet the legislative requirement that suspects understand their rights and obligations.

The analysis of a myth of threatened authority demonstrated that pio1 and pio3, in particular, appeared to harbour erroneous beliefs about the vulnerability of their own authoritative voice. Whereas the analysis found that the most successful elicitation of information would be facilitated by the interviewer orienting to the role of 'information recipient' and not 'questioner', this was only attempted by pio2. In INT1 and INT3, attempts by the interviewing officers to maintain control over the discourse upon shifting from the Opening to the Information Gathering were characterised by their orientation to the role of 'questioner'. The findings of the analysis in the previous chapter indicated that the interactional resources available to the suspect are severely limited and the interactions are overwhelmingly dominated by the interviewer. Therefore police concerns that their power may be threatened by the suspect's behaviour seem remarkably misguided, especially if that behaviour consists of suspect initiations (i.e. voluntary confessions). In fact, it is clear from the analysis that such a misjudged belief in potential threats to their power exposed these officers to a failure to obtain a voluntary confession.

Finally, the way that different versions of events are constructed and negotiated by the participants was analysed in terms of a police belief in their own persuasive tactics, highlighted by Baldwin (1993). The first of these tactics to be identified involved sequences of progressively more direct elicitation devices following an initial disagreement over some aspect of the events. Not only does this discursive practice fail to persuade the suspect to align to the police version, but it has the potential to undermine the elicitation of a voluntary confession by fostering in the suspect a stronger alignment to his own version of events. The second tactic involved the use of formulations to associate the suspect's version with anti-social or violent behaviour. This too fails to persuade suspects to commit to a police version and only emphasises the conflict between the suspect and police versions without achieving a resolution. As was noted earlier, a failure to resolve conflicting versions of events may result in inconsistencies between the evidence provided by the interview and other sources of information, and this has the potential to erode the case for the prosecution in court.

In sum, three police beliefs have been shown to produce behaviour that jeopardises the success of the interview by threatening the fulfilment of three key institutional goals: ensuring the suspect understands the relevant legislative requirements; obtaining a voluntary confession; and resolving conflicts between police and suspect versions of events for the consistency of evidence.

In the next chapter, we will explore the relationship between these myths and the sociocultural setting of a police interview.

7
Institutional Power

7.1 Introduction

The analysis of myths underlying the discourse of police interviews in the previous chapter indicates that issues concerning the institutional distribution of power are central to police beliefs about the process of eliciting a confession from a suspect. It is possible to observe, for instance, that conflicts arise between the level of power available to police interviewers and the level of power actually required to conduct a successful interview. Such general observations offer a direction for further discussion of the findings, namely the relationship between the institutional features of the discourse, the construction of police power and the implications of police beliefs about power and domination for the interview as a social practice. We will first undertake a review of the findings of the initial textual analyses in Chapters 3 and 4 in relation to the construction of police power in the discourse structure. Drawing on the CDA notion of discourse constituting society and culture through 'representations, relations and identity' (Fairclough and Wodak 1997), we will investigate the construction of conflicting suspect identities by the participants, and in particular, the way that these identities are designed to address different functional requirements by each participant. Through this investigation it will be possible to clarify the social implications of the elements of the mythology identified in Chapter 6 and consider the effects of power and the diverse goals of participants on the construction of a police interview.

Finally, we will be in a position to draw together these 'lines of enquiry' into a discussion focused on the interdependent relationship between police discursive behaviour, the construction of a mythology about interviewing and policing as a social institution.

7.2   Police power and interview discourse

In this section the findings of the text analyses in the previous four chapters will be examined in relation to police power. The tri-partite framework based on the distribution of participant roles in the interview, and the turn-taking structure, or the distribution of turn types, will both be discussed in relation to the contributions they each make to the construction of a dominant police role in the interview.

7.2.1   Police power and the tri-partite framework

In a police interview, participants display their orientation to a tri-partite framework consisting of an Opening, Information Gathering and Closing, as we identified in Chapter 3. The analysis of the participation frameworks that were invoked through the language of the interview demonstrated that speakers oriented to shifts in the distribution of participant roles at two key points in the interview. The first of these points was identified as the end of the Opening and the beginning of the Information Gathering, and the second was identified as the end of the Information Gathering and the beginning of the Closing. The talk in the Opening and the Closing was found to involve 'form-filling' types of activities, regulated by legislative requirements, whereas the Information Gathering was found to require less formal speech that provided the suspect with more 'space' to produce longer, descriptive turns.

Participant roles (Goffman 1981) were intended to provide a framework that would facilitate a description of the alignment speakers take up in relation to their utterances, specifically in terms of the status that speakers assign themselves (p. 517). As such, the negotiation of participant roles can be described in terms of the speaker's control over their own utterances. For example, speakers who takes up an alignment of *author* and *principal* in relation to an utterance they produce (i.e. of which they are the *animator*) are demonstrating a level of control over the content of that utterance. As *author* they are displaying that they 'wrote' the utterance and therefore have control over the choice of words that they have used to construct the utterance. As *principal* they are taking responsibility for the effect of that utterance and as such they are constituting themelves as members of society in a position to be held responsible for their actions. Clearly, the roles of *author* and *principal* when combined with the *animator* role attribute to speakers a greater level of control over their utterances than would be attributed by the *animator* role alone.

Furthermore, where the participation framework of an interaction indicates that these three roles are aligned to by one participant and not others, then there is a clear disparity in the level of control over utterances held by one speaker compared to another. Perhaps in ordinary conversation between speakers of roughly equal social status it would be rare to find a discrepancy in the distribution of participant roles between one speaker and another. It seems likely that both speakers would align to *author, principal* and *animator* roles in relation to the bulk of their utterances. However, we have already seen that in the case of a police interview, participant roles are not equally distributed.

In the Opening and the Closing, the individual police officer conducting the interview does not align to the roles of *author* and *principal* in relation to utterances that she or he produces. These roles are assigned to the police institution in order to maximise the police interviewer's adherence to police regulations. The police officer does not, therefore, have control over her or his utterances beyond controlling their physical production. This is comparable to Bakhtin's notion of 'authoritative discourse' (Holquist 1981). Bakhtin describes the process through which another's discourse is appropriated and assimilated not freely, but so that it 'demands our unconditional allegiance' and 'permits no play with the context framing it' (p. 343). This is precisely the position of the police officers in the PI2R framework of the Opening and Closing.

During the Information Gathering, the institutional requirement to elicit a voluntary confession is best served by a participation framework where suspects align to the three roles of *author, principal* and *animator* (S3R) in relation to any utterances that contribute information about the events being discussed. In order to maintain this participation framework, the police interviewers need to avoid occupying the *author, principal* and *animator* roles in relation to any utterances that contain event information. If the police officers find they do need to produce event information, they could do so as *animators* and attempt to have the suspect align to the utterance as *author* and *principal*. This could be achieved through a direct quote, for example. However, it remains the case that event information is best introduced by the suspect voluntarily within the S3R framework if it is to be attributed to them as a confession.

It is possible to identify certain types of utterance as more critical to the fulfilment of institutional goals in the interview than others. In the Opening and the Closing parts of the interview the critical utterances are those that elicit the suspect's identification and inform the suspect of his rights and obligations. Prior analysis has demonstrated that the content of these utterances and the responsibility for their consequences is controlled not by the police officers who produce them, but by the police institution that scripts them in accordance with legislative requirements and takes responsibility if those requirements are not met by the wording used. In the Information Gathering, the utterances that most contribute to the realisation of police aims (the elicitation of a confession) are those that provide information about the events being discussed. These critical utterances are ideally controlled by the suspects with respect to their *author-* and *principalship*. Police officers should specifically avoid aligning to the *author* and *principal* roles in relation to such utterances, if they produce them at all.

If, at the local level of speaker utterances, we consider power expressed as control over the discourse, then the distribution of participant roles throughout the interview indicates that police interviewers are allocated very little power over the utterances most critical to the achievement of institutional goals. Rather, the power over the content of these utterances is divided between the police institution (in the Opening and Closing) and the suspect (in the Information Gathering). We will continue to use the term 'tri-partite framework' to refer to the alignment of participation frameworks and institutional goals that form the Opening, Information Gathering and Closing of the police interview. However, from this point, the term additionally implies a particular distribution of power, expressed as control over utterances at a local level. Thus, in a tri-partite police interview, power is distributed in favour of the institution (in the Opening and Closing) and the suspect (in the Information Gathering). It is important to realise, however, that controlling the content of utterances does not necessarily equate to a powerful role in the interview. To further our understanding of police power as it is allocated to and exercised by individual officers, we will turn to the findings of Chapter 4.

7.2.2   Power and the allocation of interactional resources

The analysis of turn types and their distribution in a police interview in Chapter 5 found that turns that constitute first pair parts of adjacency pairs are routinely allocated to police interviewers. The recurrent nature of this arrangement from one adjacency pair, typically a question–answer pair, to the next was identified as a 'Q-A chain rule'. That is, first and second pair parts recognisable as questions and answers are produced by the police interviewer and the suspect respectively to form chains of such pairs across the longer sequences that make up the interview.

The effect of this arrangement on the interaction is to limit access to interactional resources by the suspect while at the same time maximising the police interviewer's access to these resources. Thus police interviewers have access to resources (i.e. first pair parts) that enable them to introduce, maintain or suppress topics whereas suspects are constrained to devices such as stepwise transitions to introduce new topics within second pair parts and have no resources available to maintain or suppress topics.

A further dimension to this issue is added by consideration of the allocation of turn types in relation to the level of obligation placed on the recipient by a particular turn type. According to the 'hierarchy of obligatingness' proposed by Thomas (1989), the turn types available to the police interviewers, which comprise mainly direct questions and direct requests, are placed at the highly obligating end of the hierarchy. The turn types allocated to suspects, on the other hand, are generally assertions about information that is known to the speaker, which are considered minimally obligating (Thomas 1989: 152–3).

The findings of the analysis in Chapter 5 indicate that interactional resources used to control important aspects of the discourse are distributed in favour of the interviewing officer. The resources needed to control the topic of talk, for instance, are largely inaccessible to the suspect and those resources that are accessible, such as stepwise topic transitions, do not obligate the police interviewer to maintain the topic that has been initiated by the suspect. Resources such as first pair parts and interruptions provide the police interviewer with the potential to maintain a great deal of control over the discourse by constraining the topic and length of suspect's contributions, for example. Therefore, the distribution of turn types and interactional resources grant the interviewers a level of power over the interaction that is unattainable by the suspect. In earlier parts of the analysis (see Chapter 4) this distribution of resources was labelled a 'deference structure' (Frankel 1990) and this term will continue to be used to refer to the allocation of power, in the form of access to interactional resources, that favours the police interviewer.

7.2.3   Conflicting structures of power

To summarise the discussion so far, we have seen that the distribution of participant roles provides the police interviewer with few if any opportunities to produce important utterances over which they can be said to have complete control. However, this arrangement appears contradictory to the distribution of interactional resources that grants police interviewers a very substantial amount of control over both their own utterances and those of the suspect. In other words, within the tri-partite framework, the police officer as an individual experiences a reduced level of power in the discourse in favour of the institution and the suspect, but within the deference structure, the interviewing officer occupies a potentially powerful position having access to resources that control the contributions of all participants.

The key to resolving this apparent conflict is the issue of choice. Police officers as individuals can choose to align to particular participant roles just as they can choose to access interactional resources of discourse control available to them. We have already begun to explore the impact that these choices can have on the interview through the analysis of police beliefs about interview practice in Chapter 6. In particular, there is a relatively straightforward relationship between this conflict and the discourse that produces the myth of threatened authority, discussed in section 6.3. It was found that the shift from the formal introductory part of the interview to the information-seeking part of the interview is marked by participants with an attempt to realign the participant roles to a participation framework which will best facilitate the confessional narrative of the suspect. However, this realignment is itself problematised by the police participants in some cases as, through their negotiation of the shift, they feel they must maintain their authoritative role.

Police interviewers pio1 and pio3 demonstrate that they are reluctant to choose a 'powerless' participation framework at the start of the Information Gathering and instead maximise their power by using the most highly obligating features of the interactional resources available to them, such as interruptions and direct questions. In the terms of this discussion, pio1 and pio3 are unwilling to align to the tri-partite framework and minimise the inherently powerful police position provided through the deference structure. Their unwillingness appears to be the manifestation in the discourse of these officers' belief that the tri-partite framework comprises a threat to their power. Their failure to recognise the importance of the tri-partite framework in eliciting a voluntary confession is exacerbated by an apparent scepticism that the deference structure will provide them a sufficiently powerful role in the discourse.

Pio2, however, chooses to align to a participation framework that will minimise the inherent power of the deference structure, although he is able to draw on the resources provided by the deference structure at other stages of the interview and realign to participant roles that provide him with more control over his utterances than afforded by the tri-partite framework. This demonstrates that the threat to police power posed by suspects aligning to an S3R framework is a myth. Additionally, by comparing the police-suspect interviews with the police child witness interviews we saw that police interviewers can indeed choose an interactional approach that de-emphasises their authoritative voice when they are specifically trained to do so.

It is interesting that the myth of comprehension involves the contrary position – reluctance of police interviewers to take up a more powerful role in order to clarify misunderstandings. In the Opening and Closing, the tri-partite structure distributes most of the control over the utterances to the police institution. Nonetheless, the deference structure is still enabled and the police interviewers can select turn types to respond to the needs of the interview. This is demonstrated by the fact that pio1 initiates a clarification sequence when she perceives that there is a problem with SPT1's refusal to consent to the fingerprinting procedure. However, despite the resources available to pio1, she still fails to adequately articulate the issue in order to identify the problem. As we observed in the previous chapter, the police interviewers orient to the PI2R participation framework in the Opening and Closing so comprehensively that they appear unable to address serious misunderstandings by the suspects.

Thus a directly proportional relationship between counterproductive police behaviour and the distribution of power suggested by the myth of threatened authority is problematised by the myth of comprehension. While the myth of threatened authority suggests that police behaviour that undermines the success of the interview is a result of an unnecessary recourse to powerful discourse, the myth of comprehension indicates that the problem is a failure by police officers to take more control of the discourse.

Conflicting distributions of power at the local level of discourse production also underlie the police behaviour that results from the 'myth of persuasion'; however, the relationship is more complex as this myth is not based directly on issues of power negotiation. In the following section we will identify the relevance of power negotiations to the myth of persuasion through an examination of the construction and deconstruction of criminality by the police and suspects respectively.

7.3   A negotiated suspect identity

In section 6.4 above, it was found that one of the police discursive practices used when negotiating competing version of events is to produce formulations that associate the suspect's version with criminal or anti-social behaviour. It was found that this practice is not successful in persuading the suspect to shift their alignment towards the police version of events. However, this discursive practice is characterised by an attempt to construct an identity for the suspect, which, it will be shown, conflicts with the identity constructed by the suspects themselves.

The construction of the suspect's identity through the discourse is an important tool in the negotiation of 'criminality' and the apportionment of blame, concepts that are discussed by Watson (1983). We will begin this discussion by examining the features of the varying suspect identities constructed by the participants. The police construction of a suspect identity will be discussed in terms of the construction of criminality and the imposition of moral judgements. The suspect construction of their own identity will be considered in relation to the mitigation of criminal activity and blame. Throughout the discussion, we will also draw on the notion of 'representations of reality' and 'social relations', which together with 'people's social and personal identities' are described by Fairclough and Wodak (1997) as 'three broad domains of social life' constituted through discourse (p. 273; cf. CA-based research into identity, e.g. Antaki and Widdicombe 1998). While the focus will be the construction of identity, an examination of representations and relations will contribute to our understanding of both mitigating and criminalising discursive activities.

Finally, it is important to recognise that in addition to constructing the suspect's identity as a participant in past events that are being described (an 'event-participant identity', cf. 'situated identities': Zimmerman 1998: 94–6), both police and suspects are involved in constructing identities for themselves as participants in the interview ('interview-participant identities') through their discursive behaviour (cf. 'discourse identities': Zimmerman 1998: 91–4). Although the constitution of an 'interview-participant identity' through the discourse is important to this study generally (for instance the police construction of their identity as 'listeners' or 'questioners' at the start of the Information Gathering is crucial to the consideration of the myth of threatened authority), here we are concerned primarily with the issues relating to 'event-participant identities'.

7.3.1 Imposed moralising

We have already discussed to a large extent the police use of language in general and formulations in particular as a means of representing the behaviour of the suspect in an unfavourable light. We have seen how the police officers variously represent the suspect's behaviour as negligent, violent or motivated by some further criminal motive (e.g. 518/ pio3: *(0.5) ah (0.4) do you um (1.0) do you um (.) sell that* [marijuana] *to anyone else↑*). For the purposes of this discussion, we will focus on police discourse that constitutes an 'irrationally violent' criminal identity for the suspect, but the conclusions presented below will draw on a range of findings relating to aspects of police discursive behaviour.

In relation to the construction of the suspect identity mentioned above, both pio1 and pio2 present descriptions of the suspects as irrationally enraged and overreacting to essentially non-threatening circumstances. This is achieved by emphasising the inactivity or relative helplessness of their targets. In the extract below, we see that pio1 reiterates an earlier comment by SPT1 that Ian (referred to by the pronoun *he* in the extract) backed away during the assault.

Extract 7-1 INT1

354.   pio1:   what was he <u>doing</u> while you were
355.   SPT1:   (0.8) <u>nothing</u> (0.3) <u>nothing</u> at all↓
356.   pio1:   (0.6) so he wasn't <u>fighting</u> back or <u>defending</u> himself ∧
357.   he was just <u>standing</u> there⇒
358.   SPT1:   just <u>standing</u> there↓
359.   pio1:   and <u>backing</u> back towards the <u>fridges</u>↓

By returning the focus of talk to Ian's actions during the assault, a topic that was discussed at an earlier stage in the interview, pio1 emphasises the disparity between SPT1's actions and Ian's response.

Pio2 is engaged in a similar practice when he concentrates on the physical difference between SPT2 and Leila (273–4/pio2: *(1.2) she's not a (.) <u>big girl</u>↓ (.) you're a rather large <u>fellow</u>↑ (0.2) // fair*⇒ bit <u>bigger</u> than her↓*) to assert the inappropriateness of the assault. In both cases the police interviewers express a disproportional relationship between the suspect's behaviour relative to the circumstances and in doing so, attribute to a suspect the identity of an irrational and unreasonable criminal. In INT12, which also relates to an assault, the suspect is cast as a habitual fighter throughout the interview and in INT11 the interviewing officer uses language which implies that SPT11 knowingly brought the victim to the place where he was assaulted. In INT8, the suspect is indirectly accused of being a negligent mother, as we can see in Extract 7-2 where pio8 asks whether she has *fed the children*.

Extract 7-2 INT8

137.   pio8:   <u>prior</u> to the <u>children</u> coming here <u>today</u> ⇒
138.   (3.4) um have <u>you</u> ah fed the children ↑
139.   (1.0) <u>today</u>↑
140.   SPT8:   yes ⇒
141.   pio8:   you <u>have</u>↓
142.   what did you <u>feed</u> them ∧
143.   SPT8:   ((with vehemence)) no <u>comment</u> ↓

In line 142, as if to verify SPT8's answer, pio8 asks what they were fed. This information has absolutely no bearing on the case, which concerns an alleged burglary, but because the goods stolen were prescription drugs, anything which adds to the suspect's image as a desperate drug addict will support the police version that she is likely to have committed the crime.

It is important to recognise that these expressions that distinguish appropriate from inappropriate behaviour are a form of moral judgement presented as 'commonsense assumptions'. For instance, pio2 follows his comment about the relative size of SPT2 and Leila, with the question 276/pio2: *(0.6) um↓ (.) was there any reason why you had to e::rm↓ (.) <u>treat</u> 'a this way at all↓*. There is no further elaboration on the implications of his prior observations about physical size, but the place of the question in line 276 as subsequent to those observations automatically make them relevant to the question. Thus the assumption that it is inappropriate to physically assault a smaller person under any circumstances (*treat 'a this way at all*) is embedded in this sequence of adjacency pairs. This is a judgement based on a particular moral view of the world – 'it is wrong to hit women and those smaller than you'.

Furthermore, from an interactional perspective, the use of formulations to construct these judgements places a high degree of obligation on the suspect to respond and take some position in relation to their own morality. In this sense, the police activity illustrated in the above examples comprises an imposition of a moral framework by the police officers on the suspects. We will return to this issue in order to explore how it relates to the power relations discussed above, but first we will examine suspect discourse in relation to criminality and identity.

7.3.2   Mitigation, blame and the suspect's identity

We have mentioned as a part of the analysis in section 4.3.1 that suspects are engaged in the construction of an identity of a reasonable, rational person, responding to provocation or general life circumstances in a predictable fashion. This is achieved both through the use of descriptions relating directly to their own character and relations with others, and through discourse that makes representations about their circumstances.

Thus, SPT1 produces a large amount of talk providing evidence of his good relationship with Betty (102/SPT1: *and we get on <u>all right</u> just as <u>friends</u> ⇒*), and his usual placid character (384/SPT1: *I've never <u>been</u> like that before↓*). These assertions contribute to a view of SPT1 as a placid and reasonable person who is able to sustain a mature friendship with his ex-de facto partner. He also provides details of the threatening phone call and why it was threatening to him at that time (112–113/ SPT1: *(0.8) then I was thinking about the <u>kids</u> ∧ I said <u>jeez</u> like what happens* *if something <u>does</u> really happen*∧). Through this description, SPT1 in fact constructs himself as a victim of criminal behaviour.

Similarly, SPT2 identifies himself as a victim of betrayal by his girl-friend and his *best mate*. He elaborates on this identity later by describing himself as a person who has difficulty controlling his anger, but this is moderated by an implication that he is also a responsible person who has taken steps to seek professional help for his condition (342–5/SPT2: *e:um*∧ *(0.6) I've <u>tried</u> t'↓ (1.8) do what <u>I</u> can about it*∧ *b'n⇒ (0.2) <u>nothing</u> seems to <u>work</u>⇒ so↓ (0.8) e'jus gotta keep on <u>goin</u> an'↓ (0.2) go back n' see the people <u>again</u>*∧ *(0.2) I'd'no↓ (1.8) // (like)**).

SPT7 responds to questions about his consumption of cannabis with substantial turns at talk emphasising that he does not have an addiction to the drug, for instance 296/SPT7: *I get by without it and 299/SPT7: I don't think I'm a addict.*

These identities are not, of course, created in a vacuum, but in the context of a criminal enquiry. They are therefore designed to provide a specific response to the police investigation of the suspect's alleged (and, in the case of most of the interviews, admitted) criminal behaviour. This response by the suspects comprises a mitigation of their involvement in criminal activities in a number of ways, some of which may appear contradictory in their implications. For example, SPT1 constructs himself as a normally calm and rational person who committed one abnormal act of violence. However, such aberrant behaviour, even on one occasion, could be construed as indicative of an irrational character, which might imply future recidivism. Consciously or not, SPT1 demonstrates that he is sensitive to this interpretation and, as we have seen, takes pains to describe the telephone threats he received as a motive for his behaviour. In this way, SPT1 represents the assault as a defensive response to a threat of violence made against him. Furthermore, by refusing to acknowledge either his own social relation of familiarity with Ian (210/SPT1: *(0.4) I don't <u>know</u> him↓*) or a social relation of intimacy between Ian and Betty (213: SPT1: *//just a <u>friend</u> ⇒**), SPT1 is avoiding representations of his actions as an attack on his ex-de facto's new partner in an irrational fit of jealousy.

Through his discourse, SPT1 constructs a complex set of identities, representations and relations that all contribute to an overarching aim of mitigating the criminality of his actions. If we accept the view that blame can be conceived of in zero-sum terms (Watson 1976), and that 'the degree to which one party (or parties) is blamed is the degree to which another party or parties cannot be so blamed' (Watson 1976: 65), then SPT1's claim of victim status in relation to the threatening phone call is a way of reducing his own responsibility for assault. This is probably the most important aspect of SPT1's narrative in terms of its function in mitigating his role in the assault. All SPT1's discursive work to establish himself as a non-violent person supports the argument that he was provoked, and in being provoked, was himself a victim, which would call for a renegotiation of blame.

SPT2 also mitigates his actions by reference to his status as a victim; however, the argument for mitigation is weaker since there was no physical threat against which he could be defending himself. SPT2 instead focuses on representing the events after the assault as a resolution to the conflict with Leila and thereby constitutes relations of intimacy, or at least friendship, as enduring between them. This combination of representations and relations recasts the assault as a regrettable moment of disharmony within the relationship, rather than as a violent and permanent end to the relationship. In this sense, SPT2 works towards a mitigation of his actions by minimising the harm caused to the victim.

In the other two interviews that relate to allegations of assault, INT11 and INT12, the suspects either deny their involvement entirely (SPT11) or claim that they only acted in self-defence (SPT12). Nonetheless, SPT11 is careful to say that he was not actually watching as his friend attacked the victim and SPT12 emphasises that he *wouldn't do that* when asked about particularly violent acts. In other words, they may be prone to fighting but they have a sense of honour.

It is interesting that INT3 does not feature the same kind of behaviour on the part of the suspect, which may be due to the absence of a 'victim-offender' relationship. For instance, Watson (1976) suggests that in the case of 'victimless acts', notions of blame and guilt may not be relevant (p. 66). As SPT3 does not have access to any mitigation involving an *agent provocateur*, we see that he works mainly to mitigate the criminality of his actions by reference to issues related to intention. We have already seen that SPT3 is concerned to represent his involvement in the cultivation of the marijuana crop and his possession of unregistered firearms as minimally organised. In this sense, his discourse is directed towards the act of mitigating the degree to which his actions could be considered premeditated. This is also true of SPT7, who is charged with possession and use of cannabis, and who focuses on emphasing that his drug cultivation is personal and not connected with dealing.

There are a great many other observations that might be made about the use of language by the suspects, but the main focus of this enquiry is the language use of police officers, and in particular the negotiation of power by police interviewers. It is necessary, therefore that this discussion be confined to features of the suspect's language that are relevant to the deconstruction of criminality through mitigation.

To summarise this discussion, we have established that suspects use their turns at talk to constitute identities, representations and relations that function interdependently to mitigate their involvement in criminal activities.

7.3.3 Police power and moral impositions

We have already observed that some of the discursive practices of police officers when negotiating competing versions of events involve the imposition of a moral framework on the suspect. In order to do this, police officers draw on resources made available to them through the deference structure, such as direct questions and formulations. It is interesting to compare this behaviour to the observations that Bergmann (1992) makes about discursive practices of psychiatrists in interviews with candidate patients of a hospital. In particular, he finds that by being 'discreet' about candidate patients' behaviour, psychiatrists imply 'some improper, deviant, or morally questionable' quality pertaining to the candidate patients' actions so that these actions require discretion when mentioned (p. 156). Bergmann (1992) goes on to demonstrate that in response, 'many candidate patients do not join the insinuation game but choose instead to turn against the psychiatrist' (p. 157). This is consistent with the findings of this study, and even though the police interviewers do not employ discretion to imply a moral judgement, suspects, like the candidate patients in Bergmann's study, resist this imposition. Furthermore, as our earlier discussion of police power in the discourse has shown, police discursive practices that impose a moral framework on the suspect's story conflict with the requirements of the tri-partite framework. It is therefore relevant to consider what might motivate such behaviour, and in doing so, we might also begin to explore some of the effects of institutional requirements on the discourse of the interview.

The discussion above suggested that a key function of suspect-produced talk in an interview is to deconstruct the criminality of the suspect's actions through mitigation. For instance, a suspect may highlight any circumstances that may have acted to provoke the criminal act and imply that these circumstances warranted the actions of the suspect to some extent. The initial analysis of police attempts to associate the suspect's version with violence or anti-social behaviour suggested that such practices function as indirect attempts to persuade the suspect to change his or her story. However, consideration of the discourse as social practice, constituting identities, representations and relations, suggests that these discursive practices constitute a direct challenge to the mitigating discourse of suspects. In other words, imposing a moral framework on a suspect is a way of challenging the suspect's assertion that their actions were in some way justified by circumstances. It is a way of obligating the suspect to take a moral stance that invalidates their own attempts to mitigate their crime.

It is clear that police officers do not merely attempt to persuade suspects to change their version of events through questions and other elicitation devices, but that they may resort to the use of inappropriate moral judgements to try to align the suspect with the police version. Not only does this behaviour fall well outside the scope of a police interviewer's legally defined role, but it exposes the interviewer to the risk of subverting the tri-partite framework through the use of highly obligating and discursively powerful resources of the deference structure.

7.4   Institutional discourse and the police interview

The discussion of power and myths has revealed that in each case of a police myth about interviewing suspects there is a corresponding conflict between the requirements of the tri-partite framework and the use of resources provided in the deference structure. In this section I will address this issue by exploring the role of institutional discourse in police-suspect interviews as it is revealed through the participant negotiation of power relations and institutional goals.

7.4.1   Understanding police behaviour

In order to explore the reasons for police behaviour that potentially undermines the success of an interview, it may be useful to consider, as other researchers have done, the relationship between the production of a police-suspect interview and its role as the key piece of evidence in any subsequent court case (see for example Coulthard 1997; Gibbons 1996; Pearse and Gudjonsson 1996; Settle 1990; Shuy 1997, 1998). A common theme of this research is that the interview process or the product (a statement or recording) may be affected or distorted due to a police concern with the outcome of the court case. This is clearly expressed by Settle (1990) who finds that a widespread motivation for the 'strengthening' of evidence is the need for ratification in the courtroom of the police officer's decision to arrest, detain and charge a suspect. Thus there is an organisational pressure on police officers to obtain a conviction, and this is considered sufficient explanation of police behaviour that 'bends the rules'.

However, the findings of this research indicate that this explanation is insufficient as it does not account for the fact that most of the behaviour thought to be responsible for 'strengthening' the evidence, or supporting the police prosecution in court, is in fact counterproductive. This is because the discursive practices of police officers in the Information Gathering when attempting to align the suspect to police versions of events rely on manipulating the tools provided by the deference structure to maximise police power over the discourse. But the tri-partite framework, designed to best support the voluntary confession by a suspect, requires the minimisation of the police power inherent in the deference structure.

In addition, explanations such as that offered by Settle (1990) do not account for the behaviour in which the myths of threatened authority or comprehension are manifested. They are limited to accounting only for tactics of persuasion or coercion. The findings of the present study suggest that we need to look beyond organisational pressures and address the root of the myths – i.e. the erroneous beliefs themselves. We must ask why police believe that the priority of an interview is to convince the suspect to align to a police version of events, why they believe that it is necessary to maintain control over their talk and constrain the suspect's contributions and why they believe that the priority of the Opening and Closing is to adhere to the police regulations rather than to the spirit of the legislation guiding those regulations. In each case, the answer lies in the discourse, or more accurately, in the order of discourse and the discourse type.

7.4.2   The role of institutional orders of discourse

In a brief study of a police-witness interview from a CDA perspective, Fairclough (1989) finds that

> although it is the prerogative of the more powerful participants, in this case the police interviewers, to determine which discourse type(s) is/are the 'appropriate' ones to draw upon in a given situation, the choice positions all participants in a determinate place in the order of discourse and the social order of police work. (p. 31)

The findings of this study have so far revealed a clear connection between choices relating to power in the discourse and discourse that embodies underlying, erroneous and potentially damaging beliefs.

Fairclough's (1989) interpretation of the relationship between power and discourse types, and in particular the notion that a powerful police role is responsible for positioning participants within a police institutional order of discourse, provides us with an additional perspective on the problem of how myths are generated and perpetuated to the detriment of the institution.

It is observable that a common feature of each myth is a failure by the police to acknowledge the role of discourse types that are unrelated to police institutional discourse in the production of a police-suspect interview. Instead, the interview is oriented to by police officers as the product of and a contribution to police institutional discourse only. Thus, the only way of interpreting the purpose of each stage of the interview is within the parameters of police institutional discourse and as a function of the institution.

This explains why police officers can behave as though the priority of the Opening and Closing were to adhere to police regulations in favour of actually providing simple explanations of the suspect's rights and obligations when they are required. The myth of comprehension is based on a belief not that everyone understands technical legal terminology or 'policespeak', but that the requirements of the Opening and Closing are best served by adhering to the legal terminology provided by the Police Manual. Such a view makes sense only if the requirements of the Opening and Closing are understood to be limited to their role as part of police institutional discourse, and not relating to their role as part of other orders of discourse, such as the discourse of justice and civil rights, for example.

Similarly, if the Information Gathering is understood only in terms of its role in police institutional discourse – that is, as a tool for the construction of police evidence – and its role as part of other discourse types, such as defence discourse or even therapeutic discourse, is ignored then it is inevitable that its purpose will be seen as the alignment of the suspect to the police version of events. A failure to treat the suspect as having concerns outside the police institution and not being motivated to contribute to that institution's discourse, would account for the police officers' perception of many suspect contributions as invalid or inappropriate. Since they are overwhelmingly concerned with the requirements of the interview from the perspective of its role in police institutional discourse, they tend not to take into account the way that their own contributions may be conflicting with the aims of the suspect. If it were better understood that the suspect's talk is largely produced as part of a discourse of defence (in a legal sense), then it might be possible to anticipate that much of their talk will function as mitigation of the criminal activity and to accept such contributions as part of the suspect's interactional role in the interview. Rather than engaging in counterproductive attempts to impose a moral framework on the suspect's mitigating turns, police officers would be in a position to recognise the value of such discourse to the suspect and choose a more effective approach.

This interpretation of the findings is consistent with research relating to institutional discourse in general (see section 2.2.4) where it is acknowledged that 'institutional talk may be associated with *inferential frameworks* and procedures that are particular to specific institutional contexts' (Drew and Heritage 1992: 22). Importantly, Drew and Heritage (1992) also find that despite an alignment by both lay and professional participants to institutionally determined tasks and functions, the conduct (or discursive behaviour) of professional participants in an institutional encounter 'is shaped by organisational and professional constraints and accountabilities which may be only vaguely known or entirely opaque to lay participants' (p. 23).

In police interviews, a conspicuous example of such *inferential frameworks* is the procedural interactions in the Opening and Closing. In all the interviews, suspects demonstrate their preparedness to comply with the particular requirements and interview procedures, irrespective of the level of co-operation displayed in the Information Gathering. However, it is clear that there are instances in the Information Gathering of police behaviour that is 'shaped by ... constraints and accountabilities' that are obscure to the suspects, such as the selective display of knowledge by police interviewers. The analysis of the participation frameworks in the Information Gathering revealed that police interviewers routinely behaved as though they were unaware of certain facts about the event, such as the names of key witnesses and the features of the locations being discussed. This behaviour has the potential to cause confusion to the suspect who may not understand the organisational motivation for asking questions to which both speaker and recipient already know the answer.

Conflict between professional and lay understandings of institutional discursive procedures is identified by Wodak (1996a) as a key issue in the origination of 'disorders of discourse'. She finds that in doctor–patient interactions 'patients are expected to comply with the explicit and implicit norms of the clinic procedures' (p. 170). However, Wodak's study shows that most people are not such 'ideal patients' and the inability of doctors to consider the requirements of non-medical discourse is the cause of many procedural 'disorders' that she identifies. Conversely,

Tannen (1993) finds that doctors who negotiate a number of different 'frames' are able to deal with the needs of multiple discourses that involve, in her terms, different 'knowledge schemas'. In this way, their behaviour is responsive to the particular needs of child patients and their attendant parents. It appears that for professionals in such institutions, successful communication with lay participants is dependent on an understanding that the interaction exists in a dialectic relationship with more than one 'order of discourse' (Fairclough 1989).

Moreover, this study has demonstrated that even the specific institutional requirements of the police interview are not best served by behaving as though a police interview exists solely as a manifestation of police institutional discourse. A police interview is by definition a point of contact between the police institution and the broader society. It is inevitable that it is produced within and contributes to many orders of discourse. The conflicts that occur in the interviews, therefore, are not so much caused by erroneous beliefs about interviewing, but rather they are caused by a failure to recognise the potential for any other beliefs about interviewing.

7.5   Conclusion

7.5.1   Summary of the findings

The primary aim of this book has been to investigate the role of police institutional discourse in the construction of a police-suspect interview, both in terms of the negotiation of power relations between participants and the successful fulfilment of institutional requirements. In order to achieve this aim, several phases of analysis were undertaken and the findings presented in Chapters 3, 4, 5 and 6.

The description of a tri-partite interview framework based on participant roles (in Chapter 3) highlighted a variance between the participation frameworks invoked in the Opening and Closing and the target participation framework of the Information Gathering. In the Opening and Closing, participants oriented to a PI2R framework (*principal* and *author* roles are attributed to the police institution) within which contributions by both police and suspects were heavily constrained. At times, this produced a conflict for police officers between the need to clarify institutional talk for the suspect and the need to use only words and phrases supplied by the institution.

The analysis of the negotiation of participant roles in the Information Gathering indicated that the institutional goals of the interview were best achieved within an S3R framework (*principal, author* and *animator* roles are attributed to the suspect), which was described as a target participation framework. The investigation revealed that conflicts exist between information known to the police interviewer and information formally recognised in the interview as known to that interviewer. Thus, information treated as common knowledge by the suspect might be treated by the police interviewer as 'new' and known only to the suspect.

The analysis of discursive practices and turn taking in interactions, examined in Chapter 4, addressed the second of the supporting research aims. A conflict was identified between the distribution of resources that provided access to topic initiation devices and the needs of participants to initiate topics. That is, suspects, who require access to topic initiations to introduce new information and usefully inform the police enquiry, are granted only minimal access to initiation devices as a result of their role as interviewees. Conversely, the interviewer role grants police access to a wide range of topic management tools through which they may guide the content of talk and display its perceived relevance to the interview. However, it is questionable as to whether this best serves the goals of the interview because it discourages the suspect from introducing potentially important information.

Analysis of the interactions between police and suspects in Chapter 4 also revealed that a great many of the turns produced by each participant contributed to the construction of a particular version of events. At several points in each interview, the police version and the suspect version contained contradictory elements and the police interviewers used the interactional resources at their disposal to attempt to reconcile these two versions in favour of the police version.

The findings of the analyses in Chapters 3 and 4 taken together were found to indicate a larger conflict between the requirements of the tri-partite framework in terms of a minimisation of police power and the inherently powerful police role embedded in the deference structure. The transition into the Information Gathering was found to be the focus of this conflict and police behaviour in two interviews at this point was indicative of a belief that moving into the S3R framework was a lesser priority than maintaining control over the discourse. However, the findings of the VATE study presented in Chapter 5 revealed that alternative forms of discursive practice exist within the framework of police institutional discourse and that it is possible for police interviewers to produce utterances that attend to both the institutional requirements of an information-seeking interview and the concerns of the interviewee.

Chapter 6 exposed the underlying beliefs or myths held by the police participants in three particular areas. The conflict between the potential for misunderstandings in the Opening and the Closing and the actual resources used to clarify such misunderstandings when they do occur was described as a myth of comprehension. This myth also encompassed the discrepancy between the assumption that only the police institutional utterances would be confusing to suspects and the actual experience of suspects that indicated that other aspects of language use might well cause confusion, as in everyday interaction.

The myth of threatened authority arises from the inconsistency between the empowering language used by some police officers in the transition from Opening to Information Gathering and the police 'disempowerment' required for a successful invocation of the S3R framework. An erroneous belief that it is necessary for the police to maintain control over the discourse was supported by the findings of the VATE study, where police interviewers displayed an orientation to the duality of discourses mentioned above.

Finally, the unsuccessful attempts by police interviewers to have suspects align to the police version of events, and abandon a competing suspect version, is symptomatic of the myth of persuasion. Further discussion of the persuasive tactics used by police officers found that attempts to cast the suspect's version in a negative light can be characterised as impositions of a moral framework on the suspect's contributions. Not only is this inappropriate behaviour for an interviewing officer, but it does not effect a realignment by the suspect to the police version in the long term.

Thus a mythology underlying particular aspects of police behaviour when interviewing suspects is based on elements of conflict. The key element of conflict was found to exist between the institutional goals of the interview and the reliance by police interviewers on police institutional discourse as a guide to their discursive behaviour. Overwhelmingly, the conflicts identified in the interviews were characterised by erroneous beliefs held by police officers about interviewing practices. The failure of police interviewers to resolve these conflicts was found to result from their understanding of the interview as existing in a dialectical relationship only with a police institutional order of discourse. Thus the primary research aim of investigating the role of police institutional discourse in the negotiation of power relations and achievement of institutional requirements was addressed through the identification of a 'mono-discoursal' view of the interview. That is, police behaviour that undermines the success of the interview is most likely to occur in conjunction with an orientation to the 'policing' order of discourse as exclusively contributing to and being constructed by a police interview.

7.5.2   Implications for police institutional discourse

The analysis here has found evidence that when police interviewers display their awareness of related discourses, such as pio2's awareness of a 'story-telling' discourse displayed in his transitional turn at the start of the Information Gathering, they do not sacrifice police goals – if anything they are able to achieve their goals more easily. Thus, it will most likely benefit the institutional processes of information gathering if police can adapt to a 'multi-discoursal' approach to interviewing. This is supported by the findings of the VATE study (Heydon 1997) presented in Chapter 5, as well as other related studies (e.g. Braithwaite et al. 1998; Shuy 1998) where it has been recommended that a more 'conversational' speech style will facilitate the elicitation of a voluntary confession without diminishing the authority of the police role. Police interviewers need to anticipate the influence of other discourses and be able to recognise how such discourses are functioning in the interview. By taking a multi-discoursal approach to the interview, police do not need to take up roles outside their institutional role as interviewer. It would not be appropriate for them to assume the role of therapist or defence counsel, for instance. However, by anticipating that the suspect is likely to engage in talk that mitigates the criminality being ascribed to him or her through the interview, police interviewers might recognise that such talk does not necessarily threaten the success of the interview. In fact, it may be part of a longer confessional discourse and thus comprise a valuable part of the interview.

The findings of this study have a number of implications for police institutional discourse, both as it is drawn upon as a resource in police interviews and as it is constructed by the interview. The mythology underlying police interviewing that this study has identified correlates with an over-reliance on police institutional discourse as the only relevant order of discourse in the construction of this type of interaction. In order to reduce the incidence of counterproductive police behaviour, it seems clear that we should start by addressing this mono-discoursal view of the interview.

What is perhaps most important for police interviewers is to understand properly what it is they are hoping to achieve through the interview. Thus, an emphasis needs to be placed on achieving compliance with the legislative requirements rather than on adhering to police institutional guidelines. This means that individual officers should feel sufficiently comfortable with the legislative requirements pertaining to the rights of the suspect that they can produce plain language explanations that clarify the 'policespeak' and still fulfil police officers' legal obligations. Police interviewers should maintain awareness throughout the interview that, as in any interaction, misunderstandings of the most mundane language, and not just specialist terminology, can occur.

Furthermore, police may need to reveal their discursive intentions to the suspect to avoid unnecessary confusion. For instance, police interviewers should avoid misrepresenting their 'knowledge state' by asking for information that the suspect might reasonably assume is 'common knowledge', such as the names of key witnesses. If this process is necessary in order to maintain an S3R framework and to demonstrate the suspect's knowledge of some fact, then that purpose should be made clear through the use of a preface like 'for the tape' or some similar device. Police interviewers should be aware that asking for confirmation of common knowledge items gives the impression of testing the recipient's knowledge, and while this practice is familiar to most people as belonging to classroom discourse, they may not be expecting it to feature as part of a police interview. However, if it were explained to suspects that they may be required to confirm some facts known to the individuals present but perhaps unknown to later listeners, questions such as 51/pio1: *w'l who's Betty*↓ might elicit a more informative response than 52/SPT1: *Fisher*∧.

Finally, though it would involve a major change to police procedures in Australian states and territories, an effective way to introduce suspect-related discourses into the interview might be to permit the suspect to have a lawyer present, as is the practice in some other countries with an adversarial system of justice. This way the discourse of defence, which the suspect is most likely to be concerned with, will be given professional representation, counteracting the representation of policing discourses by the two police officers.

7.5.3   Directions for future research

In addition to presenting the findings of an investigation of police discursive practices, this book has presented a framework for analysis which might usefully be employed in a broader study of police interviews or other institutional discursive events. In particular, the integration of tools drawn from Interactional Sociolinguistics and Conversation Analysis may be helpful in undertaking further research as suggested below.

Section 7.5.2 has identified a number of areas in which changes to police procedure might benefit the interview process and facilitate the achievement of institutional goals. In general, the analysis suggests that this might best be achieved by introducing a 'multi-discoursal' approach to the interview by police participants. However, in order to implement changes to police procedure, or to investigate the impact of a mono- or multi-discoursal approach to institutional interactions, this study should be augmented by further research in areas ranging from Discourse Analysis to forensic linguistics and criminology.

Initially, it would be helpful to identify the features of other discourses related to the police interview: an analysis of 'troubles talk' (Jefferson and Lee 1980) by suspects that positions police interviewers as 'troubles recipients' would provide the basis for a study of a 'therapeutic' discourse in the police interview; the interactional construction of the suspect's narrative would reveal the role of 'story-teller' as it is oriented to by suspects; and an investigation of the development of evidence from the police interview room to the courtroom might give some indication of the effect of police institutional discourse on the discourse of defence.

We recognised early in section 4.4.4 that research into the use of formulations in other institutional settings has found that, as an inter-actional device, formulations display a stronger orientation to the role of the audience in the discourse than question–answer sequences (Heritage 1985: 100). If we accept this relationship, then it becomes pertinent to consider the role played by formulations in the construction of the inter-view as a text to be overheard in court, or by members of the legal system.

In a broader context, a study investigating the pervasiveness of a mono-discoursal approach to police interviewing might usefully involve a comparison with interviewing in countries where legal representation is permitted or in countries that operate under a different system, such as an inquisitorial system (as in France, for instance).

Whereas this study was restricted to the analysis of the interviews in isolation, it might be fruitful to take a more holistic approach to the collection of data and analyse the interview as part of a longer interaction between the suspect and the police lasting from the time of the arrest to the time that the suspect is released on bail, if applicable. Finally, a review of training materials to ascertain their effect on mono-discoursal view of interview might also be appropriate.

In sum, this study has extended the current understanding of a police interview, both as a discursive event and as a social practice. The findings suggest that analysts in this area should continue to treat a police interview as a socially situated discursive event existing in a dialectical relationship with the police institution, the justice system and the broader society.

Appendix: Features of the Police-Suspect Interviews

Code	Location	Sex of participants				Charges
		Pio	Sio	Tio	SPT	
INT1	PS	F	M		M	Assault and criminal damage
INT2	PS	M	M		M	Assault
INT3	PS	M	M		M	Possession and use of cannabis
INT4	CIB	M	M		M	Burglary
INT5	PS	M	F		M	Car theft
INT6	CIB	M	M		M	Theft
INT7	PS	M	M		M	Possession and use of cannabis
INT8	PS	M	F	M	F	Burglary
INT9	CIB	M	M		M	Firearms
INT10	CIB	M	M		M	Indecent act
INT11	CIB	M	M		M	Assault
INT12	PS	F	M	M	M	Assault
INT13	CIB	M	M		Ml	Burglary

Notes

1. This is followed with the instruction to '[u]se the wording on the Preamble to Interview Card', a prompt for officers containing such legislatively inspired scripts, which accounts for the consistency of wording across interviews.
2. This interview, recorded in 1995, reflects a slightly different wording in use at that time, notably the use of the passive form of the verb 'oblige', which has been replaced by the active form 'have to' in the latest instructions.
3. See section 2.3.2 for a description of the conventions used in transcriptions and extracts.
4. The word 'answers' here seems anomalous – it is possible that this clause is supposed to read 'where such person makes a confession [a member of the Force shall not] attempt, by further questioning, to break down **questions** to which unfavourable replies have been received...', but this too seems less than clear.
5. Cf. Webster's definition of forensic psychiatry: 'the application of psychiatry in courts of law (as for the determination of criminal responsibility or liability for commitment for insanity)'.
6. Some of the legislative requirements have changed very slightly over the period of time in which the interviews were recorded. Most notably, the wording of the fingerprinting caution changed in 1993 to reflect the new power granted to police officers to 'use reasonable force' to obtain fingerprints from suspects who did not consent to giving them freely. Prior to this change, the officer had to apply to the magistrates' court for an order to take the suspect's fingerprints by force.
7. This situation might usefully be compared to the notion of 'knowership' proposed by Goffman (1983) as involving 'the right and obligation mutually to accept and openly to acknowledge individual identification on all initial occasions of incidentally produced proximity' (p. 13).
8. Unfortunately we are unable to ascertain why SPT1 takes this stance of ignorance – we can only speculate that he must feel it mitigates his actions in some way, perhaps because he is trying to give the impression that the assault was not premeditated – if he did not know Ian, he could not have planned to assault him. Alternatively, SPT1, having recently ended a long-term relationship with Betty, may be unwilling to give any more weight than necessary to the possibility that she has begun a new relationship with Ian. Certainly SPT1 is quick to downgrade Ian's relationship with Betty from 'boyfriend', as suggested by pio1, to 'someone who hangs around the shop' (while still claiming not to know him!) which would support this alternative. Ultimately, though, it may be a combination of these factors, and others, which motivates SPT1 to claim he does not know Ian.
9. SPT2 names a radio station, which is here given the pseudonym 3ZX.
10. Incidentally, SPT2 uses the same terminology to describe smoking marijuana in line 138/SPT2: *and I said well↓ (0.6) more like you've had too much to↓ (0.2) <u>smo:ke∧</u>.*

11. The example given by Greatbatch included cases where the interviewee began to initiate question sequences that did not return the floor to the interviewer, and the interviewer responded by noting the inappropriateness of this initiation in some way.
12. In INT3, the response 150/SPT3: *mm⇒ no↓* has already been offered in response to pio3's question but a further response is invited by pio3 in line 151/pio3: *no∧*.
13. Extracts from interviews contained in the text are preceded by a code including the Interview number, Turn number and Participant number. See Appendix I for a list of transcription conventions and codes used in the study. For the full transcriptions of the seven interviews see Appendix II in Heydon 1997.
14. See for instance Thomas (1989), who discusses the use of discoursal indicators in a disciplinary interview between two police officers of unequal rank. This is a different form of discourse from that of a police interview with a non-member of the police force; however the same feature is being used.
15. Fairclough's use of the term 'orders of discourse' – drawn from Michel Foucault's work – forms an important part of the discussion in Chapter 7 where it is examined in more detail.

References

Ainsworth, J. (1993). 'In a different register: the pragmatics of powerlessness in police interrogation'. *Yale Law Journal*, 103, 259–322.

Antaki, C. and Widdicombe, S. (eds) (1998). *Identities in Talk*. London: Sage Publications.

Atkinson, J. M. (1984). 'Public speaking and audience responses: some techniques for inviting applause'. In J. M. Atkinson and J. Heritage (eds), *Structures of Social Action: Studies in Conversation Analysis* (pp. 370–409). Cambridge: Cambridge University Press.

Atkinson, J. M. (1992). 'Displaying neutrality: formal aspects of court proceedings'. In P. Drew and J. Heritage (eds), *Talk at Work* (pp. 199–211). Cambridge: Cambridge University Press.

Atkinson, J. M. and Drew, P. (1979). *Order in Court: the Organisation of Verbal Interaction in Judicial Settings*. Atlantic Highlands, NJ: Humanities Press.

Auburn, T., Drake, S. and Willig, C. (1995). ' "You punched him, didn't you?": versions of violence in accusatory interviews'. *Discourse and Society*, 6(3), 353–86.

Austin, J. (1962). *How To Do Things with Words*. Cambridge, MA: Harvard University Press.

Baldwin, J. (1993). 'Police interview techniques: establishing truth or proof?' *British Journal of Criminology*, 33(3), 325–52.

Barthes, R. (1972). *Mythologies* (trans. A. Lavers). London: Jonathan Cape.

Bergmann, J. R. (1992). 'Veiled morality: notes on discretion in psychiatry'. In P. Drew and J. Heritage (eds), *Talk at Work* (pp. 137–62). Cambridge: Cambridge University Press.

Billig, M. (1991). *Ideology and Opinions: Studies in Rhetorical Psychology*. London: Sage.

Bilmes, J. (1988). 'The concept of preference in conversation analysis'. *Language in Society*, 17, 161–81.

Bourdieu, P. (1991). *Language and Symbolic Power*. Cambridge: Polity Press.

Braithwaite, H., Brewer, N. and Strelan, P. (1998). *Conflict Management in Police–Citizen Interactions*. Roseville: McGraw-Hill.

Button, G. and Casey, N. (1984). 'Generating topic: the use of topic initial elicitors'. In J. M. Atkinson and J. Heritage (eds), *Structures of Social Action: Studies in Conversation Analysis* (pp. 167–90). Cambridge: Cambridge University Press.

Cassell, P. (1993). *The Giddens Reader*. London: Macmillan Press.

Clayman, S. E. (1992). 'Footing in the achievement of neutrality'. In P. Drew and J. Heritage (eds), *Talk at Work* (pp. 163–98). Cambridge: Cambridge University Press.

Cooke, M. (1996). 'A different story: narrative versus "question and answer" in Aboriginal evidence'. *Forensic Linguistics: the International Journal of Speech, Language and the Law*, 3(2), 273–88.

Cotterill, J. (1998). ' "If it doesn't fit, you must acquit": metaphor and the O. J. Simpson criminal trial'. *Forensic Linguistics: the International Journal of Speech, Language and the Law*, 5(2), 141–58.

Cotterill, J. (2000). 'Reading the rights: a cautionary tale of comprehension and comprehensibility'. *Forensic Linguistics: the International Journal of Speech, Language and the Law*, 7(1), 4–25.

Cotterill, J. (2001). 'Domestic discord, rocky relationships: semantic prosodies in representations of marital violence in the O. J. Simpson trial'. *Discourse and Society*, 12(3), 291–312.

Coulthard, M. (1997). 'A failed appeal'. *Forensic Linguistics: the International Journal of Speech, Language and the Law*, 4(2), 287–302.

Coulthard, M. (2000). 'Whose text is it? On the linguistic investigation of authorship'. In M. Coulthard and S. Sarangi (eds), *Discourse and Social Life* (pp. 270–87). London: Longman.

Coupland, J., Robinson, J. D. and Coupland, N. (1994). 'Frame negotiation in doctor–elderly patient consultations'. *Discourse and Society*, 5(1), 89–124.

Danet, B. (1980). 'Language in the legal process'. *Law and Society Review*, 14, 445–564.

Davidson, A. I. (1986). 'Archaeology, genealogy and ethics'. In D. C. Hoy (ed.), *Foucault: A Critical Reader* (pp. 221–233). Oxford: Basil Blackwell.

Davidson, J. (1984). 'Subsequent versions of invitations, offers, requests, and proposals dealing with potential or actual rejection'. In J. M. Atkinson and J. Heritage (eds), *Structures of Social Action: Studies in Conversation Analysis* (pp. 102–28). Cambridge: Cambridge University Press.

Dean, M. (1994). *Critical and Effective Histories: Foucault's Methods and Historical sociology*. London: Routledge.

Drew, P. (1984). 'Speakers' reportings in invitation sequences'. In J. M. Atkinson and J. Heritage (eds), *Structures of Social Action: Studies in Conversation Analysis* (pp. 129–51). Cambridge: Cambridge University Press.

Drew, P. (1985). 'Analyzing the use of language in courtroom interaction'. In T. A. Van Dijk (ed.), *Handbook of Discourse Analysis* (Vol. 3, pp. 133–47). London: Academic Press.

Drew, P. and Heritage, J. (1992). 'Analyzing talk at work'. In P. Drew and J. Heritage (eds), *Talk at Work* (pp. 3–65). Cambridge: Cambridge University Press.

Drew, P. and Holt, E. (1988). 'Complainable matters: the use of idiomatic expressions in making complaints'. *Social Problems*, 35(4), 398–417.

Drew, P. and Sorjonen, M.-L. (1997). 'Institutional dialogue'. In T. A. van Dijk (ed.), *Discourse as Social Interaction* (Vol. 2, pp. 92–118). London: Sage.

Eades, D. (1982). ' "You gotta know how to talk...": information seeking in South-East Queensland Aboriginal Society'. *Australian Journal of Linguistics*, 2(1), 61–82.

Eades, D. (1990). 'Language and the law: an Australian introduction'. *Australian Journal of Linguistics*, 10, 89–100.

Eades, D. (1994). 'A case of communicative clash: Aboriginal English and the legal system'. In J. Gibbons (ed.), *Language and the Law* (pp. 234–64). Harlow: Longman.

Fairclough, N. (1989). *Language and Power*. Harlow: Longman.

Fairclough, N. (2000). *New Labour, New Language?* London: Routledge.

Fairclough, N. and Wodak, R. (1997). 'Critical Discourse Analysis'. In T. A. Van Dijk (ed.), *Discourse as Social Interaction* (pp. 258–84). London: Sage.

Fisher, S. and Todd, A. (1986a). 'Friendly persuasion: negotiating decisions to use oral contraceptive'. In S. Fisher and A. Todd (eds), *Discourse and Institutional*

Authority: Medicine, Education and Law (pp. 3–25). Norwood, NJ: Ablex Publishing Corporation.

Fisher, S. and Todd, A. (1986b). 'Introduction. Communication in institutional contexts: social interaction and social structure'. In S. Fisher and A. Todd (eds), *Discourse and Institutional Authority: Medicine, Education and Law* (pp. ix–xviii). Norwood, NJ: Ablex Publishing Corporation.

Fisher, S. and Todd, A. (eds) (1986c). *Discourse and Institutional Authority: Medicine, Education and Law* (Vol. XIX). Norwood, NJ: Ablex Publishing Corporation.

Foucault, M. (1980). *Power/Knowledge: Selected Interviews and Other Writings, 1972–1977*. New York: Pantheon.

Foucault, M. (1990). *The History of Sexuality: Volume 1: An Introduction*. London: Penguin Books.

Fox, G. (1993). 'A comparison of "policespeak" and "normalspeak": a preliminary study'. In S. J. M. Hoey and G. Fox (eds), *Techniques of Description: Spoken and Written Discourse* (pp. 183–95). London: Routledge.

Frankel, R. (1990). 'Talking in interviews: a dispreference for patient-initiated questions in physician–patient encounters'. In G. Psathas (ed.), *Interaction Competence* (pp. 231–62). Washington DC: University Press of America.

Garfinkel, H. (1967). *Studies in Ethnomethodology*. Englewood Cliffs, NJ: Prentice Hall.

Garfinkel, H. (1974). 'On the origins of the term "ethnomethodology"'. In R. Turner (ed.), *Ethnomethodology*. Harmondsworth: Penguin.

Genine, L. and Shuy, R. W. (1990). '*Mc-*: meaning in the marketplace'. *American Speech*, 65(4), 349–66.

Gerth, H. and Wright Mills, C. (1970). *From Max Weber*. London: Routledge & Kegan Paul.

Gibbons, J. (1990). 'Applied linguistics in court'. *Applied Linguistics*, 11(3), 229–37.

Gibbons, J. (1996). 'Distortions of the police interview process revealed by video-tape'. *Forensic Linguistics: the International Journal of Speech, Language and the Law*, 3(2), 289–298.

Giddens, A. (1982). *Profiles and Critiques in Social Theory*. London: Macmillan Press.

Giddens, A. (1984). *The Constitution of Society: Outline of the Theory of Structuration*. Cambridge: Polity Press.

Goffman, E. (1974). *Frame Analysis*. New York: Harper and Row.

Goffman, E. (1981). *Forms of Talk*. Philadelphia: University of Pennsylvania Press.

Goffman, E. (1983). 'The interaction order'. *American Sociological Review*, 48 (February), 1–17.

Goldsmith, D. J. (1999). 'Content-based resources for giving face sensitive advice in troubles talk'. *Research on Language and Social Interaction*, 32(4), 303–36.

Greatbatch, D. (1988). 'A turn-taking system for British news interviews'. *Language in Society*, 17, 401–30.

Greatbatch, D. and Dingwall, R. (1998). 'Talk and identity in divorce mediation'. In C. Antaki and S. Widdicombe (eds), *Identities in Talk* (pp. 121–32). London: Sage Publications.

Grice, H. P. (1975). 'Logic and conversation'. In P. Cole and J. L. Morgan (eds), *Speech Acts (Syntax and Semantics Volume III)* (pp. 41–58). New York: Academic Press.

Gumperz, J. (1981). 'The linguistic bases of communicative competence'. In D. Tannen (ed.), *Analyzing Discourse: Text and Talk* (pp. 323–34). Washington, DC: Georgetown University Press.

Gumperz, J. (1982). *Discourse Strategies*. Cambridge: Cambridge University Press.

Gumperz, J. (1999). 'On interactional sociolinguistic method'. In S. Sarangi and C. Roberts (eds), *Talk, Work and Institutional Order: Discourse in Medical, Mediation and Management Settings* (pp. 453–71). Berlin: Mouton de Gruyter.

Habermas, J. (1986). 'Taking aim at the heart of the present'. In D. C. Hoy (ed.), *Foucault: a Critical Reader* (pp. 103–8). Oxford: Basil Blackwell.

Hall, M. C., and Collins, A. M. (1980). 'The admission of spectographic evidence: a note on *Reg v Gilmore*'. *The Australian Law Journal*, 54, 21–4.

Heritage, J. (1984). 'A change-of-state token and aspects of its sequential placement'. In J. M. Atkinson and J. Heritage (eds), *Structures of Social Action: Studies in Conversation Analysis* (pp. 299–345). Cambridge: Cambridge University Press.

Heritage, J. (1985). 'Analyzing news interviews: aspects of the production of talk for an overhearing audience'. In T. A. V. Dijk (ed.), *Handbook of Discourse Analysis* (Vol. 3, pp. 95–117). London: Academic Press.

Heritage, J. and Watson, D. R. (1979). 'Formulations as conversational objects'. In G. Psathas (ed.), *Everyday Language: Studies in Ethnomethodology* (pp. 123–62). New York: Irvington Publishers.

Heydon, G. (1997). 'Participation frameworks, discourse features and embedded requests in police V.A.T.E. interviews with children'. Unpublished thesis, Monash University, Melbourne.

Holquist, M. (ed.) (1981). *The Dialogic Imagination: Four Essays by M. M. Bakhtin*. Austin: University of Texas Press.

Jefferson, G. (1978). 'Sequential aspects of storytelling in conversation'. In J. Schenkein (ed.), *Studies in the Organization of Conversational Interaction* (pp. 219–48). New York: Academic Press.

Jefferson, G. (1979). 'A technique for inviting laughter and its subsequent acceptance declination'. In G. Psathas (ed.), *Everyday Language: Studies in Ethnomethodology* (pp. 79–96). New York: Irvington Publishers.

Jefferson, G. (1980). 'On "trouble-premonitory" response to inquiry'. *Sociological Enquiry*, 50, 153–85.

Jefferson, G. (1984a). 'On stepwise transition from talk about a trouble to inappropriately next-positioned matters'. In J. M. Atkinson and J. Heritage (eds), *Structures of Social Action: Studies in Conversation Analysis* (pp. 191–222). Cambridge: Cambridge University Press.

Jefferson, G. (1984b). 'On the organisation of laughter in talk about troubles'. In J. M. Atkinson and J. Heritage (eds), *Structures of Social Action: Studies in Conversation Analysis* (pp. 346–69). Cambridge: Cambridge University Press.

Jefferson, G. (1985). 'On the interactional unpackaging of a "gloss"'. *Language in Society*, 14, 435–66.

Jefferson, G. (1987). 'On exposed and embedded correction in conversation'. In G. Button and J. Lee (eds), *Talk and Social Organisation* (pp. 86–100). Clevedon, Philadelphia: Multilingual Matters Ltd.

Jefferson, G. (1988). 'On the sequential organization of troubles-talk in ordinary conversation'. *Social Problems*, 35(4), 418–41.

Jefferson, G. (1989). 'Preliminary notes on a possible metric which provides for a "standard maximum" silence of approximately one second in conversation'.

In D. Roger and P. Bull (eds), *Conversation: an Interdisciplinary Perspective*. Clevedon: Multilingual Matters Ltd.

Jefferson, G. and Lee, J. (1980). *The Analysis of Conversations in which 'Troubles' and 'Anxieties' are Expressed* (SSRC No. HR 4805/2). Manchester: University of Manchester.

Jefferson, G. and Lee, J. (1992). 'The rejection of advice: managing the problematic convergence of a "troubles-telling" and a "service encounter" '. In P. Drew and J. Heritage (eds), *Talk at Work* (pp. 521–48). Cambridge: Cambridge University Press.

Jensen, M.-T. (1990). 'Differences between a written police record of interview and a tape-recorded interview of a non-native speaker of English'. *Melbourne Papers in Applied Linguistics*, 2(1), 1–18.

Jensen, M.-T. (1995). 'Linguistic evidence accepted in the case of a non-native speaker of English'. In D. Eades (ed.), *Language in Evidence: Issues Confronting Aboriginal and Multicultural Australia* (pp. 127–46). Sydney: University of New South Wales Press.

Labov, W. (1982). 'Objectivity and commitment in linguistic science: the case of the Black English trial in Ann Arbor'. *Language in Society*, 11, 165–201.

Lakoff, R. (1975). *Language and Woman's Place*. New York: Harper and Row.

Lakoff, R. (1990). *Talking Power: the Notion of Language in an Institutional Setting*. New York: Basic Books.

Ledbetter, P. J. and Dent, C. H. (1988). 'Young children's sensitivity to direct and indirect request structure'. *First Language*, 8, 227–46.

Levi, J. N. (1994). 'Language as evidence: the linguist as expert witness in North American courts'. *Forensic Linguistics: the International Journal of Speech, Language and the Law*, 1(1), 1–26.

Levinson, S. C. (1983). *Pragmatics*. Cambridge: Cambridge University Press.

Levinson, S. C. (1988). 'Putting linguistics on a proper footing: explorations in Goffman's concepts of participation'. In P. Drew and A. Wootton (eds), *Erving Goffman: Exploring the Interaction Order* (pp. 161–227). Cambridge: Polity Press.

Levinson, S. C. (1992). 'Activity types and language'. In P. Drew and J. Heritage (eds), *Talk at Work* (pp. 66–100). Cambridge: Cambridge University Press.

Linell, P. and Jonsson, L. (1991). 'Suspect stories: on perspective setting in an asymmetrical situation'. In I. Markova and K. Foppa (eds), *Asymmetries in Dialogue* (pp. 75–100). Hemel Hempstead: Harvester Wheatsheaf.

McElhinny, B. S. (1995). 'Challenging hegemonic masculinities: female and male police officers handling domestic violence'. In K. Hall and M. Bucholtz (eds), *Gender Articulated: Language and the Socially Constructed Self* (pp. 217–43). New York: Routledge.

Michaud, S. L. and Warner, R. M. (1997). 'Gender differences in self-reported response to troubles talk'. *Sex Roles*, 37(7/8), 527–40.

Milroy, J. (1984). 'Sociolinguistic methodology and the identification of speakers' voices in legal proceedings'. In P. Trudgill (ed.), *Applied Sociolinguistics* (pp. 51–72). London: Academic Press.

Pearse, J. and Gudjonsson, G. H. (1996). 'Police interviewing techniques at two South London police stations'. *Psychology, Crime & Law*, 3, 63–74.

Pennycook, A. (2001). *Critical Applied Linguistics: a Critical Introduction*. London: Lawrence Erlbaum Associates.

Perakyla, A. and Silverman, D. (1991). 'Reinterpreting speech-exchange systems: communication formats in AIDS counselling'. *Sociology*, 25(4), 627–51.

Polanyi, L. (1985). 'Conversational storytelling'. In T. A. V. Dijk (ed.), *Handbook of Discourse Analysis* (Vol. 3, pp. 183–201). London: Academic Press.

Pomerantz, A. M. (1980). 'Telling my side: "limited access" as a "fishing" device'. *Sociological Enquiry*, 50(3–4), 186–98.

Pomerantz, A. M. (1984a). 'Agreeing and disagreeing with assessments: some features of preferred/dispreferred turn shapes'. In J. M. Atkinson and J. Heritage (eds), *Structures of Social Action: Studies in Conversation Analysis* (pp. 57–101). Cambridge: Cambridge University Press.

Pomerantz, A. M. (1984b). 'Giving a source or basis: the practice in conversation of telling "how I know" '. *Journal of Pragmatics*, 8, 607–25.

Pomerantz, A. M. (1984c). 'Pursuing a response'. In J. M. Atkinson and J. Heritage (eds), *Structures of Social Action: Studies in Conversation Analysis* (pp. 152–63). Cambridge: Cambridge University Press.

Pomerantz, A. M. (1986). 'Extreme case formulations: a way of legitimizing claims'. *Human Studies*, 9, 219–29.

Pomerantz, A. M. (1987). 'Description in legal settings'. In G. Button and J. Lee (eds), *Talk and Social Organisation* (pp. 226–43). Clevedon, Philadelphia: Multilingual Matters Ltd.

Powell, M. B. and Thomson, D. M. (1994). 'Children's eyewitness-memory research: implications for practice'. *Families in Society: the Journal of Contemporary Human Services*, April, 204–15.

Pritchard, C. R. (1993). 'Supportive devices in language and paralanguage in the achievement of affiliation in troubles talk'. *Australian Review of Applied Linguistics*, 16(1), 57–70.

Pritchard, C. R. (1994). 'Analysis of structure and interaction in the construction of a program for radio'. Unpublished MA thesis, University of Melbourne, Melbourne.

Roberts, C. and Sarangi, S. (1999). 'Introduction: negotiating and legitimating roles and identities'. In S. Sarangi and C. Roberts (eds), *Talk, Work and Institutional Order: Discourse in Medical, Mediation and Management Settings* (pp. 227–36). Berlin: Mouton de Gruyter.

Sacks, H. (1972). 'Notes on police assessment of moral character'. In D. N. Sudnow (ed.), *Studies in Social Interaction* (pp. 280–93). New York: Free Press.

Sacks, H. (1974). 'An analysis of the course of a joke's telling in conversation'. In R. Bauman and J. Sherzer (eds), *Explorations in the Ethnography of Speaking* (pp. 337–53). New York: Cambridge University Press.

Sacks, H. (1987). 'On the preferences for agreement and contiguity in sequences in conversation'. In G. Button and J. Lee (eds), *Talk and Social Organisation* (pp. 54–69). Clevedon, Philadelphia: Multilingual Matters Ltd.

Sacks, H. (1992a). 'Lecture 1: rules of conversational sequence'. In G. Jefferson (ed.), *Lectures on Conversation* (Vol. 1, pp. 3–11). Cambridge, MA: Blackwell Publishers.

Sacks, H. (1992b). *Lectures on Conversation*. Cambridge, MA: Blackwell Publishers.

Sacks, H., Schegloff, E. and Jefferson, G. (1974). 'A simplest systematics for the organisation of turn-taking for conversation'. *Language*, 50(4), 696–735.

Sarangi, S. and Roberts, C. (eds) (1999). *Talk, Work and Institutional Order: Discourse in Medical, Mediation and Management settings*. Berlin: Mouton de Gruyter.

Schegloff, E. (1991). 'Reflections on talk and social structure'. In D. Boden and D. H. Zimmerman (eds), *Talk and Social Structure: Studies in Ethnomethodology and Conversation Analysis* (pp. 44–70). Cambridge: Polity Press in association with Blackwell.

Schegloff, E. and Sacks, H. (1973). 'Opening up closing'. *Semiotica*, 8(4), 289–327.

Schiffrin, D. (1994). *Approaches to Discourse*. Cambridge, MA: Blackwell Publishers.

Settle, R. (1990). *Police Power: Use and Abuse*. Northcote: Muxworthy Press.

Shuy, R. W. (1997). 'Ten unanswered questions about Miranda'. *Forensic Linguistics: the International Journal of Speech, Language and the Law*, 4(2), 175–96.

Shuy, R. W. (1998). *The Language of Confession, Interrogation, and Deception*. Thousand Oaks: Sage.

Tannen, D. (1993). 'Interactive frames and knowledge schemas in interaction: examples from a medical examination/interview'. In *Framing in Discourse*. Oxford: Oxford University Press.

Thomas, J. A. (1989). 'Discourse control in confrontational interaction'. In L. Hickey (ed.), *The Pragmatics of Style* (pp. 133–56). London: Routledge.

Tracy, K. (1997). 'Interactional trouble in emergency service requests: a problem of frames'. *Research on Language and Social Interaction*, 30(4), 315–43.

van Dijk, T. A. (1987). *Communicating Racism: Ethnic Prejudice in Thought and Talk*. Newbury Park, CA: Sage Publications.

van Dijk, T. A. (1996). 'Discourse, power and access'. In C. R. Caldas-Coulthard and M. Coulthard (eds), *Texts and Practices: Readings in Critical Discourse Analysis* (pp. 84–104). London: Routledge.

van Dijk, T. A. (1997). 'Discourse as interaction in society'. In T. A. van Dijk (ed.), *Discourse as Social Interaction* (pp. 1–37). London: Sage.

Walsh, M. (1994). 'Interactional styles in the courtroom: an example from Northern Australia'. In J. Gibbons (ed.), *Language and the Law* (pp. 217–33). Harlow: Longman.

Watson, D. R. (1976). 'Some conceptual issues in the social identification of victims and offenders'. In E. C. Viano (ed.), *Victims and Society* (pp. 60–71). Washington DC: Visage Press.

Watson, D. R. (1983). 'The presentation of victim and motive in discourse: the case of police interrogations and interviews'. *Victimology*, 8(1–2), 31–52.

Wodak, R. (1996a). *Disorders of Discourse*. London: Addison Wesley Longman.

Wodak, R. (1996b). 'The genesis of racist discourse in Austria since 1989'. In C. R. Caldas-Coulthard and M. Coulthard (eds), *Texts and Practices: Readings in Critical Discourse Analysis* (pp. 107–28). London: Routledge.

Woolls, D. and Coulthard, M. (1998). 'Tools for the trade'. *Forensic Linguistics: the International Journal of Speech, Language and the Law*, 5(1), 33–57.

Zimmerman, D. H. (1998). 'Identity, context and interaction'. In C. Antaki and S. Widdicombe (eds), *Identities in Talk* (pp. 87–106). London: Sage Publications.

Index